✳

Women in the
Latin American
Development Process

✳

WOMEN IN THE LATIN AMERICAN DEVELOPMENT PROCESS

Edited by Christine E. Bose
and Edna Acosta-Belén

TEMPLE UNIVERSITY PRESS *Philadelphia*

Temple University Press, Philadelphia 19122
Copyright © 1995 by Sociologists for Women in Society. All rights reserved
Published 1995
Printed in the United States of America

The paper used in this publication meets the minimum
requirements of American National Standard for Information
Sciences—Permanence of Paper for Printed Library Materials,
ANSI Z39.48-1984 ∞

Library of Congress Cataloging-in-Publication Data

Women in the Latin American development process / edited by Christine E. Bose and Edna
     Acosta-Belén.
         p.   cm.
     Includes bibliographical references and index.
     ISBN 1-56639-292-6 (alk. paper). — ISBN 1-56639-293-4 (pbk. : alk. paper)
     1. Women in development—Latin America.   2. Women in development—Caribbean
Area.   3. Feminism—Latin America.   4. Feminism—Caribbean Area.   I. Bose,
Christine E.   II. Acosta-Belén, Edna.
HQ1240.5.L29W67   1995
305.42'098—dc20   94-27400

Chapters 1, 5, 6, 9, and 10 are adapted, respectively, from Edna Acosta-Belén and Christine
E. Bose, "From Structural Subordination to Empowerment: Women and Development in
Third World Contexts" (pp. 299–320); Palmira N. Ríos, "Export-Oriented Industrialization and the Demand for Female Labor: Puerto Rican Women in the Manufacturing Sector,
1952–1980" (pp. 321–337); June Nash, "Latin American Women in the World Capitalist
Crisis" (pp. 338–353); Helen Icken Safa, "Women's Social Movements in Latin America"
(pp. 354–369); and Norma Stoltz Chinchilla, "Revolutionary Popular Feminism in Nicaragua: Articulating Class, Gender, and National Sovereignty" (pp. 370–397) in *Gender &
Society,* vol. 4, no. 3, September 1990, copyright © 1990 by Sociologists for Women in
Society. Reprinted by permission of Sage Publications, Inc.

*To all the Latin American
and Caribbean women who struggle
for social justice and equality*

CONTENTS

PREFACE

We hope this book helps promote the international connections and comparative perspectives that will ultimately enhance research on women in the global economy and the formulation of development policies that could truly improve women's material conditions and perhaps even undermine the structures and ideologies that perpetuate their subordinate status. This process requires moving beyond traditional disciplinary boundaries, as demonstrated by our authors, who were trained as anthropologists, sociologists, historians, political scientists, and economists. Their work reflects multidimensional theoretical approaches, connecting analyses of gender, class, race, ethnicity, and nationality into a meaningful composite framework for understanding the relationship of Latin American and Caribbean women to changing development issues across material conditions, countries, and time periods. The contributors underscore the need for increased knowledge of the key structural and ideological determinants of women's subordination in these regions, as well as their efforts for economic survival, noting the inherent relationship of such struggles to the struggles of Latinas and other women of color in the United States.

This volume emerged from our own studies of the hidden aspects of women's work, combined with our recognition of the need to advance comparative research between developing and highly industrialized societies on women's productive roles. Thus, the authors of the chapters included here are some of the leading scholars in the field of women and work.

Research on development has proliferated in the 1990s, and we have been fortunate to secure many new works concerning Latin America and the Caribbean, the regional area of our own expertise. These contributions cover the topics of gender and the political economy and strategies for change. Historical gender bias, differing cultural and class patterns, linkages between family and paid work, and varied forms of resistance and collective action are the broad themes of this book, applied to a wide range of women's economic development experiences in Latin America and the Caribbean. We have also included revised versions of several articles that originally appeared in September 1990 in a special issue of *Gender & Society,* the official journal of Sociologists for Women in Society (SWS), which we edited and which was entitled "Women and

Development in the Third World." It was clear even then that only a larger volume could do justice to this topic, and we thank Bettina Huber of SWS, who encouraged us to put one together on behalf of the Society. Thus, Chapters 6 and 9 are updated and Chapters 1, 5, and 10 are substantially revised versions of articles appearing in *Gender & Society*, volume 4, number 3, and are reprinted with the permission of both SWS and Sage Publications.

The publication of this book was facilitated by the support and resources provided by the Institute for Research on Women (IROW); the Center for Latino, Latin American, and Caribbean Studies (CELAC); and the Department of Latin American and Caribbean Studies (LACS), all at the University at Albany, SUNY, as well as by SWS. Our thanks also go to Mary Jo Smith-Parés, who provided important proofreading assistance, and to Viviana Rangil and Carol Inskip, who aided in the indexing of countries and subjects. Finally, as co-editors of this volume, we would like to recognize each other's continuous support and effort in this endeavor to promote research and writing on women in the global economy and other transnational issues.

✳

*Women in the
Latin American
Development Process*

Introduction

CHRISTINE E. BOSE AND EDNA ACOSTA-BELÉN

The roles of women in Latin American and Caribbean development, their subordination and forms of resistance, are best understood with an interdisciplinary approach, making use of a historical and international political economy framework, rather than the usual country-by-country review. The advantage of this approach is that it looks at the intertwining of economic, social, and political issues within and among the countries of the American hemisphere. In addition, it recognizes the diversity of economic structures that exist in Latin America and the Caribbean, ranging from the predominant capitalist system to socialism; the various types of markets found at the local, national, or global level; and the historical shift in international socioeconomic relations away from direct colonization and toward a development model.

Both scholarly research in women's studies and feminist political work for change have documented the need for a gendered understanding in development studies. This involves more than merely incorporating women into policy making: it requires changing the framework used and the questions traditionally asked about the goals and effects of development. Authors in this book combine these interdisciplinary political economy and gendered approaches to reframe our understanding of women's relationship to development in Latin America and the Caribbean, reflecting new insights and paradigm shifts.

Most U.S. feminist theories prevalent through the mid-1980s were too focused on other issues to integrate fully all women's experiences across class, race, ethnic, and national lines or to capture the significance of the historical, cultural, and social differences that result from the exploitation endemic to the systems and practices of colonialism and slavery that once prevailed in the regions known today as the Third World. At the same time, Latin American and Caribbean feminists were busy searching for new strategies to confront the many immediate problems facing their often impoverished nations, a task that frequently demanded more grass-roots action than theorizing.

Nonetheless, since the closing of the United Nations International Decade for Women (1975–85), feminist scholarship in Latin America and the Caribbean has promoted more holistic analyses of women's multiple oppressive conditions and developed comparative perspectives that establish the crucial connections between women's conditions in these regions and in North America. Simultaneously, feminist researchers from Europe and North America have paid increased attention to the area of women and development.

New Frameworks for Understanding Gender and the Political Economy

Early feminist (and nonfeminist) discussions of women and development generally took a dichotomous approach: women were viewed as either helped or exploited by development, integrated or marginalized, drawn into paid employment or excluded from it, relegated to traditional domestic roles. Recent authors recognize many more complexities in this process and often suggest that development simultaneously has had both positive and negative consequences for women. To reach this new understanding, it has been necessary to secure additional empirical data and to create new concepts and frameworks of analysis.

In the past it was difficult accurately to assess women's role in the development process of individual countries because much of the necessary data was missing, as statistics on labor force participation often omitted work done in the household (primarily by women) or in the informal sector of the economy. As a result, women in international development have advocated better data on home-based work, to be achieved by employing methodologies such as time use, enterprise, or household surveys (United Nations 1988; *INSTRAW News* 1989).

In addition, feminist research since the mid-1980s has emphasized the need to reconceptualize work itself, as Kathryn B. Ward and Jean Larson Pyle (this volume) suggest, to measure it on a continuum from formal paid work, to informal paid labor, to household work. This approach makes clear that development, usually thought of as activity in the productive sphere, is not separate from the reproductive sphere of the home and that the macro- and microlevels of economic analysis can and must be considered simultaneously and interactively.

Redefining work as existing on a continuum implicitly illustrates the usefulness of the household as a unit of analysis for studies of women in the political economy, both in the First World (Bose 1984) and in Latin America and the Caribbean (Acevedo, this volume). Whereas traditional economic studies focus on how individuals maximize their possible income, looking at the household brings to light the power relationships within families or kin networks and how they serve to facilitate and also segregate men's and women's potential income and occupations along gender lines (Blumberg, this volume; Rothstein, this volume). Research using this household model indicates that women simultaneously are integrated into the economy and experience marginalization, either as low-wage workers in industrial jobs or within the informal economy (Ward and Pyle, this volume). Thus, household income strategies are complexly shaped by the interaction of family and transnational corporate decisions and reflect processes at both micro- and macroeconomic levels.

A gendered perspective on development also broadens the industrial sectors that are considered part of the political economy. Most analysts agree that a new international division of labor has replaced the old one. Where developing nations once were the source of raw materials, they now are the sites of manufacturing and export processing zones whose workforces are often female-dominated, in spite of frequent national efforts to increase male employment (Ríos, this volume). The growth in the employment of Latin American and Caribbean women is due not only to their direct hiring by multinationals, however, but also to the systems of subcontracting and home outwork that generate employment indirectly (Ward and Pyle, this volume; Acevedo, this volume). Thus, industrial work and the family-based economy have grown side by side. Increasingly, women are able even to create their own home-based microenterprises (Blumberg, this volume). Of course, women's labor also takes over the subsistence work that men forsake because of employment, migration, or both. Thus, while many women continue to be employed in their traditional roles as domestics (*muchachas*) or street sellers, new trends in many countries indicate an increase in home-based, income-generating work as well as industrial employment.

Growth in Latin American and Caribbean women's employment has been integrally linked to trends in North America, especially to the role of Latinas and other women of color in the U.S. political economy (Fernández Kelly and Sassen, this volume; Nash, this volume). U.S. industrial restructuring has meant that corporations design and use multiple strategies in order to maintain flexibility, allowing firms to minimize labor costs and maximize profits. Thus, electronics and garment firms that have sent much of their long-lead-time production to Asia or Latin America are also using immigrant labor from those same regions to work in smaller U.S. firms, where a quick turn-around in production is essential. Here, too, we find heavy reliance on subcontracting systems and industrial homework, and especially the labor of ethnic or migrant women, some of whom create their own small businesses (Fernández Kelly and Sassen, this volume). Interestingly, the simultaneous decline in the ability of men to be the sole breadwinners within their families and the changing gender roles that recognize women's need for employment have made this trend possible (Safa 1995).

This parallel structure in the gendered division of labor within contemporary First and Third World countries illustrates the significance of the interconnections among class, race, ethnicity, and gender in shaping women's economic roles worldwide. State policy interacts with the first three of these features either to facilitate or to restrict women's employment opportunities. Although the role of the contemporary state is clear when it creates free trade zones, export-driven industrialization policies, or immigration laws that influence the flows of low-paid labor, the highly industrialized nations of Europe and North America, as part of the international division of power within the capitalist system, have shaped gender roles in the Latin American economy since colonial times.

The contemporary condition of Latin American and Caribbean women cannot be totally separated from the legacies of the colonial experience. In many precolonial cultures, women's position and participation in productive work was parallel to men's, rather than subservient. But, Europeans presupposed a universal subordination of women and implemented rules and laws that often deprived indigenous women of property, autonomy, and many former public roles (Etienne and Leacock 1980; Acosta-Belén and Bose, this volume). Such patriarchal policies and their inherent ideologies continued through the centuries, in part because of the neocolonial character of the relations that industrialized nations still maintain with developing countries.

Until the work of Ester Boserup (1970), classic social science literature on development, as well as development policies themselves, assumed that women did not contribute to production, thus ignoring women's labor in the household and in informal economic activities. Boserup's work opened the way for feminist scholars who, beginning in the 1970s, have reframed gender and development issues by placing women at the center of the analysis. On a theoretical level, development is no longer viewed in a dichotomous mode as either economic salvation or unrestrained exploitation of the poor, and the concept of work has been expanded into a continuum that includes the informal economy and industrial homework. In addition, a wide variety of interconnections has been recognized: the economic bond of women in the United States with those in Latin America and the Caribbean, the relationship of gender issues not only to class but also to race and ethnicity (for example, in considering the productive roles of enslaved black women), and the links between changes over time in the economy and those in role expectations for women.

Another major positive effect of the new feminist research on development is the move away from a woman-as-victim model, inherent in the marginalization thesis. In the new model, women's empowerment is recognized as simultaneously occurring with shifts in the international division of labor that nonetheless often relegate women to a secondary place. In many ways the status of women is symbolized in the writings of Maria Mies, Veronika Bennholdt-Thomsen, and Claudia von Werlhof (1988), who envision women as the last colony—a subordinate population whose underpaid work continues to be exploited but that has the potential to create change leading to increased autonomy or independence.

Strategies for Resistance and Empowerment

Women's resistance to their subordinate position is now recognized as occurring in a broad range of dimensions, some of which also empower women to varying extents. Although women's resistance can take place in the traditionally studied large-scale social movements or in union activities, new research has examined other forms of activism as well. Because of frequent extreme conditions of poverty, much of women's organized resistance in Latin America and the Caribbean is based on survival needs, often at the individual or family level as well as in the neighborhood or workplace. Many authors argue that survival itself is an act of resistance.

It is easy to assume that families only constrain women, but contemporary researchers also focus on those family aspects that benefit them. For example, one of the most common ways that households resist the marginalization of low-wage employment generated by the global economy is the use of what Frances Abrahamer Rothstein (this volume) labels multiple income strategies: pooling wages, cash, subsistence produce, and unpaid labor from a combination of work in the formal, informal, and household sectors by a variety of family members. She argues that such strategies are replacing both peasant subsistence and single-breadwinner strategies, at least in rural Mexico, as dependence on the market increases. Decisions concerning household labor allocation must be based as much on shifting work opportunities as on gender roles, and therefore women can obtain access to resources, land, family labor, or schooling through kin networks when it will aid them in generating income. For example, help with the reproductive work of cooking or childcare often allows a mother to attend school or keep a job; a contribution of livestock can start a small chicken or cattle business. Such kin support is especially advantageous to the growing numbers of female-headed households.

Viewing multiple income strategies as an economic form of resistance also substantively illustrates the significance of two theoretical points made earlier: households and kin, rather than individuals, are an important economic unit of analysis; and work needs to be redefined as occurring on a continuum that includes income sources from the formal, informal, and subsistence economies.

The 1980s' international debt crisis and concomitant structural readjustment in many Latin American countries pushed individuals and kin groups into informal sector labor, where many run or work in microenterprises. Women are not an exception to this trend, but they are concentrated in the lower, subsistence end of the range of such enterprises and are gender-segregated into garment and food products or commerce and service work (Blumberg, this volume). Although their labor in microenterprises is often undercounted and underfunded by development agencies, when women do obtain loans their payback record is as good as or better than that of men and they create more new jobs. Rae Lesser Blumberg argues that this type of employment, even though low paid and often lacking in benefits, is especially important because it generates income under a woman's control, enhancing the well-being of her children and increasing her leverage in family decisions. As women's income, rather than men's, is more closely related to children's nutrition, both survival and empowerment are at stake.

The rising usage of multiple income pooling and informal sector employment, of which microenterprises are an example, illustrates the centrality of domestic survival issues for individuals and families. Moreover, these same issues have become the basis of women's collective organizing in many Latin American and Caribbean nations. Women's struggles are grounded in neighborhood mobilization and often phrased in moral terms, rather than based on a consciousness of class struggle or worker rights (Nash, this volume). Women demand public services such as running water, electricity, health care, or transportation for squatter communities; organize self-help collectives to buy and prepare food or to provide childcare for a neighborhood; or fight for human rights in the names of their "disappeared" relatives victimized by authoritarian regimes.

Scholars disagree about the extent of empowerment brought about through such collective action. Helen Icken Safa (this volume) argues for the advantages, noting that although these movements are undertaken in defense of women's traditional domestic roles, they contribute to greater consciousness of gender subordination and to women's legitimacy in the public sphere as well as the private one. Thus, actions that directly target their demands at the state represent a new and creative political trend, especially in countries where gender restrictions are not only culturally valued but written into many laws. Other researchers note the disadvantages to such peasant or popular movements, which can easily be co-opted since often they are not connected to a conscious feminist framework or group. These movements may ameliorate an immediate condition without changing the basic structures controlling women's survival.

The state is not an easy social formation for any group to tackle, although under the 1980s Sandinista government women's groups in Nicaragua may have been among the most successful, even if only in the short term. Their achievements were made because the Sandinista leadership took on the issue of sexism in its own theory and practice and because women's activism continued both outside and inside the revolutionary party (Chinchilla, this volume). Thus, Chinchilla and others have argued that early forms of organizing around women's "practical gender interests" must be politicized and transformed into "strategic gender interests" that are articulated with class, race, ethnicity, and other national identity issues to challenge women's subordination. This form of organizing clearly empowers women but it has been hard to maintain, since the international dynamics of the global economy (surfacing in the policies of the International Monetary Fund or the World Bank) often wield more power than the state itself. This power was demonstrated in the U.S.-led campaign to sabotage economically, politically, and militarily the Sandinista government reforms in Nicaragua as well as in the restructuring and debt crisis of the 1980s.

For this reason, women are relatively unlikely to seek change in state processes through the traditional mechanism of political parties, which are still male-dominated and often corrupt, and are more likely to organize around their work-related issues—whether the work is located at home, in a *taller*, or in a *maquiladora*. Even if women are not organized in classic labor unions, resistance takes place daily in the neighborhood organizations using communal kitchens, at computer terminals, or on the shopfloor with work slowdowns, and in the informal sector through the creation of cooperatives and loan groups.

Gender and Development

Latin American and Caribbean women, like other Third World women, have remained in the bottom tier in the international division of labor of the global economy ever since the colonial system initially facilitated and legitimated what is now considered their traditional role. This position is double-edged. Women have less control of resources and lower incomes than men in their countries, but it is their labor—either through direct employment in the *maquiladoras* or indirectly through subcontracting or homework—that has been key to the growth of transnational corporations. This growth began in the 1950s, continued through the restructuring of the 1970s, and facilitated the newest international economic changes begun in the 1980s.

From the 1950s through the 1970s, U.S. corporations began "outsourcing" or "offshoring" their production, especially to countries in Latin America, the Caribbean, and East Asia, seeking lower labor costs. National corporations thus became transnationals, with much of their workforce outside the United States. On the receiving end of these changes, export processing zones, *maquilas,* and increased industrial homework characterized what became a pattern of export-led industrialization for most Latin American and Caribbean nations. This development strategy tended to draw on women directly as employees or indirectly in subcontracted work, escalating an existing trend for women to leave agriculture and enter manufacturing or the informal economy. Ultimately, the economic power of the multinational corporations transcended the political power (or willingness) of nation-states to control them, and a new international division of labor was created between countries of the First and Third Worlds, beginning what has been dubbed "the global assembly line." Latin America and the Caribbean, as well as Asia and parts of Africa, were proletarianized by this global corporate restructuring, a process that was exacerbated by a tremendous increase in the Latin American international debt.

During the 1980s, corporate strategies began to shift again. Increasingly, their emphasis has been on internationalizing the service sector rather than manufacturing, as well as on creating global markets in finance. The global assembly line is transforming into what has been described as "regional clustering," brought on by corporate attempts to lower production costs through the use of advanced computer technology, rather than by moving production work from country to country (Nanda 1994). New methods of automation are more flexible, making use of equipment such as robotic arms or programmable lathes that are replaced less often, can be used in many production processes, and usually need only computer program modification to create a new product. The only requirement is that the computerized machines for the various industrial processes be in close proximity, clustered in a given region. The impact of this new configuration on women in Latin America and the Caribbean is beginning to be noted.

As global cities such as Los Angeles enlarge their importance, so too does the labor of Latina and other immigrant women who are hired in the electronics and garment industries there. One outcome is that women's migration patterns to the United States are beginning to separate from those of their households as they enter such regional clusters seeking employment. In this sense, the passage of the North American Free Trade Agreement (NAFTA) is unavoidably tied to the work roles of women. An additional effect of these strategic corporate shifts is that the labor cost of unskilled workers in Latin American countries has become less important to corporations than that of skilled workers, such as those who can use computers in production or data entry.

These corporate strategy shifts represent a response not only to production methods and costs but also to the internal politics of the Latin American countries in which transnationals operate. In the past, development models focused on growth, often to the detriment of both the ecological environment and the needs of the population. As a consequence, many nations, especially in Central America and the Caribbean, have called for new models of sustainable development in which the use of natural and social resources would be deliberately planned to meet basic social needs in ways that are directed and evaluated by people in local communities (Lélé 1991). The rising popularity of models of sustainable development has made the shift toward services and away from ecologically damaging industries more politically attractive as well as cost-effective.

These conceptual changes in economic growth and development models, and their outcomes for women, are epitomized in Puerto Rico, which has the dubious distinction of being in the vanguard of international corporate changes (Ríos, this volume). The island, which has been a colonial possession of the United States since 1898, was heavily industrialized in the 1950s under Operation Bootstrap, a labor-intensive development program based on U.S. investment in manufacturing industries in return for low-wage labor and corporate tax exemptions. Puerto Rico was turned into the export platform for U.S. manufacturing, with early investment in labor-intensive industries later followed by capital-intensive industries, such as petrochemicals. In accord with the foreign investment and export-led development model, the industrialization of Puerto Rico created a modern infrastructure with a concomitant improvement in per capita income, literacy and educational rates, and life expectancy, as well as new occupational opportunities and increased consumption of U.S. goods. As in other countries, in spite of Puerto Rico's efforts to bring in male-dominated employment, corporate strategies ultimately drew largely on women's labor. Furthermore, the subordination of the Puerto Rican economy to U.S. corporate interests produced massive population displacements resulting in the migration of more than one-third of the total population to the continental United States and a perennial unemployment rate of over 15 percent.

In the 1970s the island lost most of its competitive advantages as it became more integrated into the U.S. economy, and wages, energy, and commercial transportation costs increased. To alleviate this ongoing economic crisis, by the 1980s the U.S. and Puerto Rican governments were attempting to restructure Puerto Rico's economy into a unique tax haven and financial center for transnational capital, facilitating the transference of profits from operations in other parts of the world to island subsidiaries. This high-finance strategy is intended to transform Puerto Rico into an international center for investment trade and services, leading to the expansion of its commercial banking sector and the promotion of service industries, which will draw women into their heavily computerized operations.

The Puerto Rican case is a good illustration of how, collectively, Latin American and Caribbean women are the site at which economic forms continue to materialize (Sassen 1994); at the same time, these women remain in the second tier both in their native countries and in the U.S. economy. Thus, the analyses in this book of how women are an integral part of the development process and the ways in which they are seeking empowerment, or at least how they are individually and collectively resisting a subordinate status, are cornerstones of a full understanding of the interplay of forces and relationships that constitute the global economic order.

REFERENCES

Bose, Christine E. 1984. "Household Resources and U.S. Women's Work: Factors Affecting Gainful Employment at the Turn of the Century." *American Sociological Review* 49 (August): 474–490.

Boserup, Ester. 1970. *Women's Role in Economic Development*. New York: St. Martin's Press.

Etienne, Mona, and Eleanor Leacock, eds. 1980. *Women and Colonization: Anthropological Perspectives*. New York: Praeger.

INSTRAW News. 1989. "Special Issue on Women's Work: The Informal Sector." 12 (Summer): 3–8.

Lélé, Sharachchandra M. 1991. "Sustainable Development: A Critical Review." *World Development* 19 (6): 607–621.

Mies, Maria, Veronika Bennholdt-Thomsen, and Claudia von Werlhof. 1988. *Women: The Last Colony*. London: Zed.

Nanda, Meera. 1994. "New Technologies/New Challenges." Paper presented at the Conference on Women in the Global Economy: Making Connections, Albany, New York, Institute for Research on Women, University at Albany, SUNY, April 22–24.

Safa, Helen. 1995. *The Myth of the Male Breadwinner: Women and Industrialization in the Caribbean*. Boulder, Colo.: Westview.

Sassen, Saskia. 1994. "Women in the World Economy, 1945 to the Present." Paper presented at the Conference on Women in the Global Economy: Making Connections, Albany, New York, Institute for Research on Women, University at Albany, SUNY, April 22–24.

United Nations, Department of International Economic and Social Affairs, Statistical Office, and International Research and Training Institute for the Advancement of Women. 1988. *Improving Statistics and Indicators on Women Using Household Surveys.* Studies in Methods Series F, no. 48. New York: United Nations.

PART I

*

From Colonization to Development and Industrialization: Gender and the Economy

CHAPTER 1

＊

Colonialism, Structural Subordination, and Empowerment

Women in the Development Process in Latin America and the Caribbean

EDNA ACOSTA-BELÉN AND CHRISTINE E. BOSE

understanding dev re of L.A.

Understanding the development of Latin America, the Caribbean, and other Third World societies requires recognizing the fundamental differences in their processes of incorporation into a global system of capital accumulation. In this complex system of economic and social relations, the subordination of women has been ideologically conceived as an integral part of the natural order of things and perpetuated by cultural praxis, religion, education, and other social institutions. Thus, understanding development also entails drawing on the continuities of power relations and ideologies rooted and molded in the era of European imperial and colonial expansion and examining the set of socioeconomic and political practices that the dominant Western nations developed for their acquired overseas territories during the colonial era. On the surface, the era of the *conquistadores* represents a thing of the past and is far different from today's multinational corporations, monopoly capital, and international division of labor. Nonetheless, it is not a far-fetched comparison if we consider which nations were the masters of the old colonial economic order and which nations control today's global economy.

(1)

(2)

Women's experience

The contemporary condition of most women in Third World nations, therefore, cannot be separated from the colonial experience, since, historically, the exploitation of both women and colonies has been fundamental to the development of world capitalism and sexism, a part of its embedded ideology (Saffioti 1978; Etienne and Leacock 1980; Mies, Bennholdt-Thomsen, and Werlhof 1988). Men and women in colonial territories and women in developed nations share the commonality of having been

15

appropriated, controlled, and placed in subordinate positions of dependency by those who own the means of production and dominate access to capital.

This chapter introduces a theoretical framework for the study of women in the development process, with a focus on Latin America and the Caribbean which stresses that the basic paradigm of power relationships, established during the era of imperialist expansion between Europe and its New World colonial territories, and between women and men, has not varied significantly since then. These relations are still recreated through contemporary mechanisms. Much too often development projects promoted by Western countries have, in the long run, better served their own interests than those of their intended beneficiaries. As a result, contrary to expectations, growth and prosperity still elude most Latin American and Caribbean countries. In addition, if we examine the international economic crisis of the 1980s, the determining role of gender is illustrated, since women's unpaid or underpaid labor was at the core of new development programs and policies and a crucial part of this phase of capitalist expansion.

Most authors cannot refer to the nations of Latin America and the Caribbean without viewing them as the dramatic setting for encounters between the powerful and the subjugated, the poor and the wealthy, the traditional and the modern, the rural and the urban. These overgeneralized dichotomies emphasize the risks of discussing the regions of the Third World without paying sufficient attention to either their complexities or their divergent national needs. Nonetheless, rather than concentrating on the wide-ranging differences among nations or regions, we offer a comprehensive feminist framework for analyzing the socioeconomic condition of women in Latin America and the Caribbean, at the same time providing a critique of the development literature.

Gita Sen and Caren Grown (1987) have convincingly argued that despite the apparent contrasts in patterns and consequences of development among Third World nations, actual differences are minimal. Sen and Grown identify a narrow spectrum of patterns and processes that bind such countries together: their unfavorable structural position in the world economy; their economic vulnerability to the changes in the world market and flows of capital; their internal inequalities in income, employment, land tenure, and control of resources; and their populations' destitution and lack of basic necessities, such as food, housing, and health care.

In addition to these structural features, found in varying degrees in all Latin American and Caribbean nations, other factors continue to aggravate these nations' position of relative disadvantage when compared to the industrialized West. Mona Etienne and Eleanor Leacock (1980, 17) have noted the importance of also considering "the particular mode of colonization, itself determined by the political and economic imperatives of the colonizer and the nature of the colonized society; the precise strategies of exploitation employed by the colonizer; and the strategies of accommodation or resistance adopted by the colonized." Within the remarkable convergences that can be found throughout diverse colonial contexts, this interplay of variables underscores the unique character of each colonial experience.

Understanding Third World Development

Development is an all-encompassing word used to summarize the overriding concerns and aspirations of advanced capitalist nations and their international agencies in undertaking initiatives and generating responses to a whole range of critical problems faced by what they categorized as the poor, "underdeveloped" countries of the world.[1] These chronic conditions include famine and malnutrition, displacement and homelessness, unemployment and underemployment, disease, the destruction of the environment, and political repression and violence. Survival problems remain historical constants for much of Latin America, the Caribbean, and the rest of the Third World, the outcome of the cumulative effects of the unequal and dependent relationships maintained for centuries. It has been accurately noted that "development would not exist without underdevelopment, wealth would not exist without poverty, and the domination of men would not exist without the subjection and submissiveness of women" (Mies et al. 1988, 3).

Until the mid-1980s the development policies promoted by Western nations were grounded on the notion that the world was divided as follows: the highly developed and more advanced capitalist industrial nations of the First World, the opposing socialist nations of the Second World (now a much smaller group), and the less developed (or developing) poor agricultural countries of the Third World. Another common distinction between the First and Third Worlds is the hemispheric division between the core countries of the North and the peripheral or semi-peripheral countries of the South. Behind these stratified views of the world is the claim that Western societies represent the ideal form of cultural, socioeconomic, and political development for Third World countries to emulate if they are to achieve progress, prosperity, and democracy. The antinomy of civilized Europe vis-à-vis its primitive colonial subjects has left a legacy of unequal power relations and ideological paradigms that still presuppose the natural inferiority of these populations.

The old argument of dependence theorists (Jalee 1964; Gunder Frank 1969), who claimed that discussion of a Third World is intended to hide the imperialism of exploiting and exploited nations, still holds some validity. In addition, the model obscures the forms of resistance and empowerment that emerge among these populations. Speaking about a Third World may wrongly imply that so many diverse countries constitute a particular entity or a world in themselves, separate from the capitalist and socialist worlds, when we are actually referring to a cluster of nations that are predominantly former colonial possessions of the present-day industrialized nations and have, therefore, always been integrated into the capitalist system of accumulation. Moreover, the term tends to mask the neocolonial relations that currently prevail between industrialized nations and their former colonial territories (Gunder Frank 1969). More recently, this commonly accepted term is being viewed not as the lower tier in a vertical ranking system but rather as a resisting nonaligned force (Minh-ha 1989). The regional integration and economic restructuring processes taking place in the 1990s will undoubtedly lead to a reassessment of these categories.

Not surprisingly, most of the development strategies and policies for Latin America and the Caribbean have been formulated from the ideological and economic perspectives and interests of the industrialized Western nations. Such plans are generally applied across the board, with scant attention to the specific national needs and realities of the territories they are intended to transform. Their overall failure is frequently attributed to the remnants of archaic forces that still loom over developing nations and supposedly keep them suspended in time, rather than to the misguided nature of the development projects. In reality, Latin American and Caribbean nations are faced with continued profound internal inequalities, the inability to meet the basic needs of their populations, rampant inflation, national deficits, and an unfavorable and vulnerable position in the international economy, exacerbated by foreign debt problems. These problems dispute the paternalistic tenets of most development policies. Although development agencies have begun to be more attentive to specific national needs, they are far from discarding profit-centered development in favor of people-centered programs. For their part, many developing countries are making concerted efforts to examine development on their own terms, in the hope that they can enhance the living conditions of larger segments of their poverty-stricken populations.

Historically, most development programs and policies have assumed that rapid industrialization and export-led economics would promote growth and reduce poverty. A secondary assumption was that modernization and economic development would result in political democracy.

The success or failure of these programs was then measured by increases in indexes of modernization—gross national product, per capita income, literacy rates, life expectancy, and fertility rates—rather than by the disappearance of authoritarian or dictatorial regimes. The prevalence of dictatorships even in the countries that have achieved a relative degree of economic development has discredited the assumed connection between development and democracy.

Industrialization and modernization projects have tended to rely on foreign investment, commercialization, and manufacturing for export rather than local consumption (Sen and Grown 1987). As a result, the development process has meant, to a large extent, the "denationalizing" of many Third World economies, because foreign industrial capital frequently interferes with or restricts the autonomy of local governments, as well as the capacity of national industries to compete in the world market. In addition, in order to promote their economies, these nations frequently become dependent on single-commodity export trade, leaving them extremely vulnerable to the fluctuations and perils of global markets. Such dependent, as opposed to self-sufficient, development strategies have been the norm rather than the exception.

A pioneering model for export-led industrialization projects in developing nations was Operation Bootstrap, an industrialization program introduced in Puerto Rico in 1948. Palmira N. Ríos's case study (1990; this volume) of Puerto Rico's industrialization process documents the resulting increased demand for female labor in the manufacturing sector. Although local governments of developing countries try to promote male-dominated industries, which they see as providing more stable jobs and higher wages than those where women workers predominate, Ríos's study shows that the foreign labor needs of multinationals are being met primarily by women.

Development policies and projects that are implemented from outside, without careful consideration of national infrastructures, internal human and natural resources, or needs for reform, can increase inequality in Latin America, the Caribbean, and other Third World regions. Agricultural development, for instance, without the precondition of agrarian reform and more equitable land distribution, has tended to benefit wealthy landowners rather than poor peasants. Moreover, it has often stimulated peasant migration from rural areas to towns and cities, disrupting the lives of families and entire communities. In some areas of Latin America and the Caribbean it is the women who were driven out of agricultural pursuits and forced to migrate, whereas in some African countries men have moved to towns and cities in search of jobs and left women to do agricultural work (Boserup 1970).

Gender and Development

A quick perusal of international data demonstrates that almost without exception, women *everywhere* in the world are worse off than men. On the whole, women have less power and money and more work and responsibility (Seager and Olson 1986, 7; Young, Fort, and Danner forthcoming). When the United Nations proclaimed International Women's Year in 1975, the data it released showed that women were performing two-thirds of the world's work and receiving only 10 percent of all income, while owning only 1 percent of the means of production (Bennholdt-Thomsen 1988b). The picture becomes even more distressing when we consider the enormous socioeconomic disparities between the highly industrialized and developing nations. First World nations constitute only one-fourth of the world's population, but they receive four-fifths of the income (Brandt Report 1980). Yet even within First World nations, women, relative to the men of their class and racial ethnic group, also tend to be disadvantaged.

The 1975 international call for integrating women into development was more a denunciation of the male-oriented biases in development policies and the invisibility to which official agencies had relegated women's participation than an acknowledgment that women had not been active participants in the development process, as they had been. Indeed, the pervasive idea that men were the primary earners had frequently led to the formulation of development policies that excluded or diminished women's productive roles and thus their status, added extra hours to their double burden when they had to replace men (now engaged in wage labor) in the subsistence activities that were performed collectively before, and often did not even account properly for women's actual participation and contributions.

It is difficult to address gender issues in the developing countries of Latin America and the Caribbean without recognizing that they are inextricably linked to a global capitalist and patriarchal model of accumulation and hence to the history of imperialist expansion and colonialism (Saffioti 1978; Mies et al. 1988). Although it is not always self-evident, both women and colonies have served as the foundations of industrial development of the economically dominant Western nations.

Colonialism, born in the fifteenth century—the gateway to discovery, exploration, and conquest—was to become the mainspring of European industrial development. Since the "discovery" of their existence by European settlers, primarily from Spain, Portugal, Great Britain, France, and the Netherlands, territories in the New World have served as the major sources of precious metals, labor, raw materials, and food products to support the commerce, consumption, and economic development of what are today's industrialized nations. The basis for the ascendancy of capitalism in Europe was the colonial exploitation of its overseas empires. Although the nature of colonization varied from one region of the world to another, the system was based on extracting the wealth of the new lands by using the labor of both the subjugated indigenous populations and that of the displaced and enslaved African populations to support the lavish lives of European aristocracies and the consumption needs of a rising bourgeoisie (Saffioti 1978; Etienne and Leacock 1980). The wealth and natural resources of the colonies were the essence of European mercantilist capitalism and, at a later stage, of its industrial revolution. The manufactured goods produced in European factories with the colonies' raw materials and labor found their way back into colonial markets. With some variations, this cycle has essentially perpetuated itself through the centuries.

In the Americas the United States emerged as a new colonial power to substitute for the Spanish, consolidating itself in the nineteenth century through the pursuit of its Manifest Destiny policies of territorial expansion and the Monroe Doctrine (1823), aimed at reducing European presence and influence in the hemisphere. After its Civil War (1861–65) the United States was determined to become the major economic and geopolitical power in the Americas.

In the twentieth century capitalism entered its new monopoly and multinational stages of development, and the neocolonial relations developed then still link the colonizing and colonized countries into a global economic network. The unequal relationship that has kept Latin American and Caribbean nations dependent helps explain the continuing internal turmoil and clamor for change emanating from most of these nations today.

It is quite evident in the colonial literature that from the beginning of the European monarchies' imperial expansion, the adventurers, missionaries, and officials who came to the New World had little regard for any patterns of communal and egalitarian relationships among the native populations subjugated during the colonial enterprise. In many precolonial societies women's position and participation in productive activities was parallel to that of men, rather than subservient (Saffioti 1978; Etienne and Leacock 1980). The imposition of European patriarchal relationships that presupposed the universal subordination of women in many instances deprived indigenous women of property and personal autonomy and restricted the productive functions and any public roles they might have played before colonization (Saffioti 1978; Etienne and Leacock 1980; Nash 1980). These policies continued through the centuries as colonial territories were integrated into the capitalist system of production, and persisted even after those countries gained independence, in part because of the neocolonial relations the industrialized nations still maintain with developing countries. The conditions of *internal colonialism* (Blauner 1972) that later emerged within Western metropolitan centers, wherein immigrant groups and racial minorities are relegated to a structurally marginal position, replicate the patterns of colonial relationships.

Before the work of Ester Boserup (1970), most of the classical development literature tended to ignore women's economic role and contributions. Assuming women were passive dependents, the literature relegated them to reproductive rather than productive roles, confining them to an undervalued domestic sphere isolated from the rest of the social structure. Little attention was paid to differences in productivity between women and men in different developing nations or to women's labor activities in the informal economy. One of Boserup's major contributions was to establish empirically the vital role of women in agricultural economies and to recognize that economic development, with its tendency to encourage labor specialization, was actually depriving women of their original productive functions and on the whole deteriorating their status. Acknowledged by many as a pathbreaker in the field of women and development (Benería 1982; Sen and Grown 1987; Bolles 1988), Boserup is also credited with documenting the existence of a gendered division of labor across nations and with showing that women's labor had not been reported in official records.

Shortcomings in Boserup's important work stem from her adherence to the modernization approach so prevalent at the time which reflected policies that encouraged the diffusion of capitalism. Boserup also did not pay enough attention to women's household labor as a basis for subordination or to the effects of capital accumulation in colonial settings on different groups (Benería and Sen 1981; Bolles 1988). Nonetheless, her research fostered an understanding of the dual aspect of colonial and contemporary development policies, which ideologically denigrated women's economic contributions while relying on and exploiting their labor.

Since Boserup's initial work, numerous studies at local, national, and international levels have documented the impact of development on women and confirmed their segregation in labor that generates the lowest wages and prestige. Among the best studies are those by Lourdes Benería (1982) and Carmen Diana Deere and Magdalena León (1982, 1987) describing the meaning and impact of development for rural women in Latin America and the Caribbean. Benería has emphasized the need to "counteract the ideological underevaluation of women's work" (1982, 135) by arguing for the inclusion of use-value as well as exchange-value production in defining active labor. She refers to the entire gamut of women's activities as ways of "making a living" rather than "earning a living," an approach that highlights the need to include a multiplicity of daily survival activities performed by Third World women that are otherwise excluded because they are not defined as waged work (also see Bose 1987; Rothstein, this volume).

Deere, Humphries, and León's (1982) theoretical model of "tiers of interaction" considers the impact of the macrosystem on different structural layers down to the household and individual units of production. Deere et al. thus establish the effects of changes in the international economy on national economies and social relations of developing countries. Deere and León (1982, 1987) concluded that in the division between productive and reproductive activities in Latin America, rural women bear a heavier burden than urban women, but the gendered division of labor within the productive sector is extremely heterogeneous. They thus confirm that in general terms, the process of development has multivaried effects on rural men and women.

One result of the conceptual evolution in the study of women and development is that feminist researchers are now paying attention to those previously ignored sectors of working women essential to Third World economies. For instance, historical studies on the New World colonial experience are beginning to examine the contribution of African enslaved women in both the productive and reproductive spheres and in those areas that made their experience so different from that of black men (Morrissey 1989; Bush 1990).

Several other key studies attempt to document the diverse roles and activities of women in the productive sphere. Elsa M. Chaney and Mary Garcia Castro (1989) describe the contemporary search of household domestic workers in Latin America and the Caribbean for a class identity, demanding both respect for their labor and legal recognition of their rights. The authors argue that these women are striving for identification as workers rather than as *muchachas* (serving girls). Ximena Bunster, Elsa M. Chaney, and Ellan Young (1985) produced a compelling study of rural, mostly indigenous, women in Peru who migrate to the cities and towns, where they find their greatest employment opportunities are as street vendors and servants. These two occupations account for one-third of all employed women in Latin America. Using what they call the "talking pictures" approach, which combines still photographs with open-ended interviews, these authors introduce an innovative, interdisciplinary technique not used by traditional development researchers in studying the working lives of women.

Through some of the studies mentioned, we can see why the feminist critique of development paradigms was a major factor in the emergence of women's studies as a field of academic inquiry in Latin American and

Caribbean higher education institutions during the 1980s. A significant body of scholarship has emerged and programmatic initiatives are being undertaken in spite of limited institutional resources and support, bureaucratic barriers, and the quasi-"subversive" character and implications of feminism, which in these countries is often regarded as a Western penetration that threatens traditional cultural values and sex roles.[2]

Women and the Economic Crisis of the 1980s

Beyond the commonalities of Third World conditions and issues outlined by Sen and Grown (1987), Latin American and Caribbean nations in the 1980s confronted significant new realities. Perhaps the most acute circumstances were the perennial foreign debt, rampant national levels of inflation, political repression and human rights violations, and continuous migration of native populations from rural areas to towns and cities or across national borders to industrialized countries, both legally or as undocumented workers. Whether these conditions are solved, contained, or worsen is heavily dependent on the multinational corporations that continue, with the help of the local ruling oligarchies, to subordinate these countries' national interests to their own growth and profit margins. Although local working-class and women's groups have organizations advocating their needs (Nash, this volume; Safa, this volume), the much-needed internal political and socioeconomic reforms have been hard to achieve, as the ruling political structures of many developing nations are frequently in alliance with foreign investment interests, sometimes at the expense of collective national interests.

In the 1980s and 1990s, the impact of the cyclical fluctuations of global capitalism has become more evident, particularly during the 1980s in Latin America and the Caribbean, where the economic crisis affected the survival potential of both authoritarian and democratic regimes. It was a major factor in bringing down military repressive governments in Argentina and Chile and in derailing the socialist reform aspirations of the Sandinistas in Nicaragua (Stallings and Kaufman 1989; Chinchilla 1990, this volume).

According to June Nash and María Patricia Fernández Kelly (1983), the 1980s' international crisis, compared by some to the Great Depression, reflects a new relationship between less developed and highly industrialized countries based on the geographic dispersion of the various stages of manufacturing production by large corporations. Attracted by low-cost labor, tax exemptions, and lax production restrictions, transnational corporate capital is radically altering the international workforce. These changes are also causing substantial transformations of families and community structures worldwide.

The growing integration of the world system of production no longer is based on the exploitation of primary sources but on offshore production, or the transfer of assembly plants, primarily in electronics, apparel, and textiles, from core to peripheral or semiperipheral countries. Nash (1983) has shown how industrial plant closings and decline in blue-collar employment in the United States are linked to the emergence of a new, cheaper industrial force in the Third World, now in direct competition with the First World labor force.

Many of the hidden aspects of offshore production occur in export processing zones. In a study of *maquiladoras* (subsidiaries of multinational corporations) on the U.S.-Mexico border, Fernández Kelly (1983) confirms that these industries are encouraging the use of young women's labor. As a development strategy, the *maquiladoras* exacerbate unemployment and underemployment and increase sex segregation in the labor force. Women's alternatives are not substantially improved because these companies offer no job security, provide minimal possibilities for advancement, and frequently expose workers to hazardous conditions. In fact, the families of women working in *maquiladoras* generally are poorer than other migrant households where the women work in service or commerce jobs (Young and Fort forthcoming). Thus, transnational corporations have contributed to the growing proletarianization of Latin American women, aptly described as working on the global assembly line.

This new international division of labor has had considerable economic and political impact on Latin American and Caribbean nations, since it keeps them at the mercy of external economic interests that determine what and how they will produce. To worsen an already detrimental situation, multinational corporations frequently generate economic havoc by moving their operations to a new port with more advantageous incentives when their "industrial peace" is threatened by labor activism or when they seek increased profit margins.

One continuing concern of both the developing and advanced capitalist nations is the increasing amount of women's poverty worldwide, associated with the rise in female-headed households. Whereas in North America and a large part of the Caribbean such households are primarily created by divorce or childbirth out of wedlock, in most Latin American countries the origin lies more in household splits due to migration of one partner from rural to urban areas or even out of the country in search of work, and in the case of several Central American countries war and violence have created large numbers of widows. The attention paid to this feminization of poverty since the 1980s' economic crisis partly stems from the increased visibility and effectiveness of women's movements around the world. Poor women in Latin America have used their responsibilities as mothers and domestic workers not only to enter the formal and informal economies but as the basis for political demands (Nash, this volume; Safa, this volume). Their organizing and advocacy on behalf of the survival of their children and families have made them as potentially explosive as the former colonies in which they live.

Women as a Last Colony

The conceptualization of women as a last colony, advanced by the work of German feminist scholars Mies, Bennholdt-Thomsen, and Werlhof (1988), has provided a valuable new interpretative model for feminist research on Third World issues. This framework underscores the convergences of race, class, and gender and recognizes one complex but coherent system of oppression. It also allows us to see that the patterns of sexism are compounded by a layer of oppression, shared by Third World men and women, brought about by the colonizing experience.

Werlhof (1988a, 25) argues that the relationship of Third World subsistence workers of both genders to First World multinationals in some ways resembles the relationship between men and women worldwide. Women and colonies are both low-wage and nonwage producers, share structural subordination and dependency, and are overwhelmingly poor. Werlhof contends that in response to its accumulation crisis, capitalism is now implicitly acknowledging that the unpaid labor of women in the household goes beyond the reproductive sphere into the production of commodities. Nevertheless, housewives are frequently and explicitly excluded from what is defined as the economy in order to maintain the illusion of the predominance of the male wage worker. The problems with this definition are increasingly obvious, as many Latin American and Caribbean households, using multiple income strategies, rely on women's informal economy activities or subsistence work (Rothstein, this volume).

Mies et al. (1988, 7) indicates there are actually three tiers in the capitalist pyramid of exploitation: (1) the holders of capital, (2) wage workers (mostly white men or the traditional proletariat) and nonwage workers (mostly women), and (3) housewives and subsistence producers (men and women) in the colonial countries. Using this model, both Werlhof (1988a) and Bennholdt-Thomsen (1988a) argue that the new international trend in the division of labor is toward the "housewifization" (*Hausfrauisierung*) of labor, namely, labor that exhibits the major characteristics of housework, and away from the classical proletariat whose labor is now being replaced. Of course, the housewife role entails different things across nations, ranging from cooking, cleaning, washing, and taking care of children and the elderly, to grinding maize, carrying water, or plowing the family plot. The determining factor is always whether or not these tasks are performed for wages. Werlhof (1988b, 173) establishes a key link between the undervalued work performed by women and that of Third World populations, which leads her to conclude that the classical proletariat is being replaced by the Third World worker and the housewife as the new "pillars of accumulation." This conclusion also points to the contradiction between any cultural or economic devaluation of women's work and the important role it actually plays.

Following this line of argument, the three authors note that, since the latter part of the nineteenth century, patriarchal capitalist practice and ideology have colonized women by the "housewifization" of their work: by attempting to isolate women in the domestic sphere and devaluing the work they perform there; by ideologically justifying it as a genetic predisposition based on their capacity for motherhood; by regarding any type of income they generate as supplementary or secondary, thus ascribing a lower status to their occupations; and ultimately, by controlling their sexuality. These power relations between men and women are thus comparable to the international division of labor between First and Third World countries. The present-day world economic crisis is not just another cycle of capitalism but rather a new phase of development relying on female forms of labor (i.e., doing any kind of work at any time, unpaid or poorly paid) wherein the industrialized powers try to force Third World nations to "restructure" or adapt their national economies to the needs of the world system for such flexible labor (Mies et al. 1988).

The analogy to housework is used at many levels. First, under some circumstances there literally has been an increase in the number of housewives in countries such as Mexico, Bolivia, and Colombia, particularly when migration or a switch to ranching from farming results in a loss of women's control over resources (Townsend 1993). Second, there is a rise in work that is like housework—especially in the informal economy and for both men and women—which is flexible and poorly paid, as well as occupationally segregated. Thus, the parallel to housework is exemplified in both the nature of the work and its dependent status.

Bennholdt-Thomsen (1988a) illustrates the practical outcomes occurring as capitalists come to view nonwage labor as a means of extracting surplus value. In a detailed analysis of current World Bank policy, she found that powerful development agencies made use of the profitability of nonwaged peasantry in Third World countries by granting credits for small-scale production, drawing peasants increasingly from subsistence to commercial production (p. 61). This development policy, promoted by the World Bank since the early 1970s, claims to attack absolute poverty through "investment in the poor" (p. 51). The real yield, however, has been increased profits for the agency from loans to the poor and increased external control over peasant subsistence work and resources. As

Bennholdt-Thomsen points out, development policy is in the hands of "a gigantic centralized apparatus of planning and administration" (1988b, 158). Any new policy trends are deliberately aimed at certain sectors of the population such as women and peasants, although the responses of those groups are not always the anticipated ones (Blumberg, this volume).

Empowerment

Women Organizing for Change

Women are not passive victims in the socioeconomic processes that maintain their lower status. Instead, they are developing creative ways in which to resist the new forms of subordination. Latin American activists expect that changes in sexist practice and ideology can be obtained during economic crises—an experience quite different from that of feminists in the core capitalist countries whose achievements were made in the context of improving material conditions. In Latin America and the Caribbean various types of resistance, solidarity, and collective action are used by women in diverse geographic regions and under different sociopolitical structures, a pattern that is beginning to be recognized in comparative studies of women's movements (Margolis 1993).

Although Latin American women's subsistence activities as peasant producers can be seen as similar to the unpaid housework of women in Europe and the United States, the resultant political strategies are different, as described by Nash (this volume), perhaps because of the class differences between them. In First World countries women have responded to cutbacks in government services to families by entering the paid labor force, especially in the service industry, and by taking over the tasks of eldercare and childcare. In Latin America and the Caribbean nations, though some women do create microenterprises (Blumberg, this volume), take jobs in export processing zones, or enter the service sector, the vast majority respond to the breakdown of their subsistence economy by organizing collective meals, health cooperatives, mothers' clubs, neighborhood water-rights groups, or their own textile and craft collectives, which produce goods both for street vending and for international markets. Thus, rather than *privatizing* their survival problems, these women *collectivize* them and form social-change groups based on social reproduction concerns. In these new terms, the political discourse and arena of struggle is not worker exploitation and control of the means of production but rather moral persuasion to place demands on the state for rights related to family survival.

Many Latin American women activists contend that their traditional roles as wives and mothers are the basis for these collective actions on behalf of their families. Although most of the groups are composed of poor women, they do not organize either explicitly on a class basis or at the workplace. Instead, they organize at a neighborhood level around a broad list of issues that they redefine as women's concerns, such as running water or transportation for squatter communities. Some feminist scholars argue that this approach constitutes a movement of women but not necessarily a feminist movement; others feel these tactics represent a form of working-class feminism that promotes consciousness of how gender shapes women's lives (Sternback et al. 1992). Safa (this volume) notes that this approach, which emphasizes women's traditional roles, is clearly different from European or U.S. women's movements, which are viewed as seeking participation in the public sphere based on the elimination (rather than the retention) of most gender distinctions. Others, such as Chandra Talpade Mohanty (1991, 28), suggest that challenging the state is not merely different but "a crucial context" for Third World women's struggles, precisely because it is the state that has created laws with implicit gender and race limitations. In fact, women did not receive even the right to vote in most Latin American countries until after 1940 (Seager and Olson 1986). On the other hand, some note that women's massive entry into this new political arena is what makes them "prime targets for cooptation by political parties, unions, and government bureaucracies" (Stephen 1993, 84), especially if no feminist or gender consciousness is involved. The multiple outcomes remain to be seen as women increase their presence in the public sphere.

Urban organizing is not the only form of empowerment. Indigenous and peasant women in rural areas find that agricultural issues are often paramount. Women's development-related activism in this setting includes struggles over land tenure, actions of landlords, and plantation working conditions—issues that link community and labor—as well as cultural concerns related to ethnic identity and survival of indigenous peoples (Chinchilla 1993). Norma Stoltz Chinchilla indicates that women's rural organizing has changed since the 1960s, when women were involved in housewives' committees, such as those of the Bolivian miners; in the 1980s more women participated in independent peasant organizations such as Mexican *ejidos* or other agrarian reform unions.

Other forms of resistance include women's participation in revolutionary movements. Not surprisingly, women on the left retained a commitment to changing the social relations of production, and many were critiqued for subordinating gender to class concerns. Early organizers saw themselves as engaged in a double militancy, carrying out both political and feminist activism in separate organizations (Sternbach et al. 1992). Nicaragua stands as an exception in that period and an example of how feminism has the potential to strengthen class struggle without being reduced by it, as exhibited in the Sandinista call for links between the women's movement and working-class organizations such as unions (Chinchilla 1990, this volume).

In many other Latin American countries the Catholic church, the left, and traditional political parties are seen as major obstacles to women's empowerment, necessitating considerable grassroots women's organizing. The result is a change in the concept of double militancy: instead of bringing class analysis to the women's movement, feminists try to bring a gender analysis to their political party, union, job, or neighborhood organization (Sternbach et al. 1992). Nancy Saporta Sternbach et al. argue that this change is reflected in the debates that occurred during the series of five feminist *Encuentros* held in Latin America, beginning in Bogotá, Colombia, in 1981 and culminating in San Bernardo, Argentina, in 1990.

New forms of feminist organizing have been generated that link the issues of nationality, race, class, and gender and whose mission is self-determined women's development. A. Lynn Bolles (1993) provides examples of such women's projects in the Commonwealth Caribbean including the Women and Development Unit (WAND), which promotes women's activities especially through income-generating projects, local technical assistance, and government advisement; Development Alternatives with Women for a New Era (DAWN), a network of activist researchers and policy makers; and the Caribbean Association for Feminist Research and Action (CAFRA), whose projects include monitoring the Caribbean Basin Initiative effects, exposing worker conditions in Jamaica's export processing zones, and aiding rural women through the Women in Caribbean Agriculture Project.

These brief examples give a sense of the wide range of alternatives used by women in Latin America and the Caribbean to achieve a measure of empowerment in the context of capitalist dependency and development.

Toward a Decolonization of Gender

Thus far, we have focused on the need to include the historical role of colonialism in understanding women's experiences in Latin America and the Caribbean. We have argued that the successful theory must not only separate us from the patriarchal and Eurocentric concepts and paradigms that have been so dominant in the traditional disciplines, but also analyze the commonalities between the various forms of women's subordination and the colonial subjugation of different populations within the capital accumulation process. The empowering theoretical and pragmatic question is, How can gender be decolonized?

The concept of decolonization was extensively discussed by Franz Fanon ([1961] 1968), who argued that to achieve the liberation of colonized peoples, it was necessary to change the whole social structure from the bottom up, creating a "new species" of human beings in substitution for the old (p. 35). He saw the historical process of decolonization as trying to "change the order of the world" and as "a program of complete disorder" (p. 36). Recognizing the antagonistic nature of the process, Fanon viewed ideological and socioeconomic decolonization as essential steps in transforming the historical relationships among the settler, the colonized, and the colonizer.

In attempting to denounce the oppressive psychological effects of colonialism and to lay the groundwork for the national liberation struggles of the African colonies, Fanon particularly did not distinguish between the ways in which colonialism might have affected the formation of men's and women's identities. Nonetheless, his work and that of Albert Memmi ([1957] 1965) provide a foundation for understanding the cumulative cultural and psychological effects of oppression on the colonized.

Etienne and Leacock (1980) were interested in analyzing the impact of colonization on women. They asserted that since the ultimate goal of the colonial system was the economic exploitation of both women and men (p. 17), it had a profound effect on personal relations between them. In some instances, the imposition of European patriarchal social structures destroyed the more egalitarian indigenous societies (Leacock 1980; Nash 1980). Since colonization systematically eroded the autonomy of women, the effects, though detrimental to both men and women, were more oppressive to women. Therefore, the understanding of the subordination of women in colonial and neocolonial contexts, both as women and as the cheapest producers of labor worldwide, requires recognition of these various layers of oppression. In these contexts, women's liberation struggles often coexist and must be balanced with other collective national liberation movements. The metaphor that in colonial and neocolonial societies women are "the slaves of slaves" (Latin American and Caribbean Women's Collective 1980) dramatizes how industrial and colonial nations have been historic allies in perpetuating a patriarchal order wherein women are subordinated and, in some cases, used as pawns or commodities (Nasimiyu 1990).

Most movements for self-determination among colonial nations have been far from advocating the liberation of women (Acosta-Belén 1986). On the contrary, women's resistance to male oppression is generally relegated to the margins, separated from other class and national struggles, and subordinated to the wider and presumed "higher" cause of national liberation. The issue is often treated as a divisive and detracting self-indulgence, rather than the result of oppressive social structures and relations. Thus, it is assumed that women can liberate themselves only after liberating all other oppressed sectors of society. Even in the best of circumstances, when women's equality is acknowledged as important by the state, as in the revolutionary experiences of Cuba and Nicaragua, token reforms become substitutes for much-needed transformations. Reconstruction in both men's and women's roles always manages to remain part of an unrealized future agenda.

Nevertheless, the efforts made by the socialist revolutions in Cuba and Nicaragua in creating different conditions for women should not be underrated (Chinchilla, this volume). In these two nations women have benefited from both general agrarian reforms and specific policies to develop cooperatives and increase women's participation in agriculture, as well as from direct state intervention on their behalf and more favorable health and working conditions (Deere and León 1987). Even in these contexts, however, women still face the power of traditional forces in their quest for achieving egalitarian relations in both the productive and household arenas.

Conclusion

If we accept the premise that the layer of subordination experienced by *any* woman because of her gender is in many ways comparable to that of any colonial subject (male or female), then, for women in Latin America, the Caribbean, and other Third World areas who historically share the commonality of the colonial experience, gender represents a compounding factor of their oppression, just as race or ethnicity does for women of color living in First World countries or indigenous, mestizo, and black populations in Latin America and the Caribbean. The concept of women as a last colony thus becomes a compelling metaphor of liberation and should be an integral part of any human rights struggle. Ultimately, therefore, we see a pressing need to focus on a worldwide project of gender decolonization that calls for profound reformulations and restructuring of the existing power relations between women and men at the domestic and societal levels.

The extent to which this process can be advanced within the dominant patriarchal capitalist system of production should frame analyses of and struggles to improve women's condition. Obviously, there are limits to the empowerment currently possible. We live in a world where the unfolding expansion of communication technology and mass culture will continue to force Western styles and concepts, with all their individualistic, competitive, hierarchical, sexist, and consumerist dimensions, on the rest of the world. While the worldwide triumph of capitalism is celebrated because of the rapid changes taking place in eastern Europe, workers in developed and developing countries continue to struggle for survival on a daily basis within a system of transnational capital linked to local capital, a system characterized by tremendous inequalities, erratic growth, intensification of conflict and competition, declining wages, greater numbers of vulnerable and marginal workers, and a general polarization of labor.

Although feminists share a universal struggle against gender subordination and for egalitarian relations, the experiences of Latin American and Caribbean women, with their compounding layers of oppression, will continue to generate a wide diversity of feminist and women's movements. Women are striving to decolonize gender through collective action reflected in the creation of worker organizations in agriculture and export processing zones, neighborhood groups challenging the state to deliver services, cultural affirmation and human rights struggles of indigenous peoples, and feminist research and activist groups, all working in the context of the agendas of international aid organizations and transnational corporations. These movements represent articulated responses from women of all classes, races, ethnicities, and nationalities who, in the midst of their socioeconomic and political difficulties, are carrying the struggle for liberation and equality forward on a variety of fronts, ranging from the home and within the family, to their communities and governments, to their international quests for peace, human rights, and a healthy environment, but most of all, for the possibility of a more just society.

NOTES

1. The term *underdevelopment* was commonly used in most of the literature before the mid-1960s. Third World intellectuals, in particular, considered the term to be value-laden and based on the notion that the Western industrialized nations were more qualified for setting the development norms and standards for the rest of the world. Beginning in the 1970s the terms *developing* or *Third World nations* have been more widely acceptable.

2. The emergence of women's studies programs in Latin American and Caribbean higher education institutions was a phenomenon of the 1980s. Among the programs established in these regions are the ones at El Colegio de México, the University of Costa Rica, the Universidad Nacional at Heredia (Costa Rica), the Confederación Universitaria Centroamericana (CSUCA), the University of Puerto Rico, the University of Buenos Aires, and the University of the West Indies.

REFERENCES

Acosta-Belén, Edna. 1986. "Puerto Rican Women in Culture, History, and Society." In *The Puerto Rican Woman: Perspectives on Culture, History, and Society,* ed. Edna Acosta-Belén, 1–29. New York: Praeger.

Benería, Lourdes, ed. 1982. *Women and Development: The Sexual Division of Labor in Rural Societies*. New York: Praeger.

Benería, Lourdes, and Gita Sen. 1981. "Accumulation, Reproduction, and Women's Role in Economic Development: Boserup Revisited." *Signs: Journal of Women in Culture and Society* 7: 279–298.

Bennholdt-Thomsen, Veronika. 1988a. " 'Investment in the Poor': An Analysis of World Bank Policy." In *Women: The Last Colony,* ed. Maria Mies, Veronika Bennholdt-Thomsen, and Claudia von Werlhof, 51–63. London: Zed.

———. 1988b. "Why Do Housewives Continue to be Created in the Third World Too?" In *Women: The Last Colony,* ed. Maria Mies, Veronika Bennholdt-Thomsen, and Claudia von Werlhof, 159–167. London: Zed.

Blauner, Robert. 1972. *Racial Oppression in America*. New York: Harper and Row.

Bolles, A. Lynn. 1988. "Theories of Women and Development in the Caribbean: The Ongoing Debate." In *Gender in Caribbean Development,* ed. Patricia Mohammed and Catherine Shepherd, 21–34. Cave Hill, Barbados: University of the West Indies, Women and Development Studies Project.

———. 1993. "Doing It for Themselves: Women's Research and Action in the Commonwealth Caribbean." In *Researching Women in Latin America and the Caribbean,* ed. Edna Acosta-Belén and Christine E. Bose, 153–174. Boulder, Colo.: Westview.

Bose, Christine E. 1987. "Devaluing Women's Work: The Undercount of Women's Employment in 1900 and 1980." In *Hidden Aspects of Women's Work,* ed. Christine Bose, Roslyn Feldberg, and Natalie Sokoloff, 95–115. New York: Praeger.

 Boserup, Ester. 1970. *Woman's Role in Economic Development*. New York: St. Martin's Press.

Brandt Report. 1980. *North-South: A Programme for Survival*. London: Pan World Affairs.

Bunster, Ximena, Elsa M. Chaney, and Ellan Young. 1985. *Sellers and Servants: Working Women in Lima, Peru*. New York: Praeger.

Bush, Barbara. 1990. *Slave Women in Caribbean Society*. Kingston, Jamaica: Heinemann; Bloomington: Indiana University Press; London: James Currey.

Chaney, Elsa M., and Mary Garcia Castro, eds. 1989. *Muchachas No More: Household Workers in Latin America and the Caribbean*. Philadelphia: Temple University Press.

 Chinchilla, Norma Stoltz. 1990. "Revolutionary Popular Feminism in Nicaragua: Articulating Class, Gender, and National Sovereignty." *Gender & Society* 4 (3): 370–397.

———. 1993. "Gender and National Politics: Issues and Trends in Women's Participation in Latin American Movements." In *Researching Women in Latin America and the Caribbean,* ed. Edna Acosta-Belén and Christine E. Bose, 37–54. Boulder, Colo.: Westview.

 Deere, Carmen Diana. 1987. "The Latin American Agrarian Reform Experience." In *Rural Women and State Policy: Feminist Perspectives on Latin*

American Agricultural Development, ed. Carmen Diana Deere and Magdalena León, 165–190. Boulder, Colo.: Westview.

Deere, Carmen Diana, Jane Humphries, and Magdalena León. 1982. "Class and Historical Analysis for the Study of Women and Economic Change." In *Women's Roles and Population Trends in the Third World,* ed. R. Anker, M. Buvenic, and N. Youssef, 87–114. Geneva: International Labour Organization.

Deere, Carmen Diana, and Magdalena León. 1982. "Peasant Production, Proletarianization, and the Sexual Division of Labor in the Andes." In *Women and Development: The Sexual Division of Labor in Rural Societies,* ed. Lourdes Benería, 29–64. New York: Praeger.

———, eds. 1987. *Rural Women and State Policy: Feminist Perspectives on Latin American Agricultural Development.* Boulder, Colo.: Westview.

Etienne, Mona, and Eleanor Leacock, eds. 1980. *Women and Colonization: Anthropological Perspectives.* New York: Praeger.

Fanon, Franz. [1961] 1968. *The Wretched of the Earth.* New York: Grove Press.

Fernández Kelly, M. Patricia. 1983. *For We Are Sold, I and My People: Women and Industry in Mexico's Frontier.* Albany: State University of New York Press.

Frank, Andre Gunder. 1969. *Latin America: Underdevelopment or Revolution.* New York: Monthly Review.

Genovese, Eugene. 1965. *The Political Economy of Slavery.* New York: Pantheon.

Jalee, Pierre. 1964. "Third World? Which Third World?" *Revolution* 1:7.

Kardam, Nüket. 1991. *Bringing Women In: Women's Issues in International Development Programs.* Boulder, Colo.: Lynne Reinner.

Latin American and Caribbean Women's Collective. 1980. *Slaves of Slaves: The Challenge of Latin American Women.* London: Zed.

Leacock, Eleanor. 1980. "Montagnais Women and the Jesuit Program for Colonization." In *Women and Colonization: Anthropological Perspectives,* ed. Mona Etienne and Eleanor Leacock, 25–42. New York: Praeger.

Margolis, Diane Rothbard. 1993. "Women's Movements around the World: Cross-Cultural Comparisons." *Gender & Society* 7 (3): 379–399.

Memmi, Albert. [1957] 1965. *The Colonizer and the Colonized.* Boston: Beacon Press.

Mies, Maria, Veronika Bennholdt-Thomsen, and Claudia von Werlhof. 1988. *Women: The Last Colony.* London: Zed.

Minh-ha, Trinh T. 1989. *Woman, Native, Other: Writing Postcoloniality and Feminism.* Bloomington: Indiana University Press.

Mohanty, Chandra Talpade. 1991. "Cartographies of Struggle: Third World Women and the Politics of Feminism." In *Third World Women and the Politics of Feminism,* ed. Chandra Talpade Mohanty, Ann Russo, and Lourdes Torres, 1–47. Bloomington: Indiana University Press.

Morrissey, Marietta. 1989. *Slave Women in the New World: Gender Stratification in the Caribbean.* Lawrence: University of Kansas Press.

Nash, June. 1980. "Aztec Women: The Transition from Status to Class in Empire and Colony." In *Women and Colonization: Anthropological Perspectives,* ed. Mona Etienne and Eleanor Leacock, 134–148. New York: Praeger.

———. 1983. "The Impact of the Changing International Division of Labor on Different Sectors of the Labor Force." In *Women, Men, and the International Division of Labor,* ed. June Nash and María Patricia Fernández Kelly, 3–38. Albany: State University of New York Press.

Nash, June, and María Patricia Fernández Kelly, eds. 1983. *Women, Men, and the International Division of Labor.* Albany: State University of New York Press.

Nasimiyu, Ruth. 1990. "Female and Child Labor in Kenya in the Twentieth Century." Unpublished manuscript.

Ríos, Palmira. 1990. "Export-Oriented Industrialization and the Demand for Female Labor: Puerto Rican Women in the Manufacturing Sector, 1952–1980." *Gender & Society* 4 (3): 321–337.

Saffioti, Heleieth I. B. 1978. *Women in Class Society.* New York: Monthly Review.

Seager, Joni, and Ann Olson. 1986. *Women in the World: An International Atlas.* New York: Simon and Schuster.

Sen, Gita, and Caren Grown. 1987. *Development, Crises, and Alternative Visions.* New York: Monthly Review.

Stallings, Barbara, and Robert Kaufman, eds. 1989. *Debt and Democracy in Latin America.* Boulder, Colo.: Westview.

Stephen, Lynn. 1993. "Anthropological Research on Latin American Women: Past Trends and New Directions for the 1990s." In *Researching Women in Latin America and the Caribbean,* ed. Edna Acosta-Belén and Christine E. Bose, 77–97. Boulder, Colo.: Westview.

Sternback, Nancy Saporta, Marysa Navarro-Aranguren, Patricia Chuchryk, and Sonia E. Alvarez. 1992. "Feminisms in Latin America: From Bogotá to San Bernardo." *Signs: Journal of Women in Culture and Society* 17 (2): 393–434.

Townsend, Janet. 1993. "Housewifisation and Colonisation in the Colombian Rainforest." In *Different Places, Different Voices: Gender and Development in Africa, Asia, and Latin America,* ed. Janet H. Momsen and Vivian Kinnaird, 270–277. London: Routledge.

Werlhof, Claudia von. 1988a. "Women's Work: The Blind Spot in the Critique of Political Economy." In *Women: The Last Colony,* ed. Maria Mies, Veronika Bennholdt-Thomsen, and Claudia von Werlhof, 13–26. London: Zed.

———. 1988b. "The Proletarian Is Dead: Long Live the Housewife!" In *Women: The Last Colony,* ed. Maria Mies, Veronika Bennholdt-Thomsen, and Claudia von Werlhof, 168–181. London: Zed.

Young, Gay, and Lucia Fort. Forthcoming. "Household Responses to Economic Change: Migration and Maquila Work in Northern Mexico." *Social Science Quarterly.*

Young, Gay, Lucia Fort, and Mona Danner. Forthcoming. "Moving from 'The Status of Women' to 'Gender Inequality': Conceptualization, Social Indicators, and an Empirical Application." *Gender & Society.*

CHAPTER 2

✳

Gender, Industrialization, Transnational Corporations, and Development

An Overview of Trends and Patterns

KATHRYN B. WARD AND JEAN LARSON PYLE

Since the middle 1980s research on global restructuring, industrialization, and gender has fundamentally altered past conceptual frameworks. In the early 1980s key theoretical and empirical issues revolved around the importance of women in development and whether women were integrated into the development process or marginalized by it (Scott 1986; Tiano 1987; Ward 1988b; Joel 1989). The dialogue often involved dichotomous approaches that analyzed advantages and disadvantages of industrialization for women or examined women's roles in production and reproduction or in the public and private spheres.

More recent research, however, has largely resolved these earlier controversies and altered the binary nature of the analyses. For example, studies have demonstrated the critical importance of women to economic development: women's labor has been essential for labor-intensive, export-oriented development (Ward 1988b; Fernández Kelly 1989; Lim 1990). Further, failure by development theorists and planners to understand the constraints on women or to incorporate women's contributions to formal, informal, and household economies into development programs has led to limited socioeconomic development in many areas and inadequate responses to numerous global crises in agriculture or the environment (Overholt et al. 1985; Sen and Grown 1987).

In addition, the newer literature on women in development reveals that women's marginalization involves more complex dimensions than envisioned in the past (Scott 1986; Tiano 1987; Joel 1989). This research shows that even women who would have been considered integrated into

37

the development process under earlier analyses, such as women employed in transnational corporations, are actually subordinated in low-level, dead-end jobs with low wages relative to men (Scott 1986). Given this measure of women's relative equality, many argue that as development has proceeded, the economic position of women has largely deteriorated (Ward 1984, 1988b; Sen and Grown 1987; Tiano 1987).

Correspondingly, dichotomous theoretical approaches have been abandoned or replaced by analyses that address these complexities and contradictions. The issue of the advantages and disadvantages of industrialization for women is now viewed as more complicated. The production/reproduction framework is employed less often because of the recognition that both processes (production and reproduction, particularly social reproduction) occur in formal and informal work as well as in the household (for a history of these debates, see Bruce 1989; J. L. Collins 1990; Gimenez 1990; Stichter 1990). Similarly, the public/private dichotomy has been replaced by more accurate depictions of the interdependent reality of women's and men's socioeconomic lives, where women's work includes some combination of formal, informal, and household labor (Ward 1990b, 1993; Hossfeld forthcoming). Here formal work refers to waged work that is regulated by the state and covered by benefits; informal work is waged and/or self-employed but unregulated work; and household labor is unregulated and receives neither wages nor benefits (Sen and Grown 1987; Portes, Castell, and Benton 1989).

The literature on women's industrial labor and its relation to informal and household work can be understood only in the larger context of changes in the world economy that have significantly affected women's economic roles. Global restructuring in the latter part of the 1980s was characterized by three trends. First, there was a movement toward market-based economies, in particular, export-oriented strategies, at the behest of international financial institutions such as the World Bank and International Monetary Fund (Mitter 1986). Second, the rapid globalization of productive and marketing activities by transnational corporations from many countries was accompanied by substantial informalization and subcontracting of work arrangements beyond state regulation (Portes et al. 1989), or what Harvey (1989) labels "flexible accumulation." Finally, various economic crises, involving periodic recessions, debt, and the environment, have occurred. As a consequence of all these changes, industrial and family-based economies now exist side by side in a mixture of factory organization and subcontracting to family sweatshops that maintains men's control over women workers (Harvey 1989).

Several themes are clear in this portion of the women-in-development literature. First, in the six years of research between 1986 and 1992, we find many similarities and some instructive differences regarding the use of women's labor and the effects of employment in export-led development and transnational corporations' production networks. As wages have risen in some areas, transnationals have cut labor costs by various combinations of relocating production to another tier of low-wage countries, increasing the use of subcontracting and/or homework (home-based assembly), or restructuring work through automation (Heyzer 1988; Elson 1989; Harvey 1989; Portes et al. 1989; Kamel 1990; Pyle and Dawson 1990). These trends reveal the growing relationship of industrial work to the informal sector and the household. Second, we note an implicit and explicit need for theoretical and empirical redefinition of "work" to capture the reality that, particularly for women, daily work often takes place in the three spheres of the formal and informal sectors and the household (Mitter 1986; Benería and Roldán 1987; Ward 1990b; Benería 1991; Hossfeld forthcoming). Third, women's resistance to unequal situations and their efforts to empower themselves involve many diverse strategies and encompass struggles in all three spheres.

Furthermore, we see the importance of the intertwining of class, race or ethnicity, and gender in shaping women's economic roles. State policy, independently or in conjunction with transnationals, plays a critical role here because it can be used to incorporate women or limit their access to opportunities. If drawn into the development process, women, people of color, and/or poor people are often restricted in their choices, and their activism is suppressed by state policy. Because of the importance of the intersection of gender, race, and class with the state, it is clear that new theoretical frameworks and praxis must be developed to incorporate these factors.

Women and Industrialization

In the early 1980s women-in-development scholars debated whether employment in transnationals was beneficial for women or if they were being exploited in yet another way, as low-wage workers, employed at most for a few years, and working under unhealthy conditions (for a review of this earlier literature, see Lim 1985; Tiano 1987; Ward 1988b; Joel 1989, 1990). Few references to this controversy have been made since then. Linda Lim (1985, 1990) continued to argue that such employment is an advantage to women, while others maintained that the net impact of such employment on women was unfavorable (Ward 1988b, 1990a).

Instead, from the mid-1980s onward, we find that this dichotomous debate has largely been replaced by analyses acknowledging the contradictions and dynamics of women's employment in transnational corporations. This newer view recognizes that transnationals have some positive and many adverse effects on women, which evolve over time because of changes in corporate strategy, state policy, geographical location, and/or worker resistance.

Although employment in transnational firms is a small proportion of women's work in the global economy, it remains a critical component for several reasons. First, women's work in these firms constitutes a growing proportion of women's work in currently developing countries (Ward 1988b; Benería 1989; Lim 1990) due to the primacy placed on the export-oriented industrial growth strategies involving transnationals by international development and financial institutions. As a result, transnationals now arise from a wider range of countries, including Japan and the newly industrializing countries (NICs) in Asia. Second, export-oriented transnational firms constitute a dynamic sector in which continual change (automation, increased use of subcontracting and homework, and movement into new tiers of countries) affects rapidly expanding numbers of women. Finally, researchers increasingly recognize the direct links of formal sector transnational employment to the many women working in the informal sector and the household.

Since the mid-1980s much research has examined women's experiences in transnational corporations and in the informalized layers of subcontracting and homework they are establishing. Such production networks span both the currently developing and the industrialized countries. In reviewing these studies, we find similarities across regions as well as unique local patterns. On the one hand, the new research has increased our understanding of the parallels that exist globally in the importance of women's labor to transnational corporations' production networks in industries such as electronics, garments/textiles, shoes/footwear, toys, plastics, and consumer products and the way gender, class, and ethnicity interact in shaping the composition of the workforce. Similarities also exist in the sometimes contradictory yet largely negative effects of transnational employment on women and how these effects persist or change over time as corporations relocate to lower-wage countries, increase their layers of subcontracting and homework, or automate. On the other hand, this research has shown how the effect of transnationals on women is mediated by preexisting cultural patterns of male dominance, state policies, and workers' resistance that can vary across countries. As a consequence, profiles of women's labor-force participation differ among some countries.

Importance of Women's Labor in Transnational Corporations

Women are employed in transnational corporations in many areas of the world: Pacific Asia, Latin America, a few areas of Africa, and throughout industrialized countries. Important differences exist by region.

Several groups of Pacific Asian countries have pursued export-oriented growth by attracting transnationals in a wide range of labor-intensive industries. Research confirms that women workers are critical to the existence of these industries throughout this region (Heyzer 1986, 1988, 1989). Since the 1960s, in the newly industrializing countries of South Korea, Taiwan, Hong Kong, and Singapore, women have provided the needed supply of low-cost labor for the remarkably rapid economic growth this region has experienced (Li 1985; Gallin 1990). The Philippines, Malaysia, Indonesia, and Thailand have relied on female workers since the 1970s; state development agencies in Thailand and Malaysia still actively advertise their availability to attract foreign investors (Pyle and Dawson 1990). In the latest group of Asian countries to establish export processing zones during the 1980s, such as Sri Lanka, Bangladesh, and areas of China and India, there is heavy reliance on the labor of women and often children (Rosa 1987; Sultana 1990). In addition, export processing zones are being planned for other developing countries as diverse as Iran, Vietnam, and Mongolia.

New studies on women's employment in transnational corporations in Latin America center on the *maquiladoras* along the United States border with Mexico and on those industries located in Mexico City, Costa Rica, Peru, Colombia, Brazil, and the Caribbean (Benería and Roldán 1987; Humphrey 1987; Peña 1987; Ruiz and Tiano 1987; Young 1987; Ríos 1990; Scott 1990; Tiano 1990; Truelove 1990; Yelvington 1993). The free trade zones along the Mexican border and in the Caribbean produce mostly garments and electronics and hire predominantly women (Gereffi 1990). In contrast to *maquiladora* production, small sweater-making workshops have expanded in rural Mexico (Wilson 1991). These backstreet shops or homesites rely extensively on women's labor. In addition, the Caribbean is the initial offshore location for newer service industry jobs in banking, airline reservations, and telemarketing (Anderson 1989; Freeman 1989; Kamel 1990).

In a few areas of Africa transnational firms employ women assembly workers. In South Africa they have used mostly black men as workers, leaving women to work as domestics (Cock 1988). Although black women were finally allowed to become factory workers, they were the last group to be employed, and a very small percentage of them work in transnationals (Seidman 1985; for a history of women cannery workers, see Berger 1990). Mauritius established the first export-oriented free trade zone on the African continent. This zone focused on textiles and garment industries and hired female workers (Hein 1986; Rosa 1987). Proximity to Europe and well-behaved workforces have made North

African countries attractive sites for production. In clothing factories established in Morocco, female labor was also preferred (Joekes 1987).

Transnational corporations have also set up operations in several countries in the western European semiperiphery, such as Greece, Spain, and the Republic of Ireland. The European textile and clothing industry has developed extensive links via coproduction or subcontracting with firms in eastern Europe and northern Africa that employ mostly women (Redclift and Mingione 1985; Mitter 1986; Elson 1989; Hadjicostandi 1990; Pyle 1990a, b). Many of these firms, such as Benetton, are marketing ventures that coordinate subcontracted production activities of family- and sweatshop-based industries (Harvey 1989).

State policies in this region have differentially affected workforce gender composition. For example, in Greece state-sponsored transnational garment manufacturing generally has employed women and structured production to take place both in the factory and at home under a piece-rate system (Hadjicostandi 1990). By contrast, the government of the Republic of Ireland designed its export-oriented development strategy to attract corporations that would employ primarily men and used discriminatory state employment and policies on family/reproductive rights to limit women's employment (Pyle 1990b).

In the United States transnational corporations operate in the same types of industries (i.e., garments and electronics) as in developing countries (Safa 1986; Lamphere 1987; Rosen 1987; Fernández Kelly and Garcia 1988, 1992; Fernández Kelly 1989; Hossfeld 1990, forthcoming; Kamel 1990). Contrary to the widespread impression that electronics and garments are declining industries, total employment in the apparel industry in the United States is greater than in the automotive, steel, and electronics industries combined (Fernández Kelly 1989).

Patterns in the composition of the labor force evolve in relation to the hiring preferences of the transnational corporations, labor shortages, state policies, and preexisting relations of male domination as well as ethnicity and class. Although the workforces in electronics consist largely of young, single women, some variation has occurred over time, and married women are employed by textiles/garment and electronics firms in countries such as Thailand and the Philippines (Lim 1990). In Ciudad Juárez, Mexico, when *maquila* employers increased job benefits to attract more workers, the proportion of men increased; but in other cities where employers did not increase benefits, this pattern did not occur (Catanzarite and Strober 1993). In Pacific Asia the state has been active in shaping the workforce via family policies and family planning programs that manipulate fertility rates either to increase the current supply of women workers or to augment the future labor supply. In Thailand and the Philippines cultural traditions have permitted women wider economic roles, whereas in Taiwan and Japan patriarchal norms have restricted women's employment in the formal sector to the period before marriage (Carney and O'Kelly 1990; Gallin 1990).

Ethnicity, class, and gender also shape the structure of the transnational corporation workforce. For example, in Taiwan in the late 1970s managers and union leaders in factories were predominantly mainland Chinese military men, whereas the workers were native Taiwanese, largely women (Arrigo 1985). Similarly, in Malaysia native Malay women are more likely to be found in assembly work than Chinese women (Salih and Young 1989). Such patterns also occur in Mexico and Latin America (Fernández Kelly and Garcia 1988, 1992; Zavella 1988; Fernández Kelly 1989). For example, Kevin Yelvington's (1993) research in Trinidad reveals that line workers are women, predominantly black, while floor supervisors are men, mainly white. Annie Phizacklea's (1990) research on the small-firm sector of the fashion industry of the United Kingdom found that production relations are conditioned by class, gender, and ethnicity. Last, in Los Angeles the labor force in garment manufacture is largely female, 91 percent of whom are minority, chiefly Hispanic (Fernández Kelly 1989).

Effects of Employment in Transnational Corporations on Women

Literature from the late 1980s and early 1990s on the effects of employment in transnational corporations on women supports two major points. First, this type of work has contradictory effects on women; positive aspects can exist even in the presence of widespread adverse impacts. Because of this recognition, the earlier dichotomous discussion regarding whether such employment was beneficial or disadvantageous for women has been replaced by a more complex analysis. Second, corporate strategies in the late 1980s increasingly involved cost-cutting measures such as relocation of production to lower-wage countries, increased use of subcontracting/homework, and/or automation, each of which has definite effects on women workers.

Female factory workers often consider transnational corporation employment a favorable option initially, because it provides them immediate earned income, material benefits, and more independence from their families than existing alternatives (Agarwal 1988; Salaff 1988). Some women in the newly industrializing countries have experienced improved working conditions and absolute wage levels over time due to worker resistance and organization. Lim (1990) argues that although wages are low in these corporations relative to industrialized countries and working conditions more adverse, in many areas transnational firms offer conditions and pay that are relatively better than those of other local employers.

On the other hand, most research since 1985 shows that, over time, women working in transnationals encounter a variety of adverse effects: occupational segregation and lack of advancement possibilities, job insecurity or loss, wages relatively lower than men's, and a variety of oppressive working conditions. Women occupy low positions on occupational ladders, and there is an absence of opportunities to gain skills and advance in the job hierarchy (Humphrey 1987). These jobs are often precarious, and in recessions, enterprises employing predominantly women are the most likely to cut back or close. For example, South Korean women remain a peripheral workforce (Phongpaichit 1988).

Relative male/female wage differentials have persisted over time and appear to be substantially due to discrimination, even in newly industrializing countries such as Taiwan and South Korea (Gannicott 1986; Amsden 1989). Subsistence or lower wage levels often prevail, and transnational corporations may rely on households to support low-wage workers. For example, in Indonesia corporations have located production in rural areas because they can pay the young women they employ less than subsistence wages since they live with their families (Mather 1985; Wolf 1990b, 1993). Cynthia Truelove (1990) argues that agribusiness transnationals in the coffee industry established rural mini-*maquiladoras* in Colombia, employing women at below-subsistence wages to produce shoes and garments for export. The year-round work of women subsidizes the wages of male agricultural workers, who are employed only seasonally.

In parts of Latin America employment in transnational corporations has little impact either on high unemployment rates for women and men or on subsistence wages, even for women with extensive labor histories (Tiano 1990; for an exception, see Catanzarite and Strober 1993). Many Latin American women display ambivalent feelings toward this type of work, because although they need money for household survival, this form of economic activity contradicts women's cultural roles (Young 1987; Tiano 1990). Transnationals in Mexico have capitalized on these contradictions to reduce unionization of Mexican women to less than 10 percent and thereby remove a source of upward pressure on wages (Kamel 1990).

Moreover, conditions of employment are often oppressive with long hours, forced overtime, increased production quotas or speedups, poor working conditions or housing, stress, and harassment from management and the state. These conditions lead to deterioration of workers' health and often to high turnover, which has been particularly documented for

Asia. Although conditions may have improved in some newly industrial-izing countries, adverse impacts persist throughout most of the region (Rosa 1987; Agarwal 1988; Heyzer 1989; Pyle and Dawson 1990; Sultana 1990). As a result, workers continue to resist and unionize (Ong 1987; Mai 1989; Kamel 1990). In the latest group of Asian countries to attract foreign investment, for example, Bangladesh and Sri Lanka, condi-tions are the worst. Furthermore, in Pacific Asia the state has always been active in controlling the workforce in transnational corporations, often at the cost of democratic movements and human rights (Agarwal 1988; Heyzer and Kean 1988; Enloe 1989). Lourdes Arrigo (1985) examines parallels between Taiwan and South Korea, the Philippines and Malaysia in terms of military dictatorships that maintained a stable economic climate for foreign investment.

In regard to the second major effect of employment in transnationals, each of the corporate cost-cutting strategies used throughout the world in the latter part of the 1980s—including relocation to lower-wage coun-tries, development of extensive networks of subcontracting and home-work, and automation—has had distinctly negative effects on women workers. As corporations relocate to lower-wage countries, women in the original country lose jobs. For example, wages in Caribbean countries are higher than in Mexico or in some Asian countries (Massiah 1989; Griffith 1990; Yelvington 1993), and employment can be shifted. Relocation is particularly disadvantageous for the original women workers if they are in low-skill jobs in a country that is restructuring its export-led economy toward higher technology products, such as South Korea (Hyo-chae 1988), or if they are in areas such as the Caribbean (or even the United States) where slow growth means few alternative job opportunities. In addition, as corporations move production into new tiers of countries, as has occurred in Asia, these firms and their local networks commonly adopt the same exploitative practices they formerly used in other coun-tries.

Subcontracting to local factories and homework (home-based assem-bly) have increased throughout the world from Mexico, the United States, and Europe to Taiwan, China, Bangladesh, and India (Arrigo 1985; Benería and Roldán 1987; Harvey 1989; Standing 1989; Sultana 1990). These extended production networks cut costs because corporations can pay lower wages than in factories, bypass provision of benefits, and avoid protective legislation. These workers are unlikely to unionize and their employment can be immediately terminated in an economic downturn. The women involved are often married or heads of households, and such work is their only option for combining home duties with participation in the wage economy. At the lowest level of the subcontracting pyramid in Taiwan, for example, mothers and children assemble components at home at piece 'rates about half the hourly wage for factory work (Arrigo 1985). In Mauritius transnational corporations locate factories throughout the country to avoid unionization efforts and to use homeworkers (Hein 1986).

Automation of existing industries or accompanying the restructuring of an economy toward more technologically complex industries has differential gender effects on employment, because it tends to reduce the number of lower-skill jobs that are primarily female. Governments in Taiwan and South Korea are deliberately altering the structure of industries in export processing zones by shifting to higher technology, automation, heavier industries, and men workers (Hyo-chae 1988; Gereffi 1990). Kamal Salih and Mei Ling Young's study of the semiconductor industry in Malaysia (1989) reveals that, although there was net growth in employment in this industry from 1977 to 1984, the proportion of women decreased. This trend is also expected to occur in the garment industry when it automates (Elson 1989).

Redefinitions of Work

Global restructuring, industrialization, and transnational corporations are increasingly linked to the growing informal sector and to unwaged work in the household, both because of these corporations' burgeoning networks of subcontracting and homework and because people are forced to find informal sector work and/or increase household subsistence activities in times of economic crisis and retrenchment. This recognition reinforces the longstanding theme in women-in-development literature that much of the work women do takes place in the informal sector and household and often is omitted from statistics on labor force participation. Because women predominate in the work done in these sectors, formal labor force data present a particularly inadequate profile of women's economic contributions (Benería 1989, 1991) and of economies that include a variety of activities such as large factories, informal sectors, and ethnic enclaves (Harvey 1989).

As a consequence, much of the research on women and work since 1984 has emphasized the need to redefine 'work' (Mies 1986; Standing 1989; Ward 1990b, 1993; Benería 1991; Hossfeld forthcoming). Women's and men's work must incorporate all three dimensions—paid labor in the formal sector, paid informal labor, and unpaid labor in the household—and should be analyzed along a continuum from formal to informal to household work, as described by Kathryn Ward (1990b). Parts of this work continuum have been suggested by others, but none has incorporated all three dimensions (Bruce and Dwyer 1987; Stichter and

Parpart 1988a, 1990; Grown and Sebstad 1989; Collins and Gimenez 1990; Nash 1990). Benería (1991) reviews the widespread efforts— conceptual, methodological, and empirical—since the mid-1970s to correct the underestimation of women's work in subsistence production, unaccounted paid work, domestic production, and volunteer work.

The majority of the world's women work in two to three of these categories, a situation Karen Hossfeld (forthcoming) has aptly called "the triple shift." For example, Joycelin Massiah (1989) describes the sixteen-hour-a-day triple shift activities of women in the Caribbean, and Noeleen Heyzer (1989) provides a detailed account for Asian women. The boundaries of the triple shift are fluid for women and relatively rigid for men (Ward 1990b). Men define work as something that takes place outside the household (Hossfeld forthcoming) and rarely engage in household labor (Hochschild 1989), whereas women's work spans all three sectors. Hossfeld (forthcoming) found that, in the Silicon Valley, women worked up to fifteen hours a day in various combinations of the triple shift, while men were often unemployed and worked far fewer hours. Caren A. Grown and Jennefer Sebstad (1989) found that poor women may spend up to sixty hours per week in unpaid household labor.

Informal Sector

Informal sector work is heterogeneous, encompassing entrepreneurial activities and wage labor that is unregulated by the state. This sector includes subcontracted industrial and service work, retail activities (street vendors), domestic service, the sex trade, and agricultural work. Although predicted to disappear over time with the expansion of the capitalist world system (Chase-Dunn 1989), the informal sector and women's participation in it have expanded dramatically (Harvey 1989). Whether this sector is part of the logic of late capitalism or represents another mode of economic organization has been debated (Harvey 1989; Portes et al. 1990; Ward 1993), but for the most part, researchers have ignored significant gender differences in informal sector activities.

Women and men enter the informal sector for different reasons. For men, the informal sector often produces more income than the formal sector and provides upward mobility during economic restructuring (Schmink 1986; Brydon and Chant 1989; Ward 1990b). In Latin America and Africa urban men make up 60 to 75 percent of the informal sector business owners and operators (Grown and Sebstad 1989). Men often become subcontractors, controlling the labor of women homeworkers.

For women, informal sector work is usually a strategy for economic survival used in addition to formal paid labor and household subsistence activities (Schmink 1986; Benería and Roldán 1987). This is particularly the case for female heads of households, who constitute an average of one-third of the world's households and as many as one-half in some countries (Nash 1988b; Bruce 1989; Moser 1989). In addition, many women seek to avoid the contradictory pulls of economic necessity, childcare and household duties, and patriarchal ideologies against women working outside the home by engaging in informal sector work in the home. The money earned may give them some power within the household (Mizan 1992).

Ethnic and gender differences are pronounced in the informal sector. For example, in the Miami garment industry most manufacturers are Jewish, the subcontractors are 90 percent Cuban men, and the workers are 95 percent Cuban women (Fernández Kelly and Garcia 1992). In addition, immigrants are central to the informalization strategy throughout the world, where they labor in subcontracting networks at manufacturing or service tasks, as domestics, or in the sex trade (Enloe 1989; Kamel 1990). Immigrants often are economically vulnerable and located in low-paid service and assembly work (Sassen 1988), although differences among immigrant groups exist. Fernández Kelly and Garcia (1988, 1992) find that women immigrants from Cuba who worked in ethnic enclaves were able to earn more than the economically vulnerable Mexican women working in garment assembly plants in Los Angeles. Cuban women's work facilitated the economic mobility and wealth of Cuban men.

Women's participation in the informal sector globally is higher than their formal participation rates and is expanding throughout the world in both rural and urban areas (Redclift and Mingione 1985; Sen and Grown 1987; Sassen 1988; Boris and Daniels 1989; Enloe 1989; Grown and Sebstad 1989; Truelove 1990; Fernández Kelly and Garcia 1992). For example, by 1980 in Chile, Brazil, and Costa Rica, about three-quarters of informal employees were women (Tokman 1989). Women in the informal sectors are marginalized, however, through job segregation and by wages that are only 45 to 74 percent of men's earnings (Scott 1986; Tokman 1989).

Women's informal industrial work takes place in clandestine assembly shops that evade protective, immigration, and wage legislation or in the household where subcontractors drop off electronic parts, garment pieces, jewelry, or envelopes for home processing. A new informal service industry involves clerical or telemarketing services subcontracted to women's homes, where workers input insurance information, airline ticket data, and medical texts at piece rates or subminimum wages (Applebaum 1987; Boris and Daniels 1989; Freeman 1989). Informal retail service activities, such as hawking produce, prepared food, or cigarettes in the streets, are also common.

Domestic service, a female occupation involving childcare, food preparation, housecleaning, and shopping, is an important component of women's informal sector work internationally and often supports the formal sector work of other women. This work is shaped by class, race, gender, and international political issues, particularly when many women domestic workers from South Asia, North Africa, and the Middle East migrate to other countries (Gowen 1988; Enloe 1989). By hiring domestic workers, middle- and upper-class women around the world can resolve conflicts with male partners over housework and childcare and engage in formal sector work (Byerly 1986; Rollins 1986; Ruiz 1987; Cock 1988; Anderson 1989; De Melo 1989; Enloe 1989; Gimenez 1990).

Many domestic workers experience particularly exploitative working conditions because their work falls outside state regulation (Chaney and Garcia Castro 1989). A hierarchy exists within the occupation (Enloe 1989). Nannies and *au pairs* (frequently white Europeans) have relatively more power than maids (often women of color or immigrant women who may be fleeing political persecution or economies plagued by underdevelopment and debt crises). The latter are more economically vulnerable and often subject to sexual harassment by men in employers' households, as documented for Filipinas in Hong Kong, Singapore, Japan, and the Middle East, and for African American and immigrant women in the United States (Rollins 1985; Gowen 1988; Paguio 1988; Heyzer 1989). At the same time, in contrast to the historical experience of industrialized countries, many currently developing countries such as Bangladesh, the Philippines, and Sri Lanka have become dependent on the wages that their migrant domestic workers remit to their home countries (Heyzer 1989).

A type of informal sector work increasingly mentioned in the late 1980s is the international sex trade, which uses patterns of racism and sexism in the prostitution of women and children in Asia (Heyzer 1986; Mies 1986; Enloe 1989; Truong 1990), the Caribbean (Levy and Lerch 1991), and Africa (Brydon and Chant 1989). These women and children often come from impoverished families in rural areas, and the numbers involved are substantial. Benería (1989), citing Thanh-dam Truong (1990), notes that in Bangkok the number of prostitutes is equivalent to 10 percent of the workers in transnational corporations. The sex trade is linked to international business investments and transnationals, the United States' military bases, and male patrons from currently developed countries. International financial institutions and some countries see the promotion of this industry as a solution to the debt crisis (Enloe 1989). Ironically, the governments of these countries play a central role in promoting this form of women's informal labor while simultaneously extolling the virtues of women factory workers (Enloe 1989).

Informalization and global restructuring also affect agricultural work. Capitalists retain flexibility during labor-intensive harvest and food-processing periods, when women and men are used in a mixture of industrial and agricultural activities to ensure that families do not migrate during slack times (Aguiar 1986; Enloe 1989; Heyzer 1989; Truelove 1990). Cynthia Enloe (1989) describes the shifting gender and race division of labor and informalization on sugar and banana plantations in Central America that seasonally employ women and use race to allocate jobs.

Many women homeworkers, other informal workers, and entrepreneurs report dissatisfaction with the arrangements because of low wages, little control over the work processes, health risks, long hours, and overhead costs (Leung 1986; Boris and Daniels 1989; Enloe 1989; Narotzky 1990). For example, Ximena Bunster, Elsa Chaney, and Ellan Young (1985) and Linda North (1988) describe the struggles of Peruvian market women who work eighteen to twenty hours a day. In Africa and Latin America women's informal businesses have lower sales revenues, asset bases, and profit margins than men's (Grown and Sebstad 1989; Jiggins 1989). M. Patricia Fernández Kelly and Anna Garcia (1988) found similar conditions for women entrepreneurs in Los Angeles. Janice Jiggins (1989), however, describes how some Sub-Saharan African women entrepreneurs have moved from survival activities to more prosperous growth-oriented enterprises. As in formal factory work, the empowerment of women is a complex process. Women homeworkers and entrepreneurs benefit immediately by the wages earned in informal sector work. In the long run, though, many women work in isolated, hazardous conditions and continue to exist at the survival level rather than experience economic mobility (Jiggins 1989; Massiah 1989).

Household Labor

As discussed above, women's household labor is integrally linked to formal and informal sector work, since the majority of women worldwide pursue some combination of these types of work to sustain their families. Transnational firms are increasingly intertwined with women and households when they subcontract assembly work as paid homework and when they pay low wages, because women's work in the household subsidizes the actual cost of family maintenance. Such relationships with transnationals intensify women's workloads. If the totality of women's work lives is not examined, this fact is obscured.

The literature since the mid-1980s has reinforced and extended research showing that women's unpaid labor in the household and agriculture is critical. As producers and consumers, women provide food, clothing, and energy and maintain the family in time-consuming activities. For poor households in many countries, such work contributes at least half the household subsistence (J. L. Collins 1990; Narotzky 1990; Stichter 1990). Women's household labor is intensified in times of economic crisis and global restructuring (Friedmann 1990).

Another major development in scholarship regarding women's roles in the household is the movement beyond earlier research that treated household members as having a unity of interests (Smith, Wallerstein, and Evers 1984). New studies show how the roles of individuals in the household vary by gender, race, and class (Bruce and Dwyer 1987; Acker 1988; Lever 1988; Stichter and Parpart 1988b, 1990; Blumberg 1989; Bruce 1989; Fernández Kelly 1989; Collins and Gimenez 1990; Wolf 1990a, b, 1993; Amott and Matthaei 1991; Mizan 1992).

For example, women contribute far more of their earnings and unpaid labor to the household, in some cases up to 100 percent, whereas men may use most earnings for personal consumption. This is illustrated in rural Spain (Narotzky 1990) and in Mexico City, where male partners often do not pool money or information with spouses (Benería and Roldán 1987). In some cases, poor and minority men share fewer resources and devote less money and effort to the household than more economically advantaged men do (Blumberg 1989; Hochschild 1989). To maintain status and power within the household, men may devalue women's economic contributions or resort to domestic violence.

Resistance

The new scholarship on women's industrial labor and its connections to the informal and household sectors reveals broader dimensions of women's resistance to their subordinate positions than had formerly been recognized (Dill 1986, 1988; Bookman and Morgen 1988; Ward 1988a; Westwood and Bhachu 1988; P. H. Collins 1990; Talwar 1990). In the past many labor unions viewed women workers as unorganizable. Earlier accounts depicted women as passive victims of the consequences of development, transnational corporations, and various types of marginalization.

New research has illustrated the need to examine forms of resistance other than large-scale social movements or union activities. Like the commonalities noted in women's experiences in transnational employment and the informal sector around the world, similarities exist among women's resistance strategies. Bettina Aptheker (1989, 173–174) proposes examining women's daily resistance: "To see women's resistance is to also see the accumulated effects of daily, arduous, creative, sometimes ingenious labors, performed over time, sometimes over generations." She suggests that since much resistance is based on the need to survive, survival itself is a form of resistance. Resistance strategies fall into three categories: (1) making use of traditional structured organizations along with spontaneous daily resistance in the formal workplace, (2) household transformation, and (3) the act of survival itself, which may involve various combinations of activities in the formal, informal, and household sectors. Contradictions may be inherent in these strategies.

Despite barriers placed by governments and corporations, women workers in both developed and developing countries organize and strike for better wages and working conditions and against plant closures. Women workers are among the most militant union members, particularly in South Korea, the Philippines, and South Africa. Increasing international connections between women workers and unions in different countries facilitate communication of ways to support workers and strikes and to fight runaway plants, de-skilling, low wages, and other transnational corporation tactics (Arrigo 1985; Byerly 1986; Rosa 1987; Jayakody and Goonatilake 1988; Pineda-Ofreneo and Del Rosario 1988; Elson 1989; Enloe 1989; Heyzer 1989; Mai 1989; Berger 1990; Kamel 1990).

This resistance takes place daily at the computer terminals, on the shopfloor, and at other worksites around the world (Byerly 1986; Bookman and Morgen 1988; Zavella 1988). In Barbados women workers entering data for airlines reprogram their computers to record higher than actual output (Freeman 1989). Women workers in the United States' Silicon Valley use managers' racist and sexist biases to acquire more power and control over their working conditions on the shopfloor. For example, women workers may tell their male managers that they need frequent "hormone" or menstrual rest breaks (Hossfeld 1990). Sallie Westwood (1985) and Westwood and Parminder Bhachu (1988) show how immigrant women workers in England have used a variety of strategies such as wedding and baby showers to control interaction on the shopfloor. Devon Peña (1987) describes the "turtle" or slowdown strategy of workers in Mexican *maquiladoras*. Finally, Malaysian women factory workers have sought control over their work by spirit possession (Ong 1987).

Self-employed and informal sector workers are also organizing (Sen and Grown 1987; Bhatt 1989). In India the success of the Self-Employed Women's Association (SEWA) demonstrates how previously isolated women in the informal sector can achieve some power over their work situation. Loan groups based on the Grameen Bank model provide supportive contexts for women's education, economic development, and empowerment vis-à-vis men in the household (Mizan 1992; Blumberg, this volume). Nash (1988a) describes how market women in Lima, Peru, organize *comedores populares*, or communal kitchens, to ease household burdens. Migrant domestic workers in Europe organize to counter the increasing growth of transnational cleaning corporations (Gowen 1988).

New research indicates that for women around the world, some combination of work in the formal, informal, or household sector is a survival strategy and one way to resist marginalization from low-wage employment. For example, homemakers whose households' survival is threatened by the debt crisis take to the streets in alliances with unions and formal sector workers to challenge austerity programs in Latin America (Nash 1988a, b, this volume; North 1988) or governmental violence (Bunster-Burroto 1986). Bonnie Thornton Dill (1986, 1988) argues that survival itself is resistance and discusses how women of color in the United States pass skills along to their children, ensuring their survival and resisting negative socioeconomic forces (see also P. H. Collins 1990).

Aptheker (1989) describes how household relationships can be transformed by women's resistance activities. In the United States Barbara Kingsolver (1989) describes permanent transformations of gender relationships in households after Chicana and Mexicana family members and workers formed their own support organizations during the Arizona copper mine strike in 1983.

This resistance, however, contains ambivalence as women seek to reconcile the cultural and religious contradictions among their work, resistance, and the structures of male dominance in which they live (Bookman and Morgen 1988; North 1988; Freeman 1989; Hossfeld 1990; Ward 1990b). As Fernández Kelly and Garcia (1992) note, some women rationalize their need to work without questioning their particular cultural ideology.

Often women's resistance only temporarily mediates their immediate, individual situation without generating changes in the structures or institutions that control their labor. Although the triple shift strategy may ensure survival, it can reinforce the global economy that made such a strategy necessary. As a consequence, large numbers of women remain exhausted in a survival mode, and only a privileged handful experience economic mobility via this strategy.

Conclusion

Significant developments since the mid-1980s in the literature on women's role in industrialization and its relation to the informal and household sectors have added immeasurably to our understanding of women's subordinate roles. They have provided an invaluable foundation of knowledge for developing more relevant theoretical frameworks and building political and economic strategies to improve women's positions in developing and developed countries. Clearly, much theoretical, empirical, and political work is needed. This literature review and the trends we highlight starkly reveal the need for theoretical models that incorporate gender, class, ethnicity, the changing strategies of transnational corporations, the totality of work, and the role of the state in analyzing women's roles in economic development. Our review also shows that theories focusing only on work in the formal capitalist sector with little consideration of gender are simply inadequate (Mies 1986; Benería 1991; Ward 1993).

Accordingly, much more empirical research is needed. First, longitudinal and cross-national studies must be made at the firm and industry level to examine women's job histories, wage trends, differences in working conditions, and the range of economic choices women working in transnationals have in selecting employment. For example, more information is needed on the length of time women spend in such employment. Estimates from the 1970s speculated that women in electronics worked an average of only two years. If this trend remains, then any benefits for women of employment in transnationals would be short-lived. The relationship between layoffs by gender and business cycles also should be more thoroughly examined.

Changes in wages for women, at an absolute level and relative to men, should be studied to determine the effects on education levels, work experience, uninterrupted work history, support from the household, and discrimination. In addition, working conditions can be more closely examined to ascertain differences within a country between transnationals and indigenous firms or between different firms in the same industry internationally. Interviews can be conducted to provide more information regarding structural constraints versus personal choice and the economic options these women had when selecting transnational jobs. This type of information must be collected for those directly employed in such firms as well as for those working in extended subcontracting networks. Data can be gathered regarding what proportion of women's work lives are spent in factories compared with other types of work in the formal, informal, and household sectors.

Second, researchers can extend examination of women's and men's multifaceted experiences of work along the continuum of formal, informal, and household labor. More comparative and longitudinal research is needed to document commonalities and differences in women's experiences in these three sectors and the racial and class patterns that prevail. These proposed comparative work histories would require a movement away from reliance on formal labor force statistics to a combination of macrostudies and microsurveys of time use that incorporate gender, race, and class. Innumerable aspects of this work continuum can be examined. For example, ties among women's work in factories, informal assembly, and participation in the sex trade constitute an important area for new research.

Third, scholars and organizers must more fully study and understand all forms of women's resistance and the contradictions that may accompany them, recognizing that the increasing informalization of work makes effective organizing difficult. As David Harvey notes in regard to women workers (1989, 153), "struggling against capitalist exploitation in the factory is very different from struggling against a father or uncle who organizes family labour into a highly disciplined and competitive sweatshop that works to order for multinational capital." Women workers and community groups can develop new organizing strategies that encompass women's everyday acts of resistance as well as unionization. For example, local-based groups such as SEWA or the Grameen Bank projects can empower women workers relative to their immediate environment and families. In addition, researchers must more extensively analyze the international connections between gender and work in developing and industrialized countries, identifying the many parallels that exist as well as the differences. Women's groups can work toward cross-national coordination of and support for strikes and contract negotiations (Kamel 1990). Thus, scholars and activists can formulate effective strategies for change that empower women workers while facilitating socioeconomic development.

Finally, in conjunction with these dimensions of analysis, future research must more systematically and completely study the role of state policy and the intertwining of gender, race, and class. With respect to state policy, for example, scholars can examine, via case studies or comparative analyses, how the state determines the conditions of women's work by attracting investments on the basis of gender; by weakening state regulations to attract investment, thereby creating hazardous working conditions or informalizing work processes; by using police or military power to suppress workers' resistance activities; by promoting and using women workers in the tourist or sex trade; or by influencing fertility patterns with labor-supply objectives in mind. In many cases, states have sought short-run development without looking at the long-run socioeconomic and political costs of competing with other states for transnational corporations' investment. Understanding the way the state shapes women's economic lives is critical for the development of strategies for effective change.

Scholars and activists should build on these predominant themes in the women-in-development literature to create a new theoretical framework and to extend empirical research. In so doing, they will establish a solid basis for understanding women's roles in economic development and for innovating strategies that more efficiently and equitably incorporate women into this process, thus eradicating their subordinate status.

NOTES

Acknowledgments: The authors contributed equally to the preparation of this chapter. We acknowledge the comments of Linda Grant, Rachel Rosenfeld, Rita Gallin, and the New England Women in Development group. Mary Lou Fuller, Julie Gast, Carrie Forshner, and William Winders provided valuable research assistance. Laura Whistle Cates and Sue Treece patiently handled the word-processing tasks. Judith Barnes-Long at the Interlibrary Loan desk at the University of Massachusetts/Lowell provided excellent assistance.

REFERENCES

Acker, Joan. 1988. "Class, Gender, and the Relations of Production." *Signs: Journal of Women in Culture and Society* 13:473–497.

Agarwal, Bina, ed. 1988. *Structures of Patriarchy.* London: Zed.

Aguiar, Neuma. 1986. "Research Guidelines: How to Study Work in Latin America." In *Women and Change in Latin America,* ed. June Nash and Helen Safa, 22–34. South Hadley, Mass.: Bergin and Garvey.

Amott, Teresa, and Julie Matthaei. 1991. *Race, Gender, and Work: A Multicultural Economic History of Women in the United States.* Boston: South End Press.

Amsden, Alice H. 1989. *Asia's Next Giant: South Korea and Late Industrialization.* New York: Oxford University Press.

Anderson, Patricia. 1989. "Domestics and Their Employers." *Connexions* 30:20–21.

Applebaum, Eileen. 1987. "Restructuring Work." In *Computer Chips and Paper Clips: Technology and Women's Employment,* vol. 2, ed. Heidi Hartmann, 268–312. Washington, D.C.: National Academy Press.

Aptheker, Bettina. 1989. *Tapestries of Life.* Amherst: University of Massachusetts Press.

Arrigo, Lourdes. 1985. "Economic and Political Control of Women Workers in Multinational Electronics Factories in Taiwan." *Contemporary Marxism* 11:77–95.

Benería, Lourdes. 1989. "Gender and the Global Economy." In *Instability and Change in the World Economy,* ed. Arthur MacEwan and William K. Tabb, 241–258. New York: Monthly Review.

———. 1991. "Accounting for Women's Work: Assessing the Progress of Two Decades." Paper presented at UNRISD, Meeting on Social Development Indicators, Rabat, Morocco, April.

Benería, Lourdes, and Martha Roldán. 1987. *The Crossroads of Class and*

Gender: Industrial Homework, Subcontracting, and Household Dynamics in Mexico City. Chicago: University of Chicago Press.

Berger, Iris. 1990. "Gender, Race, and Political Empowerment: South African Canning Workers, 1940–1960." *Gender & Society* 4 (3): 398–420.

Bhatt, Ela. 1989. "Toward Empowerment." *World Development* 17:1059–1065.

Blumberg, Rae. 1989. "Toward a Feminist Theory of Development." In *Feminism and Sociological Theory*, ed. Ruth Wallace, 161–199. Beverly Hills, Calif.: Sage.

Bookman, Ann, and Sandra Morgen, eds. 1988. *Women and the Politics of Empowerment.* Philadephia: Temple University Press.

Boris, Eileen, and Cynthia R. Daniels, eds. 1989. *Homework: Historical and Contemporary Perspectives on Paid Labor at Home.* Urbana: University of Illinois Press.

Bruce, Judith. 1989. "Homes Divided." *World Development* 17:979–991.

Bruce, Judith, and Daisy Dwyer, eds. 1987. *A Home Divided: Women and Income in the Third World.* Stanford: Stanford University Press.

Brydon, Lynne, and Sylvia Chant. 1989. *Women in the Third World.* New Brunswick, N.J.: Rutgers University Press.

Bunster, Ximena, Elsa M. Chaney, and Ellan Young. 1985. *Sellers and Servants: Working Women in Lima, Peru.* New York: Praeger.

Bunster-Burotto, Ximena. 1986. "Surviving beyond Fear: Women and Torture in Latin America." In *Women and Change in Latin America,* ed. June Nash and Helen I. Safa, 297–325. South Hadley, Mass.: Bergin and Garvey.

Byerly, Virginia. 1986. *Hard Times Cotton Mill Girl.* Ithaca, N.Y.: ILR Press.

Carney, Larry, and Charlotte O'Kelly. 1990. "Women's Work and Women's Place in the Japanese Economic Miracle." In *Women Workers and Global Restructuring,* ed. Kathryn Ward, 113–145. Ithaca, N.Y.: ILR Press.

Catanzarite, Lisa, and Myra Strober. 1993. "Gender Recomposition of the Maquiladora Workforce." *Industrial Relations.* 32:133–147.

Chaney, Elsa, and Mary Garcia Castro, eds. 1989. *Muchachas No More: Household Workers in Latin America and the Caribbean.* Philadelphia: Temple University Press.

Chase-Dunn, Christopher. 1989. *Global Formations.* Cambridge, Mass.: Basil Blackwell.

Clark, Roger, Thomas W. Ramsbey, and Emily S. Alder. 1991. "Culture, Gender, and Labor Force Participation: A Cross-National Study." *Gender & Society* 5 (1):47–66.

Cock, Jacklynn. 1988. "Trapped Workers: The Case of Domestic Servants in South Africa." In *Patriarchy and Class: African Women in the Home and the Workforce,* ed. Sharon Stichter and Jane L. Parpart, 205–219. Boulder, Colo.: Westview.

Collins, Jane L. 1990. "Unwaged Labor in Comparative Perspective." In *Work without Wages,* ed. Jane L. Collins and Martha Gimenez, 3–24. Albany: State University of New York Press.

Collins, Jane L., and Martha Gimenez, eds. 1990. *Work without Wages.* Albany: State University of New York Press.

Collins, Patricia Hill. 1990. *Black Feminist Thought*. Boston: Allen and Unwin.

De Melo, Hildete Pereira. 1989. "Feminists and Domestic Workers in Rio de Janeiro." In *Muchachas No More: Household Workers in Latin America and the Caribbean,* ed. Elsa M. Chaney and Mary Garcia Castro, 245–267. Philadelphia: Temple University Press.

Dill, Bonnie Thornton. 1986. *Our Mothers' Grief: Racial Ethnic Women and the Maintenance of Family.* Research Paper no. 4. Memphis: Center for Research on Women, Memphis State University.

———. 1988. " 'Making Your Job Good Yourself': Domestic Service and the Construction of Personal Dignity." In *Women and the Politics of Empowerment,* ed. Ann Bookman and Sandra Morgen, 33–52. Philadephia: Temple University Press.

Elson, Diane. 1989. "The Cutting Edge: Women's Employment and Multinationals in the EEC Textiles and Clothing Industry." In *Women's Employment and Multinationals in Europe,* ed. Diane Elson and Ruth Pearson, 80–110. London: Macmillan.

Enloe, Cynthia. 1989. *Bananas, Beaches, and Bases: Making Feminist Sense of International Politics.* Berkeley: University of California Press.

Fernández Kelly, M. Patricia. 1989. "Broadening the Scope: Gender and International Economic Development." *Sociological Forum* 4:11–35.

Fernández Kelly, M. Patricia, and Anna Garcia. 1988. "Economic Restructuring in the United States." In *Women and Work #3,* ed. Barbara Gutek, Laurie Larwood, and Ann Stromberg, 49–65. Beverly Hills, Calif.: Sage.

———. 1992. "Power Surrendered, Power Restored: The Politics of Home and Work among Hispanic Women in Southern California and Southern Florida." In *Women and Politics in America,* ed. Louise Tilly and Patricia Guerin, 130–149. New York: Russell Sage.

Freeman, Carla. 1989. "High-Tech and High Heels: Barbadian Women in the Off-Shore Information Industry." Paper presented at the 15th Annual Conference of the Caribbean Studies Association, Trinidad and Tobago.

Friedmann, Harriet. 1990. "Family Wheat Farms and Third World Debts." In *Work without Wages,* ed. Joan L. Collins and Martha Gimenez, 193–214. Albany: State University of New York Press.

Gallin, Rita. 1990. "Women and the Export Industry in Taiwan: The Muting of Class Consciousness." In *Women Workers and Global Restructuring,* ed. Kathryn Ward, 179–192. Ithaca, N.Y.: ILR Press.

Gannicott, Kenneth. 1986. "Women, Wages, and Discrimination: Some Evidence from Taiwan." *Economic Development and Cultural Change* 34:721–730.

Gereffi, Gary. 1990. "Rethinking Development Theory: Insights from East Asia and Latin America." *Sociological Forum* 4:505–535.

Gimenez, Martha E. 1990. "The Dialectics of Waged and Unwaged Work." In *Work without Wages,* ed. Jane L. Collins and Martha Gimenez, 25–46. Albany: State University of New York Press.

Gowen, Susan. 1988. "Invisible Workers." *Isis: International Women's Journal* 17:34–36.

Griffith, Winston H. 1990. "CARICOM Countries and the Caribbean Basin Initiative. " *Latin American Perspectives* 17:33–54.

Grown, Caren A., and Jennefer Sebstad. 1989. "Introduction." *World Development* 17:937–952.

Hadjicostandi, Joanna. 1990. " 'Facon': Women's Formal and Informal Work in the Garment Industry in Kavala, Greece." In *Women Workers and Global Restructuring,* ed. Kathryn Ward, 64–81. Ithaca, N.Y.: ILR Press.

Harvey, David. 1989. *The Condition of Post-Modernity.* Oxford: Basil Blackwell.

Hein, Catherine. 1986. "The Feminization of Industrial Employment in Mauritius: A Case of Sex Segregation." In *Sex Inequalities in Urban Employment in the Third World,* ed. Catherine Hein, 277–311. New York: St. Martin's Press.

Heyzer, Noeleen. 1986. *Working Women in South-East Asia.* Milton Keynes, England: Open University Press.

——, ed. 1988. *Daughters in Industry: Work, Skills, and Consciousness of Women Workers in Asia.* Kuala Lumpur, Malaysia: Asian and Pacific Development Centre.

——. 1989. "Asian Women Wage Earners." *World Development* 17:1109–1124.

Heyzer, Noeleen, and Tan Boon Kean. 1988. "Work, Skills, and Consciousness of Women Workers in Asia." In *Daughters in Industry: Work, Skills, and Consciousness of Women Workers in Asia,* ed. Noeleen Heyzer, 3–32. Kuala Lumpur, Malaysia: Asian and Pacific Development Centre.

Hochschild, Arlie. 1989. *The Second Shift.* New York: Viking.

Hossfeld, Karen. 1990. " 'Their Logic against Them': Contradictions in Sex, Race, and Class in Silicon Valley." In *Women Workers and Global Restructuring,* ed. Kathryn Ward, 149–178. Ithaca, N.Y.: ILR Press.

——. Forthcoming. *Small, Foreign, and Female: Immigrant Women Workers in Silicon Valley.* Berkeley: University of California Press.

Humphrey, John. 1987. *Gender and Work in the Third World: Sexual Division in Brazilian Industry.* London: Tavistock.

Hyo-chae, Lee. 1988. "The Changing Profile of Women Workers in South Korea." In *Daughters in Industry: Work, Skills, and Consciousness of Women Workers in Asia,* ed. Noeleen Heyzer, 329–355. Kuala Lumpur, Malaysia: Asian and Pacific Development Centre.

Jayakody, Soma, and Hema Goonatilake. 1988. "Industrial Action by Women Workers in Sri Lanka." In *Daughters in Industry: Work, Skills, and Consciousness of Women Workers in Asia,* ed. Noeleen Heyzer, 292–307. Kuala Lumpur, Malaysia: Asian and Pacific Development Centre.

Jiggins, Janice. 1989. "How Poor Women Earn Income in Sub-Saharan Africa and What Works against Them." *World Development* 17:953–963.

Joekes, Susan. 1987. *Women in the World Economy.* New York: Oxford University Press.

Joel, Susan. 1989. "An Assessment of the Integration/Exploitation Framework for Understanding Women in the International Division of Labor." Master's thesis, Michigan State University, East Lansing.

——. 1990. "Female Factory Workers in Less Developed Countries: A Bibliography." *Women in International Development Working Paper.* East Lansing: Office of Women in Development, Michigan State University.

Kamel, Rachel. 1990. *The Global Factory: Analysis and Action for a New Economic Era.* Philadelphia: American Friends Service Committee/Omega Press.

Kingsolver, Barbara. 1989. *Holding the Line.* Ithaca, N.Y.: ILR Press.

Lamphere, Louise. 1987. *From Working Daughters to Working Mothers.* Ithaca, N.Y.: Cornell University Press.

Leung, Trini W. Y. 1986. "The Dark Side of Industrialization." *Multinational Monitor* 7:22–30.

Lever, Alison. 1988. "Capital, Gender, and Skill: Women Homeworkers in Rural Spain." *Feminist Review* 30:3–24.

Levy, Diane E., and Patricia B. Lerch. 1991. "Tourism as a Factor in Development." *Gender & Society* 5 (1):67–85.

Li, K. T. 1985. "Contributions of Women in the Labor Force to Economic Development in Taiwan, the Republic of China." *Industry of Free China* (August): 1–8.

Lim, Linda. 1985. *Women Workers in Multinational Enterprises in Developing Countries.* Geneva: International Labor Office.

———. 1990. "Women's Work in Export Factories: The Politics of a Cause." In *Persistent Inequalities: Women and World Development,* ed. Irene Tinker, 101–119. New York: Oxford University Press.

Mai, Kimori. 1989. "Malaysia's Workers: Jolting the Electronics Industry." *Multinational Monitor* 10:11–13.

Massiah, Joycelin. 1989. "Women's Lives and Livelihoods: A View from the Commonwealth Caribbean." *World Development* 17:965–977.

Mather, Celia. 1985. " 'Rather than Make Trouble, It's Better Just to Leave.' " In *Women, Work, and Ideology in the Third World,* ed. Helen Afshar, 153–180. London: Tavistock.

Mies, Maria. 1986. *Patriarchy and Accumulation on a World Scale: Women in the International Division of Labour.* London: Zed.

Mitter, Swasti. 1986. *Common Fate, Common Bond: Women in the Global Economy.* London: Pluto Press.

Mizan, Ainon. 1992. "Rural Women's Economic Participation and Decision-Making Power in the Family: A Study on Grameen Bank in Bangladesh." Ph.D. dissertation, Southern Illinois University at Carbondale.

Moser, Carol. 1989. "Gender Planning in the Third World: Meeting Practical and Strategic Gender Needs." *World Development* 17 (Nov.): 1799–1826.

Narotzky, Susana. 1990. " 'Not to Be a Burden': Ideologies of the Domestic Group and Women's Work in Rural Catalonia." In *Work without Wages,* ed. Jane L. Collins and Martha Gimenez, 70–88. Albany: State University of New York Press.

Nash, June. 1988a. "The Mobilization of Women in the Bolivian Debt Crisis." In *Women and Work* #3, ed. Barbara Gutek, Laurie Larwood, and Ann Stromberg, 67–86. Beverly Hills, Calif.: Sage.

———. 1988b. "Cultural Parameters of Sexism and Racism in the International Division of Labor." In *Racism, Sexism, and the World System,* ed. Joan

Smith, Jane Collins, Terrence Hopkins, and Akbar Muhammad, 11–36. Westport, Conn.: Greenwood.

———. 1990. "Latin American Women in the World Capitalist Crisis." *Gender & Society* 4 (3): 338–352.

North, Linda. 1988. "The Women Poor of Peru." *Isis: International Women's Journal* 17:12–14.

Ong, Aihwa. 1987. *Spirits of Resistance and Capitalist Discipline: Factory Women in Malaysia.* Albany: State University of New York Press.

Overholt, Catherine, Mary B. Anderson, Kathleen Cloud, and James Austin. 1985. *Gender Roles in Development Projects.* West Hartford, Conn.: Kumarian Press.

Paguio, B. 1988. "No Bed of Roses for Filipinas Abroad." *Isis: International Women's Journal* 17:37, 42.

Peña, Devon. 1987. "*Tortuosidad*: Shop Floor Struggles of Female *Maquiladora* Workers." In *Women on the U.S.-Mexico Border: Responses to Change,* ed. Vicki L. Ruiz and Susan Tiano, 129–154. Boston: Allen and Unwin.

Phizacklea, Annie. 1990. *Unpacking the Fashion Industry: Gender, Racism, and Class in Production.* London: Routledge.

Phongpaichit, Pasuk. 1988. "Two Roads to the Factory: Industrialisation Strategies and Women's Employment in Southeast Asia." In *Structures of Patriarchy,* ed. Bina Agarwal, 151–163. London: Zed.

Pineda-Ofreneo, Rosalinda, and Rosario Del Rosario. 1988. "Filipino Women Workers in Strike Actions." In *Daughters in Industry: Work, Skills, and Consciousness of Women Workers in Asia,* ed. Noleen Heyzer, 308–326. Kuala Lumpur, Malaysia: Asian and Pacific Development Centre.

Portes, Alejandro, Manuel Castells, and Lauren Benton, eds. 1989. *The Informal Economy: Studies in Advanced and Less Developed Countries.* Baltimore: Johns Hopkins University Press.

Pyle, Jean Larson. 1990a. "Export-Led Development and the Underemployment of Women: The Impact of Discriminatory Development Policy in the Republic of Ireland." In *Women Workers and Global Restructuring,* ed. Kathryn Ward, 85–112. Ithaca, N.Y.: ILR Press.

———. 1990b. *The State and Women in the Economy: Lessons from Sex Discrimination in the Republic of Ireland.* Albany: State University of New York Press.

Pyle, Jean Larson, and Leslie Dawson. 1990. "The Impact of Multinational Technology Transfer on Female Workforces in Asia." *Columbia Journal of World Business* 25 (4): 40–48.

Redclift, Nanneke, and Enzo Mingione, eds. 1985. *Beyond Employment: Household, Gender, and Subsistence.* Oxford: Basil Blackwell.

Ríos, Palmira N. 1990. "Export-Oriented Industrialization and the Demand for Female Labor: Puerto Rican Women in the Manufacturing Sector, 1952–1980." *Gender & Society* 4 (3): 321–337.

Rollins, Judith. 1985. *Between Women: Domestics and Their Employers.* Philadephia: Temple University Press.

Rosa, Kumudhini. 1987. "Organizing Women Workers in the Free Trade Zone,

Sri Lanka." In *Third World, Second Sex,* ed. Miranda Davies, 159–164. London: Zed.

Rosen, Ellen. 1987. *Bitter Choices: Blue-Collar Women In and Out of Work.* Chicago: University of Chicago Press.

Ruiz, Vicki L. 1987. "By the Day or the Week: Mexicana Domestic Workers in El Paso." In *Women on the U.S.-Mexico Border: Responses to Change,* ed. Vicki L. Ruiz and Susan Tiano, 61–76. Boston: Allen and Unwin.

Ruiz, Vicki L., and Susan Tiano, eds. 1987. *Women on the U.S.-Mexico Border: Responses to Change.* Boston: Allen and Unwin.

Safa, Helen. 1986. "Runaway Shops and Female Employment." In *Women's Work: Development and the Division of Labor by Gender,* ed. Eleanor B. Leacock and Helen I. Safa, 58–71. South Hadley, Mass.: Bergin and Garvey.

Salaff, Janet W. 1988. *State and Family in Singapore: Restructuring an Industrial Society.* Ithaca, N.Y.: Cornell University Press.

Salih, Kamal, and Mei Ling Young. 1989. "Changing Conditions of Labour in the Semiconductor Industry in Malaysia." *Labour and Society* 14:59–80.

Sassen, Saskia. 1988. *Mobility of Labor and Capital.* Cambridge: Cambridge University Press.

Schmink, Marianne. 1986. "Women and Urban Industrial Development in Brazil." In *Women and Change in Latin America,* ed. June Nash and Helen Safa, 136–164. South Hadley, Mass.: Bergin and Garvey.

Scott, Alison MacEwen. 1986. "Women and Industrialisation: Examining the 'Female Marginalisation' Thesis." *Journal of Development Studies* 22:649–680.

———. 1990. "Patterns of Patriarchy in the Peruvian Working Class." In *Women, Employment, and the Family in the International Division of Labour,* ed. Sharon Stichter and Jane L. Parpart, 198–220. Philadelphia: Temple University Press.

Seidman, Ann. 1985. *The Roots of Crisis in Southern Africa.* Trenton, N.J.: Africa World Press.

Sen, Gita, and Caren Grown. 1987. *Development, Crises, and Alternative Visions.* New York: New Feminist Library.

Smith, Joan, Immanuel Wallerstein, and Hans Evers, eds. 1984. *Households and the World Economy.* Beverly Hills, Calif.: Sage.

Standing, Guy. 1989. "Global Feminization through Flexible Labor." *World Development* 17 (7): 1077–1095.

Stichter, Sharon. 1990. "Women, Employment, and the Family: Current Debates." In *Women, Employment, and the Family in the International Division of Labour,* ed. Sharon Stichter and Jane L. Parpart, 11–71. Philadelphia: Temple University Press.

Stichter, Sharon, and Jane L. Parpart. 1988a. "Introduction: Towards a Materialist Perspective on African Women." In *Patriarchy and Class: African Women in the Home and the Workforce,* ed. Sharon Stichter and Jane L. Parpart, 1–26. Boulder, Colo.: Westview.

———, eds. 1988b. *Patriarchy and Class: African Women in the Home and the Workforce.* Boulder, Colo.: Westview.

————, eds. 1990. *Women, Employment, and the Family in the International Division of Labour*. Philadelphia: Temple University Press.

Sultana, Hazera. 1990. "The Violation of Garment Workers' Human Rights." *SAMACHAR* 3:3–7.

Talwar Oldenburg, Veena. 1990. "Lifestyle as Resistance: The Case of the Courtesans of Lucknow, India." *Feminist Studies* 16 (2): 259–287.

Tiano, Susan. 1987. "Gender, Work, and World Capitalism." In *Analyzing Gender*, ed. Beth Hess and Myra Marx Ferree, 216–243. Beverly Hills, Calif.: Sage.

————. 1990. "*Maquiladora* Women: A New Category of Workers?" In *Women Workers and Global Restructuring*, ed. Kathryn Ward, 193–223. Ithaca, N.Y.: ILR Press.

Tinker, Irene, ed. 1990. *Persistent Inequalities: Women and World Development*. New York: Oxford University Press.

Tokman, Victor E. 1989. "Policies for a Heterogeneous Informal Sector in Latin America." *World Development* 17:1067–1076.

Truelove, Cynthia. 1990. "Disguised Industrial Proletarians in Rural Latin America." In *Women Workers and Global Restructuring*, ed. Kathryn Ward, 48–63. Ithaca, N.Y.: ILR Press.

Truong, Thanh-dam. 1990. *Sex, Money, and Morality: Prostitution and Tourism in Southeast Asia*. London: Zed.

Ward, Kathryn. 1984. *Women in the World System: Its Impact on Status and Fertility*. New York: Praeger.

————. 1988a. "Female Resistance to Marginalization: The Igbo Women's War of 1929." In *Racism and Sexism in the World System*, ed. Joan Smith, 121–136. Westport, Conn.: Greenwood.

————. 1988b. "Women in the Global Economy." In *Women and Work #3*, ed. Barbara Gutek, Laurie Larwood, and Ann Stromberg, 17–48. Beverly Hills, Calif.: Sage.

————, ed. 1990a. *Women Workers and Global Restructuring*. Ithaca, N.Y.: ILR Press.

————. 1990b. "Introduction and Overview." In *Women Workers and Global Restructuring*, ed. Kathryn Ward, 1–24. Ithaca, N.Y.: ILR Press.

————. 1993. "Reconceptualizing World System Theory to Include Women." In *Theory on Gender/Feminism on Theory*, ed. Paula England, 43–68. Hawthorne, N.Y.: Aldine.

Westwood, Sallie. 1985. *All Day, Every Day: Factory and Family in the Making of Women's Lives*. Champaign: University of Illinois Press.

Westwood, Sallie, and Parminder Bhachu. 1988. *Enterprising Women: Ethnicity, Economy, and Gender Relations*. London: Routledge.

Wilson, Fiona. 1991. *Sweaters: Gender, Class, and Workshop-Based Industry in Mexico*. New York: St. Martin's Press.

Wolf, Diane. 1990a. "Linking Women's Labor with the Global Economy: Factory Workers and Their Families in Rural Java." In *Women Workers and Global Restructuring*, ed. Kathryn Ward, 25–47. Ithaca, N.Y.: ILR Press.

————. 1990b. "Daughters, Decisions, and Domination: An Empirical and

Conceptual Critique of Household Strategies." *Development and Change* 21:43–74.

———. 1993. *Factory Daughters, Their Families, and Rural Industrialization in Central Java.* Berkeley: University of California Press.

Yelvington, Kevin A. 1993. "Gender and Ethnicity at Work in a Trinidadian Factory." In *Women and Change in the Caribbean: A Pan-Caribbean Perspective,* ed. Janet Momsen, 263–277. London: Methuen.

Young, Gay. 1987. "Gender Identification and Working-Class Solidarity among *Maquila* Workers in Ciudad Juárez." In *Women on the U.S.-Mexico Border: Responses to Change,* ed. Vicki L. Ruiz and Susan Tiano, 105–128. Boston: Allen and Unwin.

Zavella, Patricia. 1988. "The Politics of Race and Gender: Organizing Chicana Cannery Workers in Northern California." In *Women and the Politics of Empowerment,* ed. Ann Bookman and Sandra Morgen, 202–224. Philadelphia: Temple University Press.

CHAPTER 3

*

Feminist Inroads in the Study of Women's Work and Development

LUZ DEL ALBA ACEVEDO

The study of women and development in Latin America focuses on the impact of the processes of economic development on the status of women. One of the recurrent themes in this literature is the participation of women in the labor force, which is generally viewed as a measure of economic status and well-being. This is not surprising, since salaried work constitutes a necessary condition to affirm women's autonomy from men. Through paid employment women generate monetary income, which serves to enhance their family's economic well-being and their bargaining power within the household. Women's work and economic activities are crucial elements in the investigation of the relationship between the sexual division of labor and the overall process of economic and social change.

One of the central questions examined in these studies is how industrial development improves women's economic opportunities in terms of employment and wages vis-à-vis men. The literature has displayed considerable explanatory power in describing the differential gender impact, but answers to this question vary according to the paradigm that informs the empirical research. Susan Tiano (1986, 1987a) classified the answers provided in the literature of the 1970s and early 1980s into three competing theses: integration, marginalization, and exploitation. The integration thesis claims that the development process brings women's integration to the modern labor market and promotes their economic autonomy from men. Conversely, the marginalization thesis claims that women become marginal to the centers of production and power during the course of economic development. The exploitation thesis, for its part, holds that women are integrated into the modern economy as cheap labor, which does not necessarily ensure their autonomy. The research that produced the building blocks for the elaboration of these three theoretical currents has a strong basis in feminist theory, as they form part of a feminist critique of social organization and traditional modes of explanation that have excluded or marginalized women from the processes of economic development and of the production of knowledge.

Although the three theses have provided interesting guidelines to the study of women and development, research in the late 1980s called into question some of their premises and their mechanistic interpretation of women's economic activities in the process of development. This new research shifted our attention from the analysis of female labor force participation in the market economy to the analysis of the complexities and dynamics involved in women's work in and out of the household. Such studies use gender as an analytical category that bridges women's economic activities in the productive and reproductive spheres of society. In this same vein, other studies elaborate interesting analyses of the relationship between paid and unpaid productive activities and the role of gender in structuring the labor market or establishing differences in the labor process.

This new research has added important knowledge to our understanding of women's work and development and has important theoretical and methodological implications for furthering the dialogue between development studies and feminist theorizing. At the theoretical level, new findings concerning women's productive work in nontraditional industries contest earlier theories of women's marginalization during industrialization. This provides the space for a reformulation of the concept of work in light of an analysis of the process of social reproduction during capitalist development. Further, the literature demystifies the theory that the growth in women's employment is mostly due to the export processing industrialization strategies promoted by multinationals.

From a methodological point of view, the gender perspective that guides these studies allows for the interrelated analysis of macrolevel processes of production and work and of microlevel analysis of the role of women's work in social reproduction. Women's work at these levels of analysis is best examined by making the unit of analysis the household or the factory rather than the individual.

Finally, underlying this new literature are implicit critiques both of the dualistic approaches that plague prior studies of gender and development and of the uncritical use of totalizing categories such as "women" that has its roots in Western feminist thought. This critique is articulated from the standpoint of Third World women, who are naming differences and defining development needs and interests from their own context. It calls for a development of a feminist theory that could be based on a differentiated conception of gender and could recognize the different needs of women and men as well as distinguishing between the needs of different groups of women.

Women's Work and Development in Latin America

As previously stated, the recent research in the field of women and development begins to challenge common assumptions about the impact of development on women and the nature of their participation in the macroprocesses of economic and social change. The vast majority of the literature published since the mid-1980s focuses primarily on the study of the crises of survival faced by Latin American women and the household strategies they created to confront the burden inflicted by the debt-induced recession in the region (Bolles 1983; Antrobus 1989; Cariola et al. 1989; DAWN/MUDAR 1990; Deere et al. 1990).[1] Some studies, however, continue to explore issues of women's work and the role of gender in structuring the productive and labor processes (MacEwen Scott 1986a; Benería and Roldán 1987; Humphrey 1987; García de Fanelli, Gogna, and Jelin 1989; Acevedo 1990; Safa 1990; Truelove 1990; Ríos, this volume). From these latter studies I identify two key contributions, mentioned above, that further the dialogue between development studies and feminist scholarship. First, the marginalization hypothesis becomes a contested terrain as new evidence disputes its underlying assumptions.[2] Second, this literature demystifies the notion that the growth in women's employment is mainly due to the export processing strategies promoted by multinationals.

Reexamining and Redefining Marginalization

The process of industrialization in developing societies has been accompanied by an increase in women's share of formal sector employment (Joekes 1987; Brydon and Chant 1989). Since 1960, for example, women's labor force participation in Latin America has grown twice as fast as women's worldwide participation. Between 1950 and 1980 worldwide participation of women increased 10 percent, whereas for Latin America it was up 23 percent (Lycette and White 1988, 38). It is estimated that by the year 2000 the female labor force in Latin America will expand from 40 to 53 million, which is more than one-fourth of the region's total workforce (Inter-American Development Bank 1990, 247). The increase of women in the labor force has been directly associated with the implementation of trade liberalization policies and export-promoting strategies that tend to increase women's participation in productive activities

(Standing 1989). This tendency has been observed in countries such as Puerto Rico, Mexico, the Dominican Republic, El Salvador, and Honduras, which have pursued export-led development. This trend in women's employment has shifted the focus of research from a concern with the extent of women's economic participation to interest in the nature of their incorporation into capitalist development in general and the labor market in particular. The analysis has centered on the impact of the new international division of labor on women and the types of jobs in which they work. For example, many studies (Fernández Kelly 1983; Nash and Fernández Kelly 1983; Kelly 1986, 1987; Pearson 1986a, 1991; Safa 1986a; Peña 1987; Tiano 1987b, 1990; Hirata 1989) explore women's work in world market factories and analyze how multinational capital uses Third World women as a source of cheap labor to keep a competitive edge in the world economy. Few studies (Chinchilla 1977; Schmink 1977), however, have investigated women's work in local industries or in the locally owned sector of the economy.[3] All these studies have concluded, although through different analytical routes, that the process of capitalist development has marginalized women. The specificity of this marginalization ranges from the exclusion of women from productive employment, to their concentration on the margins of the labor market, to the feminization or segregation of economic sectors, industries, and occupations, and to economic inequality on the basis of wage differentials and other working conditions.[4]

The most recent analyses, rather than studying the varying dimensions of marginalization, concentrate instead on the role of gender in the construction of workers' identities within the labor process and in the structuring of gender differences in the production process and the labor market. The findings of this research clearly dispute the central tenet of the marginalization thesis: exclusion from productive employment.[5] Case studies from various countries in Latin America demonstrate the growing importance of female employment in nontraditional manufacturing activities in both the formal and informal sectors of the economy. Women were employed quite extensively in blue-collar production work, and the range of industries involved extended well beyond those areas considered traditional in women's industrial work (textiles and clothing) to include pharmaceuticals, toiletries, light chemicals, plastics, motor components, leather goods, and electrical products. According to evidence from the state of São Paulo, Brazil (Humphrey 1987), for example, women are not overwhelmingly concentrated in traditional sectors of female employment as prior studies indicated (Vasques de Miranda 1977; Saffioti 1986; Schmink 1986), nor are they confined to secretarial and clerical occupations. A similar trend was observed in Puerto Rico, where women are concentrated in the fastest growing manufacturing industries: electronics and professional and scientific instruments (Ríos, this volume). In Mexico the subcontracting of women's work for home-based production exists in nongarment industries such as toys, plastics, electronics, cosmetics, and metals (Benería and Roldán 1987). Moreover, women are rapidly being incorporated into production jobs in nontraditional agroindustry. For example, in Colombia and Peru women's labor is used by large-scale horticultural enterprises in the growing, cutting, and packaging of flowers exported to the U.S. market (Cuales 1981 as cited in Pearson 1986a, 78); in Mexico women are employed picking and processing strawberries for export (Arizpe and Aranda 1986).

Acknowledging the rapid growth of women's labor market incorporation in developing countries, the new literature scrutinizes the nature of this process, focusing on the extent and rigidity of gender hierarchies in both domestic and market production. Inquiries using occupational segregation as a central aspect of inequality between women and men show considerable explanatory power. For example, studies of such segregation in the Peruvian labor market (MacEwen Scott 1986a) and of export-led and locally oriented industries in Puerto Rico's manufacturing sector (Acevedo 1993) reveal that women are employed at the bottom of the occupational hierarchy and men are at the top. The pervasiveness of the hierarchical structure of work is also found in public administration employment. In Argentina a study of the occupational structure in a national bank found that women are overwhelmingly employed as tellers and accountants, occupations that characterize the lowest echelons of banking (García de Fanelli et al. 1989). These case studies provide new perspectives for the analysis of gender differences by focusing on the specificity of women's forms of integration into the productive process and simultaneously including traditional concerns such as development and employment policies, as well as the newer issues of women's economic roles within the household. Overall, this literature suggests that women's employment and the sexual division of labor in developing societies are as complex in Latin America as in other regions of the world and cannot be viewed only in terms of the impact of external economic development factors.

The microlevel analysis introduced in these studies helps refine our understanding of gender differentiation in employment during economic development and the pervasiveness of economic inequalities, segregation, and the gendered hierarchies of status, power, and rewards that perpetuate women's subordination in patriarchal societies. It also contributes to the reassessment of the theoretical potential of the marginalization hypothesis. Clearly, the analytical objective is no longer to validate the marginalization model but to examine the feminization of the labor force and the economic inequalities inherent in a gendered hierarchical occupational structure in developing societies. The existence of the sexual division of labor throughout the development process raises some fundamental questions about the institutionalization of a gendered labor force, questions that are only beginning to be explored in the new research on women's work and development.

Export Processing and Work in the Informal and Formal Sectors

Although the studies discussed above were successful in challenging the common perception of women's labor as marginal to the national production of developing societies (see Lavrin 1987), they led to the elaboration and diffusion of some key misleading assumptions. First, that women were integrated in the industrial workforce mostly, if not solely, in export processing activities. Second, that they were integrated mostly in labor-intensive light industries, many of which were in areas of "traditional women's skills" such as apparel, textiles, or food processing. Third, that, by and large, the transnationals involved in these activities recruited mostly young, single women who lived with their families and whose income was viewed as supplemental by the family and the women themselves.

By contrast, the literature that uses the household as a unit of analysis to study women's work indicates that there is a greater variety of forms of organization of production for the world market than prior studies recognized. This new research begins to identify the different locations of women's work. Alongside factory production, where women are mainly employed for the processes that require the repetitive application of manual skill, are various domestic-based industries linked by different contractual arrangements with the factory sector producing for the urban or local market (Benería and Roldán 1987).

The new forms of organizing productive activities that rely heavily on women's work range from subcontracting, sweatshops, and small workshops to home-based production. Within each of these forms there is variation in the ways production is organized and labor accommodated. For example, within subcontracting two different forms of organization have been identified: between international industries and independent local contractors, and between international industries and their local subsidiaries.

Some of these organizational forms are beginning to be explored in case studies from Colombia and Mexico. In Colombia, Cynthia Truelove (1990) found that women's labor is subcontracted by both multinational and national industries through a system of rural assembly factories, or "mini-*maquilas*," engaged in the production of cloth shoes, bathing suits, and other garment items for local and international markets. A multitiered subcontract system, or domestic *maquila,* is operating in Mexico, where women's homework penetrates spheres of production that extend beyond the garment and textile industries (Benería and Roldán 1987). This system is another form of organizing production in which the formal sector in manufacturing tapers off into the informal sector, where women's work has become increasingly important. According to Lourdes Benería and Martha Roldán (1987), industrial homework responds to accumulation and income-generating strategies for capital and workers, respectively, in which gender plays a significant role for both. In terms of accumulation, women homeworkers represent the cheapest source of labor. In terms of income generation, homework provides a source of money that contributes to the economic survival of women's households as well as to reducing women's dependence on men. This type of women's industrial homework is at the intersection of the formal and informal sectors of the economy, making the household an intermediate point where labor, capital, and gender relations are negotiated to accommodate changing production requirements.

Diversity in the organization of production under the new dynamics of capitalist accumulation cuts across the boundaries of the formal and informal sectors of the economy. The greatest variety of forms of organizing productive activities is found in the informal sector, where women's employment has grown considerably. In Peru, for example, 53 percent of the urban labor force works in the informal sector, 40 percent are women, and 61 percent of them are self-employed. In Brazil 50 percent of the informal sector labor force is female; in Ecuador half of those employed in the urban labor markets are women (Lycette and White 1988, 39); and in Jamaica the percentage of women working in the informal sector is 38 percent, which is much higher than the 12 percent for men (Deere et al. 1990). This significant women's role in informal sector activities should not, however, reinforce the common characterization of a dualistic labor market where men dominate employment in the formal sector and women dominate in the informal sector. As Alison MacEwen Scott (1991) points out, in the Peruvian urban labor market, women are overrepresented in the informal sector in relation to their share of employment and in comparison to men, but they do not dominate it; men are still the majority workforce there. This finding suggests the need to investigate the patterns of segregation and differences in work activities between men and women within the informal sector before uncritically accepting characterizations about the "informalization" of women's work.

Although the rapid expansion of an export manufacturing sector has certainly been a key factor in the increased participation of women in the labor market, women were integrated into industrial work before the proliferation of export industries.[6] Several trends have occurred: many women shifted from agriculture to manufacture; many were thrust into informal urban work because of the displacement of the rural population by the increased internationalization of economic life; and local and international industries sought to take advantage of the skills, flexibility, and low cost of women's labor in factories and at home both in local and export-oriented production. It could be said that women's work became connected to various levels and sectors of production as blood vessels are interconnected to the cardiovascular system of the human body. Women's work is performed in different sites, plays varying roles in the process of capitalist accumulation, and is tied in numerous forms and with diverse levels of productivity to the national and international economy; similarly, the blood vessels, arteries, and capillaries have different forms, carry out different functions, and are ultimately all connected to the heart.[7]

By taking the analysis of women's work from the macro- to the microlevel, the new research has dispelled what I call the *export processing fallacy,* that is, the notion popularized by some dependency and world-systems theories that the massive integration of women into the labor force is directly caused by export processing industrialization strategies promoted by multinationals. Studies on Brazil (Humphrey 1987) and Mexico (Benería and Roldán 1987), and to some extent my own work on Puerto Rico (Acevedo 1993), suggest that women's large-scale entry into industrial employment is not necessarily dependent on assembly-type, export-oriented manufacturing (*maquila*), as many of the proponents of the marginalization and the exploitation theses suggest. Indeed, Ruth Pearson (1991) points out that Mexican women participated in the industrial labor force before the establishment of the *maquiladoras.* This fact has been blurred by the increased visibility since the 1970s of women working in *maquiladora* plants operating along the Mexican border, which Pearson argues are declining in the 1990s. Conversely, female employment in industries whose production is mostly oriented toward the domestic market, and where national capital plays an important role and coexists with multinational investment, is on the rise (Humphrey 1987; Acevedo 1993). One of the electronics factories John Humphrey (1987) studied was organized as a joint venture between Brazilian and multinational capital, and an automotive factory was solely owned by Brazilian capital; both were assumed to be producing goods for the local as well as the international market. In Puerto Rico women's employment in manufacturing activities is concentrated in industries whose levels of export (as measured by value of shipment) is lower than that of industries dominated by men (Acevedo 1993). This research demonstrates that women can be significantly integrated as cheap labor in nonexport manufacturing as well as in industries with different owner-ship arrangements.

The connections between transnational capital and female employment are more complex than marginalization proponents argued, as the studies of women's industrial work in Brazil, Puerto Rico, and Mexico suggest. The new research indicates that the conditions for the integration of women into the industrial labor force have more to do with the women's costs of reproduction and with the division of labor within the firm than with the firm's market orientation or the origin of capital. The role that women play in the productive structure of a firm seems to be contingent on two key factors: the logic of international and/or local competitiveness and the sociological makeup of the labor market in a given country. That is, political, ideological, cultural, institutional, technological, and mana-gerial elements interact to produce the necessary conditions required by the process of production and to create the necessary labor force.

Units of Analysis: Shifts in Methodology

Research in the area of women and development has made important contributions to the methodological debate over the adequacy of social science research tools for the meaningful understanding of the socioeco-nomic context in which women function and the forces that shape their lives and experiences. Two issues are of most interest here: the unit of analysis and the simultaneous use of alternative methodologies in the pursuit of research goals. Research in the 1980s shifted the unit of analysis from the individual woman or the labor market to the household (Merrick and Schmink 1983; Benería and Roldán 1987; Roldán 1988) or the factory. This change in the level of analysis provides an opportunity for a comparative assessment of the usefulness of the household or the factory as the locus of research. The most important contribution to this debate comes from major research undertakings in Brazil and Mexico. These countries traditionally have been the sites of well-funded, in-depth research in which methodological issues are central.

The Household

The use of the household as a unit of analysis is justified by the argument that it is a mediating structure in women's position in the labor market (Jelin 1982). The methodological potential of the study of the household as a descriptive and analytical tool for bridging the social and individual levels of analysis is best supported in Benería and Roldán's

(1987) case study of industrial homework and subcontracting in Mexico. The authors defined the household as "a set of people that share a living space and budget usually, although not necessarily, on the basis of kinship relations" (Benería and Roldán 1987, 20). This conceptualization allows them to follow a deconstructionist strategy to uncover the linkages between the micro- and macrolevels of experience. Methodologically, this process entails the decomposition or disaggregation of the household into its parts and its analysis in relation to the individual and interacting activities of the members that constitute it. Finally, the decomposed whole is reconstituted so that individual behavior can be related to the broader structural and social processes of capital accumulation. The objective of such a strategy is to capture the autonomous actions of each individual by gender and locate them in the context of larger economic and ideological structures (capitalism and patriarchy). In this sense, "the household constitutes both an intermediate level of analysis as well as a convenient unit for the collection of empirical data" (Schmink 1984, 88). Since the household in itself is theoretically meaningless, the criteria for its decomposition depend on the research goals pursued. The analysis of the interplay between class and gender dictates the type of ideological and material components to be explored within the household. For example, the choice to study the ideological basis of the marriage contract (as it is expressed in women's lived relations as mothers and wives) (Benería and Roldán 1987), household budgets (Bolles 1986; Roldán 1988), or the mechanisms of control in the allocation of money are empirically relevant to the theoretical goal of integrating two levels of analysis (micro and macro) into a single conceptual framework.

The use of this methodological approach has important theoretical implications. First, the disaggregation of households and families on the basis of gender allows for the recognition and systematic analysis of the continuous and multiple work activities performed by women. Women's work includes the reproductive tasks of childbearing and rearing and productive work in both the formal and informal sectors, as well as in family enterprises located in the home, carried out through subcontracting or piece work, or found at the neighborhood level.[8] The recognition of the multiple dimensions of women's work as seen from the perspective of a household analysis has led to the rethinking and elaboration of the concept of work as traditionally understood in development theory (Tiano 1984; Draper 1985; Ward and Pyle, this volume).

Second, the assessment of the internal dynamics of the family and the household provides the basis for understanding gender differences in the patterns of work. This analysis serves to challenge the stereotyped view of the male as the only or primary productive worker and breadwinner.[9]

Third, the analysis of households demonstrates that family structures are not homogeneous. They range from nuclear family, to extended family (Gilbert and Ward 1985; Brydon and Chant 1989), to households headed by women (Merrick and Schmink 1983; Massiah 1984; Bolles 1986; Gómez 1990). This finding challenges the standard conception against which households in developing societies are evaluated. The growing majority of the households in developing societies cannot be characterized along the lines of the Western ideal of a nuclear family with a productive male breadwinner.[10] By focusing on the household structure (in terms of its composition by age, gender, and marital status), researchers reveal important differences among groups that share the common characteristics of poverty, low income, poor health and nutrition, and lack of basic necessities. Differences in household structures contribute to understanding differences in the patterns of work not only between women and men but also among women.

Fourth, this approach allows the researcher to examine the ideological and material components of gender relations within the household and to uncover any existing asymmetry of rewards (resources) and disunity of interests among household members.

Aside from these theoretical implications, it is important to recognize the policy implications of this methodological approach to the study of women's work and development. The analysis of the household serves to identify the diversity of women's work activities, the multiple roles women play, and their practical and strategic gender needs.[11] Research using this approach could serve as the basis for the formulation of policies and the implementation of programs that address gender needs as defined by women's experience in the process of development.

The Factory

The overall utility of the household as a unit of analysis can be contrasted with the methodological strategies followed in studies (Fernández Kelly 1983; Kelly 1986; Safa 1986b; Humphrey 1987; Tiano 1990) whose unit of analysis is the individual woman or the factory or establishment. Almost all the case studies that use the factory as a unit of analysis focus on the employment of women in manufacturing establishments owned by multinational corporations, especially labor-intensive, export-oriented industries. Significant knowledge is derived from that research, showing that the characteristics of a specific workforce (women) are closely related to the size and form of capital investment in developing countries, type of industry, and patterns of ownership (directly owned, subsidiaries, subcontracted firms, etc.). Moreover, such research allows an inquiry into the differences among women factory workers of multinational industries according to age, education, marital status, and household composition (Fernández Kelly 1983; Safa 1986b; Tiano 1990). These studies were used to elaborate and/or substantiate the marginalization and exploitation hypotheses.

Humphrey's (1985, 1987) case study of manufacturing firms in Brazil highlights the potential of the factory or establishment as an even more meaningful unit of analysis for unraveling the selective ways in which women are excluded, marginalized, or incorporated into the labor market in the course of industrialization. His theoretical goal was to analyze the construction of gender both in society and in the workplace through a concrete examination of the ways in which the gender of workers struc-ture employment, labor markets, and the organization of work. To reach this goal, Humphrey studied the sexual division of labor and its impact on labor markets through an analysis of the processes of segregation, task specifications, and recognition of skills in seven manufacturing establish-ments. The interrelationship between the workers' domestic situation and paid employment was used to illustrate the role that familial ideology played in structuring management strategies concerning recruitment, wage rates, training, and promotion of female and male workers.[12] Hum-phrey substantiated the argument that the general parameters of gender identities are established in the domestic sphere where they are shaped by power relations within families, ideologies, and practical necessities. These identities, however, are created, structured, and recreated in the workplace according to management's perception of women's and men's work and home situations and not merely transferred from one sphere to the other.

The Brazilian case study (Humphrey 1987) also went beyond prior research that used the factory as a unit of analysis since it explored the microlevel dimensions of the labor process and the role of gender in segmenting markets. It deconstructed the labor market and the workplace as totalizing units of analysis to provide a different explanation of the impact of development and to show the complexities of women's indus-trial employment.

The use of the factory as a unit of analysis has limitations, however, unless women's lives outside the factory are integrated into the research. In Latin America the majority of women do not work in factories, even though export processing has raised their overall participation in indus-trial employment. They are most likely to be engaged in paid domestic service (Jelin 1977; Souza 1979; Chaney and Garcia Castro 1989), informal sector activities (Arizpe 1977; Merrick and Schmink 1983; Babb 1986; Berger and Buvinic 1988), and/or paid work in the home where women can reconcile familial ideologies with paid employment (Beuchler 1986; Chant 1987; Brydon and Chant 1989). In this sense, restricting the analysis to factory workers excludes the work experience of an important number of women whose economic activities have been transformed by the development of capitalism.

Research Methods

In addition to the unit of analysis, it is important to examine the research methods used in women-and-development studies. They range from formal and informal interviews to participant observation, surveys and statistical analysis, participatory action research, women's personal narratives, and ethnography.[13] Despite the multiple use of interdisciplinary research methods, most of these studies incorporate the distinct methodological features identified with feminist research, including: (a) the recognition of women's needs, interests, and experiences as legitimate sources of social analysis; (b) doing research for women, not just on women, with a commitment to the improvement and empowerment of women's lives; and (c) "conscious partiality," which implies that research subjects must be conceived not only as parts of a social whole but as entities who, like the researchers themselves, have particular values, emotions, and feelings.[14] For example, in Benería and Roldán's (1987) study, the authors provide an account of the economic precariousness of the lives of the many women they interviewed and share with the reader the fears and distress that form part of poor women's daily lives. This compassionate profile of women's life experiences, however, does not obscure their courageous character and agility in strategizing for their own survival and that of their families. The women in this case study are portrayed not as passive victims of development but as active agents, albeit in contradictory ways, in the making of their lives.

Despite the creative use of alternative research methods, such studies may have shortcomings. Most of the literature has the implicit or explicit objective of analyzing gender relations at work, implying the inclusion of women and men and the interaction between them. Yet in most of the development research the data preclude the examination of the relational dimension in the definition of gender. By limiting the research to women's experiences, the studies provide a one-dimensional view of the relational aspect of gender. For example, in the case studies from Mexico (Benería and Roldán 1987; Roldán 1988), men's experiences are captured indirectly as statistics brought to the analysis only in passing to highlight the differences in educational levels and class insertion of husbands and wives or to make reference to the marital expectations of each. The discussion of such expectations, moreover, derives from the information provided by wives rather than from the combined analysis of information obtained from both wives and husbands. This shortcoming is obvious in the discussion of the important theme of the renegotiation of gender relations within the household, but it is also evident in other feminist studies on women's participation in and contribution to the informal economy (Babb 1986; Buecheler 1986). Although such research has contributed significantly to our understanding of women's paid and unpaid work and its relationship to the economy, and to challenging and correcting the male bias inherent in previous informal sector studies, it tends to reverse the gender bias. As MacEwen Scott (1991, 108) indicates, the "bias can now go in the other direction" of solely recognizing women's work without uncovering the gender asymmetries that take place in the informal sector.

In summary, this literature demonstrates the usefulness of focusing on households or the immediate working environment (the factory) when analyzing gender and development. These units of analysis offer a more complex approach to the power dimension of gender relations in society and the construction of gender hierarchies and inequalities in the labor market. They also demonstrate, however, that a household focus does not replace the need to study patterns of gender inequality at other levels of analysis and that studies of gender must include men's as well as women's experiences.

Class and Gender

Research on women's work and development has shown that an analysis of class relations within the household has enriched gender analysis by locating women's role in the household division of labor within the broader context of social relations. Implicit in this approach is the need to examine the processes whereby gender and class relations are simultaneously or mutually constructed. These propositions have renewed the discussion of the assumptions about gender and the locus of women's subordination and have stimulated the discovery of new ways of thinking about issues of class and gender.

The connection and interplay between class and gender raises a long-unresolved question that has haunted feminist theory about the relationship between the economic system and the subordination of women. For traditional Marxist feminists, the oppression and subordination of women are rooted in the material fabric of society, in the sphere of production, or in the capitalist economic system in Latin America. In these analyses women are inserted into the class structure under the argument that their paid and unpaid work is essential to meet the needs of capital accumulation. Gender inequalities, therefore, are subsumed under class inequalities. For radical feminists, women's subordination is based on male control of women's sexuality, procreative capacity, and ideology.

In these analyses women's subordination is anchored in an ideological system of male domination and privilege, named patriarchy. In this patriarchal system the sources of women's oppression are located in the sphere of reproduction or the household.

An assessment of the epistemological framework guiding recent research clearly shows these theoretical tensions, as well as the analytical pains involved in the reformulation of a concept of class that could be integrated in a gender analysis without subsuming gender relations under a predefined system of class relations. The reconsideration of the definitions of the social relations of class found in this literature suggests that classes are structured through relations of production, reproduction, and distribution.

Gender and the Productionist View of Class

The interplay between class and gender is not the focus of most contemporary research. But in many studies class relations provide the background against which women's subordination takes place. In case studies from Brazil (Humphrey 1987) and Puerto Rico (Safa 1986b), for example, an explicit definition of the concept of class is not offered, although the arguments made provide the bases from which to infer that these studies assume a concept of social class grounded in a Marxist view. In this view, social class is based on economic and structural criteria, that is, according to the principles of economic ownership and possession of the means of production. Economic ownership of the means of production refers to control over investment and productive resources; possession refers to control over the organization of the productive and labor processes. The essential factor for class definition is the common location of individuals within the process of production. The application of this formal criterion makes it possible to identify contradictory economic interests that define social classes.

Despite the androcentric bias in that conceptualization of class, the basic argument in these works is that the relations of production are gendered. That is, the concrete relations of production experienced in the process of work are permeated with the ongoing social construction of gender. Gendering occurs in the sex segregation of jobs within work organizations that usually locate women in some jobs and men in others. In his study of automotive and electrical plants, as well as pharmaceutical and toiletries manufacturing establishments, Humphrey (1987) found that women were concentrated in low-grade production jobs grouped mainly in one of two broadly defined occupations, production assistant or assembler. Furthermore, in most factories male and female workers were segregated into single-sex production departments. The social con-

struction of gender in the labor process also was expressed in the hierarchical structures of work organizations (MacEwen Scott 1986a; Benería
and Roldán 1987; Humphrey 1987; Presser and Kishor 1991; Acevedo
1993). Workers' identities based on gender are further maintained in the
workplace by the establishment of differences among gendered workers
in terms of skill, competence, and discipline. These differences have
far-reaching implications for the relationships established between workers and management and among workers, relationships that shape their
attitudes, authority relations, and career pursuits. Moreover, employment policies are constructed differently by employers for the male and
female labor force (Humphrey 1987) as well as among females at different stages in the life cycle (Fernández Kelly 1983; Safa 1986b; Lim 1990).
The literature on the work experience of women and men and the role of
gender in the organization of work in the factory clearly demonstrates
that production relations determining class locations are gender-specific,
not neutral or gender-blind, processes.

The view of relations of production as gendered processes represents a
significant departure from prior studies that identified differences in the
work experience of women and men but used macrolevel explanations of
the economic and/or ideological sources of women's oppression. This
new perspective requires a microlevel study of the social construction of
gender that is specific to particular industries, occupations, and localities.
It also requires an understanding of the ways in which gender is used to
structure the labor market and organize the labor process at different
points in the course of development.[15] Although the construction of
gender in the labor process cannot be assumed to be identical to the
general gender relations in society, this perspective recognizes women's
productive role in reproduction and reproduction's influence on women's
productive activities. In this sense, the determinants of women's class
location are expanded to include the gamut of women's productive
activities in the household and in the formal and informal sectors of the
economy.

Relations of Reproduction and Distribution

Other studies assume an approach to the definition of social class that
gives primary attention to the historical, cultural, social, and psychological factors that influence class identity and solidarity. Benería and
Roldán (1987, 13) best exemplify this perspective when they state,
"Classes are formed historically by their relationship to the economic
foundation of society and also by coherent cultural existence, common
social identity, and life-styles, features expected to originate from shared
historical experiences through generations." This conceptualization of

social class facilitates the inclusion of gender in the analysis as it expands the sphere of class construction beyond the workplace by considering social perceptions and values, beliefs, and forms of consciousness. Nonetheless, there are two problems in this approach. First, it pays little attention to the analysis of concrete production processes and their significance for class formation. Second, it has an androcentric bias that does not consider the specific gender relation to the class system arising from women's reproductive roles and family dynamics. To overcome these limitations, Benería and Roldán (1987) include an economic criterion of ownership and possession of the means of production and modes of remuneration, as well as study the sexual division of labor in the workplace and in the household. In a similar vein, Marianne Schmink's (1986) study of household members' availability for work in Bello Horizonte, Brazil, and Lynn Bolles's (1986) analysis of differences in household formation and income-generation strategies in Jamaica show how gender relations, marital status, and kinship networks inform and shape class formation in the process of capitalist development in peripheral societies. The inclusion of these criteria allow these authors to distinguish changes in the class position of women before and after marriage and to address the relations of distribution among household members.

From a feminist point of view, this is an interesting way of rethinking the concept of class and its interplay with gender. This reformulation is predicated on the notion that wage relations are built on gender-based assumptions that construe women as economically dependent on men (e.g., males are breadwinners, and women are secondary wage earners who have lower human capital and are less skilled). Such a construct implies the need to transfer or distribute economic resources (wages) from the male salaried worker (or the state) to the economically dependent women (mothers, wives, daughters).[16] Marriage and kin relations provide an important site for the distribution of wages to the "unwaged."[17] Through the analysis of intrahousehold patterns of money flows and allocation and control of resources, Benería and Roldán (1987) show how women, although in different and precarious ways, receive money from men in exchange for managing family life. With this money women cover part of the cost of their reproduction. According to this logic, men's wages are linked to relations of production, and women's social existence is fundamentally determined by the social relations of distribution. Within the same system of relations of production and distribution, women and men are involved in the system of class relations in their own right. They experience different class identities and interests.

Overall, the analysis of the interconnectedness of gender and class seems to privilege a socialist-feminist perspective over the traditional Marxist and radical feminist views. The empirical literature shows that class and gender analysis requires a framework that integrates labor market inequalities and gender inequalities within households and marital relations. What is needed is a theoretical synthesis that could lead to a reformulation of the relationship between class and gender and that also incorporates the multiple cultural, ideological, economic, political, and structural factors of women's subordination (including its reproductive and productive components). This entails an understanding of the patterns of participation in production, reproduction, and distribution that vary among women and among men as well as over a lifetime. These patterns are shaped by the historical specificity of women's own life experiences and the cultural and political processes that lead to different perceptions of class interests between women and men as well as among women and men. In this conceptual reformulation, gender and class are viewed as mutually constructed and open to constant redefinition in the course of social practice. These are the insights derived from the suggestive empirical literature the 1980s produced in the area of women and development, insights that are still in an embryonic form and are far from being clearly articulated. Nonetheless, they provide important building blocks for the theoretical endeavor that lies ahead.

Theorizing Gender and Development

The literature produced in the 1980s on women's work in Latin America has contributed to the theorizing of gender and development in three significant ways: (1) it recognizes the gendered character of the work process at all levels, (2) it reformulates the concept of social reproduction, and (3) it creates a women-centered standpoint in development studies. These contributions are the result of a challenging debate among feminists of different persuasions about the nature of women's incorporation and participation in capitalist development. Underlying the theoretical debate are analytical tensions rooted in the conceptual limitations of North American and European feminist thought, in which dualistic approaches have guided the research and self-contained and totalizing categories have been used as an "object" of analysis to produce and claim knowledge. This is the case of the conceptual definition of the category "women," which is fundamentally based on the white, middle-class, European and North American experience. The contributions mentioned above have provided the terrain for contesting traditional feminist assumptions and modes of explanations that have relied on gender stereotypes. Implicit in these contributions is a critique of past feminist epistemology from the perspective of the work experiences of women in the course of industrial development in Latin America. This critique has infused fresh blood into the theorizing of gender as well as the theorizing of gender and development.[18]

The Social Construction of Gender

In the early literature on women and development, gender implicitly was treated in a dualistic way and invoked in the analysis as a dichotomous variable, woman or man. By focusing exclusively on women, this research began to elaborate a conceptual category named "women" that compressed the multiple dimensions in the construction of women's identity into a single experiential model and produced a simplistic explanation of the relationship between gender and development. The tendency was to treat women as individuals without other competing identities or as individuals with uniform interests and concerns. The definitional referent for the category "women" was found either in North American and European feminist writings or in the generalization of the working experience of women in developing societies employed in similar jobs, occupations, and sectors of the economy.

The most illustrative example of this generalizing is found in the elaboration of the category *"maquila* women," which refers to Third World women workers employed by multinational corporations producing manufactured goods for the world market as part of the new international division of labor.[19] The growing number of women working in *maquiladoras* spurred a proliferation of studies from which an ideal and universal image of *maquila* women emerged. In the construction of this image, as Ruth Pearson (1986b, 75) points out, "the Third World was coalesced into a single undifferentiated country where women factory workers are young, single, childless, lack experience, and are passive and industrious." Underlying this image are the assumptions that the women's integration into the development process is based on the low price of their labor and on the "natural" qualities of their character: patience, dexterity, and submissiveness (MacEwen Scott 1986c).

This stereotyped image of the *maquila* women was challenged by numerous case studies that used gender as an analytical category.[20] The new research showed the existence of considerable variation in the characteristics of the workers recruited (Fernández Kelly 1983; Kelly 1986; Safa 1986b; Peña 1987; Tiano 1987b; Pineda 1990; Acevedo 1993). It was clear that, although women were the preferred labor force for multinational industries involved in export processing internationally, there were large differences between the types of women who were hired for this work in different parts of the developing world. These differences rested on sociodemographic factors such as age, marital status, education, family structure, and family composition. The discovery of differences among women in different employment situations provided a better understanding of the complexities involved in the social construction of gender in the process of production and labor. A gender analysis revealed that the reasons for paying low wages for women's labor vary from one society to another, concomitant not only with economic factors but with ideological, cultural, and political ones as well. Two significant lessons were derived from the findings of this research that have significant implications for theorizing gender and development. First, women's labor power has to be negotiated for with forms of patriarchal control and with childbearing and reproductive roles in each context. Second, different production processes and industrial branches require different kinds of labor power that may be supplied by different subsectors of the female labor force (Fernández Kelly 1983; Pearson 1986b).

The shift in the research focus from an exclusive analysis of women to an examination of how gender shapes and is implicated in all kinds of social phenomena marks a significant theoretical change in the development literature.[21] The new approach emphasizes the social (rather than the biological) character of differences between women and men. Gender differences are shaped and determined by the interconnection of ideological, historical, ethnic, economic, regional, and cultural factors. The investigation of gender differences has shown that the social construction of people's identities varies according to their position in locality, class, race, society, nation, region, time, and space. The social construction of gender is historical, personal, and structural. Gender relations are power relations that take place within different macro- and microspheres such as the state, the labor market, the law, the household, and interpersonal relations. They are crosscut by life cycles, marital status, and family ties. Hence, gender differences cannot be itemized in a checklist originating in a universal and totalizing concept of "women" (or "men"). They have to be investigated through an inductive analysis of specific situations and contexts.

These formulations of gender represent a step forward in thinking about the subordination of women in a historically concrete and socioeconomic way, as they present a more complex view of what constitutes gender and the institutionalization of asymmetric relations in which women are subordinated to men. Through a gender analysis we come to understand that subordination and domination are current outcomes of dynamic and interactive political, economic, social, and ideological processes in constant flux and definition (Bourque 1989).

Using a deconstructionist approach, researchers in this area of inquiry are moving away from the dualistic analyses (man/woman, culture/nature, gender/class, capitalism/patriarchy) that reduce the study of women's issues to the economic or ideological elements of women's lives and are moving forward to a more integrated analysis of the multiple interrelated elements that mediate the social construction of gender. This approach to the study of women's work and development builds a theory of gender from the bottom up, one that allows for the historical analysis of the specific mechanisms of women's subordination in concrete social formations.

Social Reproduction

The concept of social reproduction has been reformulated to include an analysis of the organizations of activities and relations that make possible human survival. Three levels in the analysis of reproduction and gender inequalities have been distinguished by Felicity Edholm, Olivia Harris, and Kate Young (1977): social reproduction, reproduction of labor, and human or biological reproduction. The study of these interrelated aspects has uncovered certain regularities associated with gender difference. Women working in the household and in the informal and formal sectors are overwhelmingly engaged in economic activities linked to the daily maintenance of laborers and households. The literature that addresses the impact of the Latin American debt crisis is particularly illustrative of this (Cariola et al. 1989; Aguiar 1990), as it shows how daily life and reproduction are shattered and sometimes reconstituted by capitalist transformation.

Despite these regularities, the conceptual distinction of the processes involved in reproduction has led to the understanding that the sexual division of labor, domestic practices, and reproductive strategies vary significantly with changing relations of production in the course of development. This constitutes a significant departure from the dualistic thinking that underlies the question of determinacy, which emphasizes the spheres of production and reproduction as separate socioeconomic activities. By moving reproduction to the center of the analysis, we can see production and reproduction as a dialectical unit: each has relative autonomy from the other, but at the same time, their intersection shapes the whole. The linkages between productive and reproductive work as well as their reliance on each other is shown in the studies of women's work and development that have focused on both the household and the factory. On the one hand, women's informal work, subsistence household activities, and salaried work in the formal sector are different forms of labor "played out in a variety of different ways as part of the expansion and contraction of capitalism" (Redclift 1985, 122). On the other hand, these relations of production are shown to be based on covert but crucial assumptions about gender and reproduction.

The Women's Standpoint

The third key contribution coming out of the studies on women's work and development is the elaboration of a feminist standpoint, which results from putting women at the center of the analysis. This women's standpoint is related to the broader question addressed in the feminist literature regarding knowledge claims (Harding 1987). A women's standpoint anchors its claim to know in the lives of people and focuses on the processes and relations outside their immediate daily lives that help create the conditions for those lives. This method proposes to understand social relations from the perspectives of women who themselves define the problematic, interpret the sources of their oppression, and construct an alternative vision about society, the economy, and gender relations. The alternative visions of diverse sources of oppression, however, are grounded in specific analyses of the multiple ways in which gender relations, the sexual division of labor, development strategies, and women's work are manifested and contested at different historical locations and according to particular (im)balances of power (Mohanty 1991). The epistemological claim that emerges from such a women's standpoint is contextually elaborated, based on a recognition of difference and a rigorous analysis of the interrelations of different sites of oppression based on class, race, nation, and sexuality. Through this strategy women in developing countries are reclaiming a space from which to speak about their oppression and their vision of feminism (Sen and Grown 1987). From their standpoint, women, positioned in similar localities (geographical, structural, discursive, historical), are voicing a critique of development strategies, programs, organizations, and institutions (Antrobus 1986, 1988; Buvinic 1986; Yudelman 1987a, 1987b) in particular and of "Western" (European and North American) feminist discourse in general (Amos and Parmar 1984; Lazreg 1990; Johnson-Odim 1991; Mohanty 1991). This constitutes a change from earlier stages of theorization when "Latin American women were put in the strange position of making their own acquaintance through the medium of an internationally recognized image of themselves which they played little part in constructing" (Zabaleta 1986, 97). The development of a women's standpoint serves "to un-develop the women in development discourse" (Salazar 1992, 454) and, more important, to decolonize knowledge at the same time that it contributes to building an oppositional theory and practice that seeks to empower the poorest and most oppressed groups of people.

The best attempt at theorizing gender and development from the standpoint of women is found in the collective effort of DAWN (Development Alternatives with Women for a New Era).[22] DAWN addresses the multiple sources of oppression with which women must engage by virtue of their different positions in sexist, racist, and imperialist conflicts. As Gita Sen and Caren Grown (1987, 23) point out, this analysis must be viewed from the vantage point of women who "constitute the majority of the poor, the unemployed and the economically disadvantaged in most societies . . . [and] suffer . . . gender-based hierarchies and subordination." Ironically, the different forms of women's work in developing societies are underpaid and undervalued but still are vital to the survival and ongoing reproduction of the peoples of these countries.

Although a complete theory of gender and development has not yet materialized, the existence of a women's standpoint from which to evaluate development strategies and programs is a significant step forward, is useful in the assessment of the adequacy of theories, and represents a challenge to the traditional, ethnocentric, and androcentric development paradigms (Fernández Kelly 1989). The focus on poor and oppressed women, rather than on dominant or intermediary groups, provides a unique and powerful vantage point from which to examine and judge the impact of development strategies on different activities crucial to the socioeconomic development and human welfare of the majority of the population (Sen and Grown 1987). From this standpoint, women's socioeconomic experiences constitute the ground against which any theoretical claim about development strategy ought to be tested. This analytical strategy recognizes that women's and men's experiences provide different, but not equally reliable, guides to the production and formulation of social research and policy (Goetz 1991; Moser 1991) and that the women's perspective more accurately reflects grassroots needs and concerns (Brydon and Chant 1989; Moser 1991).

As this perspective evolves into theory, more discussions and analyses of the choices and constraints of development alternatives and the power dimensions involved in the processes of social change and economic transformation are needed to assess critically the grounding of women's claim to know. So far, the feminist knowledge explosion in the study of women's work and development has opened new inroads for research and theory building.

Conclusion

The research on women and development is pointing toward a new research agenda and theoretical-methodological perspectives. It suggests the adoption of a methodological approach whose central conceptual framework is that of gender analysis. This approach allows for the incorporation of microeconomic phenomena (e.g., household dynamics) into a macroeconomic framework (class analysis), which in turn permits the adequate treatment of concepts such as gender, class, and race as fundamental aspects of the economic system, not simply as a characteristic of the individuals. The studies that use the division of labor in the household and the factory as the unit of analysis have shed light on a range of crucial issues concerning the construction of workers' identities and the effects of gender on the structure of the household as well as on industrial structure. Moreover, this approach contributes to a better understanding of the role of women in the process of development, as women cease to be an undifferentiated totality that is a victim in the process.

As these studies demonstrate, gender analysis facilitates the holistic study of the material and ideological bases of women's subordination in a concrete historical situation. Moreover, gender analysis contributes to identifying the mechanisms involved in the creation and maintenance of gender hierarchies in the social division of labor. It also provides the key to understanding the differential impact of development on people (women and men with different social profiles) and could lead to the formulation of a new development paradigm: a feminist theory of development that can provide a richer understanding of the complexities of the development process.

NOTES

Acknowledgments: I wish to thank Kathleen S. Crittenden and Margaret Strobel for their advice and stimulus in drafting the first version of this chapter. My gratitude also goes to Christine Bose and Edna Acosta-Belén for their editorial comments and support.

1. Along with the emergence of the literature on women and the economic crisis, women's political participation and their role in the transition to democracy has received considerable attention (Charlton, Everett, and Staudt 1989; Jaquette 1989; Alvarez 1990; ISIS Internacional 1990).

2. The marginalization thesis, first proposed by Ester Boserup (1970), dominated the study of women in the labor force in Latin America during the 1970s and 1980s. One of the main proponents was Heleieth Saffioti (1978), who reformulated it within the categories of dependency theory. For studies using different versions of this perspective, see the collection of essays gathered by the Wellesley Editorial Committee (1977) and the book edited by June Nash and Helen I. Safa (1980). For an example from Africa, see Nici Nelson 1981.

3. When this issue is addressed, it is discussed only in terms of the effects that monopoly capital and the new international division of labor have on women's work and the national economy.

4. See MacEwen Scott 1986b for a discussion of the different dimensions of

marginalization of women during the course of development and an assessment of the theoretical and methodological limitations of the marginalization thesis.

5. Here productive employment is taken to be all salaried work in the formal sector of the economy traditionally performed outside the household.

6. Import-substitution industrialization was said to have a negative impact on women's employment. According to leading marginalization proponents, the jobs created under this development strategy were taken mostly by men (Saffioti 1978; Ward 1984). But in fact, studies show that women were active in manufacturing activities in a variety of ways (Rivera 1986; Humphrey 1987, chap. 1; Baerga 1993).

7. For this point, I am grateful to Emilio Pantojas-García (1992), who used this metaphor to explain the interconnections between the formal and informal sectors and national and international productive activities.

8. The growing body of literature that focuses on the role of women in the new social movements documents the community dimension of women's work through the provision of items for collective consumption (Blondet 1990; Pieres de Río Caldeira 1990).

9. Safa's (1986b) research on Puerto Rico points to the fact that in the context of high male unemployment, women's productive work becomes an important economic source for the maintenance and subsistence of all household members. A case study on women's work in Mexicali also found that many *maquila* women are primary breadwinners or support others in their households (Tiano 1990).

10. The trend in Latin America and the Caribbean is toward an increase in the number of households headed by women. This increase is associated with the postwar processes of industrial and urban development (Massiah 1984; Brydon and Chant 1989).

11. Here I refer to the distinction made by Maxine Molyneux (1986) between types of gender interests. Strategic gender interests (needs) are those derived from an analysis of women's subordination to men (e.g., abolition of the sexual division of labor); practical interests are those derived from the concrete conditions women experience. See also Caroline Moser 1991, 88–92.

12. To assess the impact of the construction of gender identities in the household on gender relationships in the factory, Humphrey (1987) constructed a succinct and simple empirical scheme to measure the division of domestic responsibilities of women and men in the household (washing clothes and dishes, ironing, cooking, cleaning the house, and shopping) and in childcare and education.

13. A comprehensive assessment of the significance of these research tools for feminist analysis is found in Reinharz 1992.

14. These guidelines are discussed at length in Duelli Klein 1983, Mies 1983, and Harding 1987. For a feminist assessment, see Reinharz 1992.

15. Empirical studies on the role of gender in the segmentation of the labor market, occupational segregation, and the construction of job hierarchies from developing societies appear to be scarce, the exceptions being reports on Venezuela (Schmink 1977), Peru (MacEwen Scott 1986a), Puerto Rico (Presser and Kishor 1991; Acevedo 1993) and Brazil (Humphrey 1987). The level of analysis

in these studies varies from the national economy, to economic sectors, to the factory.

16. Joan Acker (1988) points out, referring to the experience of African American women in the United States, that the patterns in the personal relations of income distribution are not only from men to women within marriage but also from networks of support and nurturing. In the Caribbean context this idea is reflected in the research on strategies of survival among working-class women in a Puerto Rican shantytown (Safa 1980) and among women heads of households in the context of Jamaica's economic crisis (Bolles 1986).

17. This line of argument concerning gender and work has been found problematic in the context of industrialized societies on two counts. First, female labor is confused with married women's labor, and this makes it difficult to apply the model to an analysis of specific categories of women. For example, it can be argued that the labor process is not only gender specific but also marital-status specific. Safa (1986b) and Fernández Kelly (1983) seem to provide empirical evidence for this argument in their investigation of women's work and the life cycle. Second, the assumption of dependency on a male wage raises many questions about measures of women's dependency on men as well as questions about the advantages of women's work for capitalism and their status in society; female labor is advantageous because women are economically dependent, and they are dependent because they are low paid! (Redclift 1985).

18. In response to the challenge posed by the diversity in women's experiences, two models of feminist theory of knowledge are dominating the theoretical discussion: cultural feminism and feminism and the postmodern discourses (Alcoff 1988; Nicholson 1990; Ebert 1991). For suggestive assessment of these approaches in the context of the women-and-development literature, see Ann Marie Goetz 1991. Interesting hypotheses for the construction of a gender and development theory are also found in Blumberg 1989, Blumberg in this volume, and McFarland 1987.

19. The tendency to use the category "women" in an undifferentiated way is also observed in the feminist literature that focuses on technology and development (see Bourque and Warren 1987).

20. Other valuable studies in the general area of economic development relevant to the theorization of gender are Deere and León de Leal 1981 and Jelin 1977. Of similar importance are the essays in Leacock and Safa 1986 and Nash and Safa 1986.

21. The theoretical base for the conceptualization of gender in Benería and Roldán's case study (1987), for example, was inspired by the works of Michèle Barrett (1980), who attempted to provide a synthesis of radical and Marxist analyses of the subordination of women. Seemingly, Humphrey's (1987) theoretical framework is based on the work of Gayle Rubin's (1975) sex/gender system analysis in which two contrasting types of life and behavior for women and men are defined as well as the relations between them.

22. DAWN was formed in 1984 by a group of Third World feminist and political activists who had become disenchanted with both the mainstream and radical development prescriptions for Third World women. They called for a

broader, more comparative approach to women's development problems that could lead to short-term development planning sensitive to women's needs and interests and to long-term realistic strategies for change. Their objective is to incorporate gender and class perspectives into the analysis, formulation, and implementation of macroeconomic and social policies in developing societies.

REFERENCES

Acevedo, Luz del Alba. 1990. "Industrialization and Employment: Changes in the Patterns of Women's Work in Puerto Rico." *World Development* 18 (2): 231–255.

————. 1993. "Género, trabajo asalariado y desarrollo industrial en Puerto Rico: La división sexual del trabajo en la manufactura." In *Género y trabajo: La industria de la aguja en Puerto Rico y el Caribe,* ed. María del Carmen Baerga, 161–212. Río Piedras, Puerto Rico: University of Puerto Rico Press.

Acker, Joan. 1989. "Class, Gender, and the Relations of Production." *Signs: Journal of Women in Culture and Society* 13 (3): 473–497.

Aguiar, Neuma. 1990. "Las mujeres y la crisis latinoamericana." In *Mujer y crisis,* ed. DAWN/MUDAR, 11–30. Caracas, Venezuela: Editorial Nueva Sociedad.

Alcoff, Linda. 1988. "Cultural Feminism vs. Post-Structuralism: The Identity Crisis in Feminist Theory." *Signs: Journal of Women in Culture and Society* 13 (3): 405–436.

Alvarez, Sonia E. 1990. *Engendering Democracy in Brazil.* Princeton: Princeton University Press.

Amos, Valerie, and Pratibha Parmar. 1984. "Challenging Imperial Feminism." *Feminist Review* 17:3–19.

Antrobus, Peggy. 1986. "New Institutions and Programs for Caribbean Women." In *Women of the Caribbean,* ed. Pat Ellis, 131–134. London: Zed.

————. 1988. "Crisis and Challenge: The Experiences and Responses of Caribbean Women's Organizations in the 1980s." Paper presented at the consultation/symposium to mark the tenth anniversary of the Women and Development Unit (WAND). Bridgetown, Barbados: Extra Mural Department, University of the West Indies.

————. 1989. "Gender Implications of the Debt Crisis." In *Development in Suspense: Selected Papers and Proceedings of the First Conference of Caribbean Economists,* ed. George Becford and Norman Girvan, 145–160. Kingston, Jamaica: University of the West Indies.

Arizpe, Lourdes. 1977. "Women in the Informal Labor Sector in Mexico City." *Signs: Journal of Women in Culture and Society* 3 (1): 24–37.

Arizpe, Lourdes, and Josefina Aranda. 1986. "Women Workers in the Strawberry Agribusiness in Mexico." In *Women's Work: Development and the Division of Labor by Gender,* ed. Eleanor B. Leacock and Helen I. Safa, 174–193. South Hadley, Mass.: Bergin and Garvey.

Babb, Florence E. 1986. "Producers and Reproducers: Andean Marketwomen in the Economy." In *Women and Change in Latin America,* ed. June Nash and Helen I. Safa, 53–64. South Hadley, Mass.: Bergin and Garvey.

Baerga, María del Carmen. 1993. "Las jerarquías sociales y las expresiones de resistencia: Género, clase y edad en la industria de la aguja en Puerto Rico." In *Género y trabajo: La industria de la aguja en Puerto Rico y el Caribe,* ed. María del Carmen Baerga 103–137. Río Piedras, Puerto Rico: University of Puerto Rico Press.

Barrett, Michèle. 1980. *Women's Oppression Today.* London: Verso.

Benería, Lourdes, and Martha Roldán. 1987. *The Crossroads of Class and Gender: Industrial Homework, Subcontracting, and Household Dynamics in Mexico City.* Chicago: University of Chicago Press.

Berger, Marguerite, and Mayra Buvinic, eds. 1988. *La mujer en el sector informal, trabajo femenino y microempresa en América Latina.* Caracas, Venezuela: ILDS-Quito and Editorial Nueva Sociedad.

Blondet, Cecilia. 1990. "Establishing an Identity: Women Settlers in a Poor Lima Neighborhood." In *Women and Social Change in Latin America,* ed. Elizabeth Jelin, 12–46. London: Zed.

Blumberg, Rae Lesser. 1989. "Toward a Feminist Theory of Development." In *Feminism and Sociological Theory,* ed. Ruth Wallace, 161–199. Beverly Hills, Calif.: Sage.

Bolles, Lynn. 1983. "Kitchens Hit by Priorities: Employed Working-Class Jamaican Women Confront IMF." In *Women, Men, and the International Division of Labor,* ed. June Nash and M. Patricia Fernández Kelly, 138–160. Albany: State University of New York Press.

———. 1986. "Economic Crisis and Female-Headed Households in Urban Jamaica." In *Women and Change in Latin America,* ed. June Nash and Helen I. Safa, 65–83. South Hadley, Mass.: Bergin and Garvey.

Boserup, Esther. 1970. *Women's Role in Economic Development.* New York: St. Martin's Press.

Bourque, Susan. 1989. "Gender and the State: Perspectives from Latin America." In *Women, the State, and Development,* ed. Sue Ellen M. Charlton, Jana Everett, and Kathleen Staudt, 114–129. Albany: State University of New York Press.

Bourque, Susan, and Kay B. Warren. 1987. "Technology, Gender, and Development." In *Learning about Women, Gender, Politics, and Power,* ed. Jill K. Conway, Susan C. Bourque, and Joan W. Scott, 173–198. Ann Arbor: University of Michigan Press.

Brydon, Lynne, and Sylvia Chant. 1989. *Women in the Third World.* New Brunswick, N.J.: Rutgers University Press.

Buechler, Judith-Maria. 1986. "Women in Petty Commodity Production in La Paz, Bolivia." In *Women and Change in Latin America,* ed. June Nash and Helen I. Safa, 165–188. South Hadley, Mass.: Bergin and Garvey.

Buvinic, Mayra. 1986. "Projects for Women in the Third World: Explaining Their Misbehavior." *World Development* 14 (5): 653–664.

Cariola, Cecilla, Miguel Lacabana, Luisa Bethencourt, Gregorio Darwich, Beatriz Fernández, and Ana Teresa Gutiérrez. 1989. *Crisis, sobrevivencia y sector informal.* Caracas, Venezuela: ILDIS-CENDES and Editorial Nueva Sociedad.

Chaney, Elsa M., and Mary Garcia Castro. 1989. *Muchachas No More: Household Workers in Latin America and the Caribbean.* Philadelphia: Temple University Press.

Chant, Sylvia. 1987. "Family Structure and Female Labor in Querétaro, Mexico." In *Geography of Gender in the Third World,* ed. Janet Momsen and Janet Townsend, 227–293. London: Hutchinson.

Charlton, Sue Ellen M., Jana Everett, and Kathleen Staudt. 1989. *Women, the State, and Development.* Albany: State University of New York Press.

Chinchilla, Norma Stoltz. 1977. "Industrialization, Monopoly Capitalism, and Women's Work in Guatemala." *Signs: Journal of Women in Culture and Society* 3 (1): 38–56.

DAWN/MUDAR. 1990. *Mujer y crisis: Respuesta ante la recesión.* Caracas, Venezuela: Editorial Nueva Sociedad.

Deere, Carmen Diana, Peggy Antrobus, Lynn Bolles, Edwin Melendez, Peter Phillips, Marcia Rivera, and Helen Safa. 1990. *In the Shadows of the Sun: Caribbean Development Alternatives and U.S. Policy.* Boulder, Colo.: Westview.

Deere, Carmen Diana, and Magdalena León de Leal. 1981. "Peasant Production, Proletarianization, and the Sexual Division of Labor in the Andes." In *Women and Development: The Sexual Division of Labor in Rural Societies,* ed. Lourdes Benería, 65–93. New York: Praeger.

Draper, Elaine. 1985. "Women's Work and Development in Latin America." *Studies in Comparative International Development* 20 (1): 3–30.

Duelli Klein, Renate. 1983. "How To Do What We Want To Do: Thoughts about Feminist Methodology." In *Theories of Women's Studies,* ed. Gloria Bowles and Renate Duelli Klein, 88–104. New York: Routledge and Kegan Paul.

Ebert, Teresa L. 1991. "The 'Difference' of Postmodern Feminism." *College English* 53 (8): 886–904.

Edholm, Felicity, Olivia Harris, and Kate Young. 1977. "Conceptualizing Women." *Critique of Anthropology* 3 (9–10): 101–130.

Fernández Kelly, M. Patricia. 1983. *For We Are Sold, I and My People: Women and Industry in Mexico's Frontier.* Albany: State University of New York Press.

———. 1989. "Broadening the Scope: Gender and International Economic Development." *Sociological Forum* 4:11–35.

García de Fanelli, Ana, Mónica Gogna, and Elizabeth Jelin. 1989. *El empleo de "cuello rosa" en la Argentina: El caso de un banco estatal.* Buenos Aires, Argentina: Centro de Estudios de Estado y Sociedad.

Gilbert, Alan, and Peter Ward. 1985. *Housing, the State, and the Poor: Policy and Practice in Three Latin American Cities.* Cambridge: Cambridge University Press.

Goetz, Ann Marie. 1991. "Feminism and the Claim to Know: Contradictions in Feminist Approaches to Development." In *Gender and International Rela-*

tions, ed. Rebecca Grant and Kathleen Newland, 133–157. Bloomington: Indiana University Press.

Gómez, Carmen Julia. 1990. *La problemática de las jefas de hogar: Evidencia de la insubordinación social de las mujeres.* Santo Domingo, Dominican Republic: CIPAF, Editora Taller.

Harding, Sandra. 1987. "Introduction: Is There a Feminist Method?" In *Feminism and Methodology,* ed. Sandra Harding, 1–14. Bloomington: Indiana University Press.

Hirata, Helena. 1989. "Production Relocation: An Electronics Multinational in France and Brazil." In *Women's Employment and Multinationals in Europe,* ed. Diane Elson and Ruth Pearson, 129–143. London: Macmillan.

Humphrey, John. 1985. "Gender, Pay, and Skill: Manual Workers in Brazilian Industry." In *Women, Work, and Ideology in the Third World,* ed. Haleh Afshar, 214–231. London: Tavistock.

———. 1987. *Gender and Work in the Third World: Sexual Division in Brazilian Industry.* London: Tavistock.

Inter-American Development Bank. 1990. *Economic and Social Progress in Latin America: 1990 Report.* Washington, D.C.

ISIS Internacional. 1990. *Transiciones: Mujeres en los procesos democráticos.* Ediciones de las Mujeres no. 13. Santiago, Chile.

Jaquette, Jane S. 1989. *The Women's Movement in Latin America.* Boston: Allen and Unwin.

Jelin, Elizabeth. 1977. "Migration and Labor Force Participation of Latin America Women: The Domestic Servants in the Cities." *Signs: Journal of Women in Culture and Society* 3 (1): 129–141.

———. 1982. "Women and the Urban Labor Market." In *Women's Role and Population Trends in the Third World,* ed. Richard Anker, Mayra Buvinic, and Nadia Youssef, 239–267. London: Croom Helm.

Joekes, Susan. 1987. *Women in the World Economy.* New York: Oxford University Press.

Johnson-Odim, Cheryl. 1991. "Common Themes, Different Contexts: Third World Women and Feminism." In *Third World and the Politics of Feminism,* ed. Chandra Talpade Mohanty, Ann Russo, and Lourdes Torres, 314–327. Bloomington: Indiana University Press.

Kelly, Deirdre. 1986. "St. Lucia's Female Electronics Factory Workers: Key Components in an Export-Oriented Industrialization Strategy." *World Development* 14 (7): 823–838.

———. 1987. *Hard Work, Hard Choices: A Survey of Women in St. Lucia's Export Oriented Electronics Factories.* Cave Hill, Barbados: Institute of Social and Economic Research, University of the West Indies.

Lavrin, Asunción. 1987. "Women, the Family, and Social Change in Latin America." *World Affairs* 150 (20): 109–128.

Lazreg, Marnia. 1990. "Feminism and Difference: The Perils of Writing as a Woman in Algeria." In *Conflicts in Feminism,* ed. Marianne Hirsch and Evelyn Fox Keller, 326–348. New York: Routledge.

Leacock, Eleanor, and Helen Safa, eds. 1986. *Women's Work: Development and the Division of Labor by Gender.* South Hadley, Mass.: Bergin and Garvey.

Lim, Linda Y. C. 1990. "Women's Work in Export Factories: The Politics of a Cause." In *Persistent Inequalities: Women and World Development,* ed. Irene Tinker, 101–119. New York: Oxford University Press.

López Cavalcanti de Oliveira, Zuleica. 1990. "Crisis, situación familiar y trabajo urbano." In *Mujer y crisis,* ed. DAWN/MUDAR, 40–74. Caracas, Venezuela: Editorial Nueva Sociedad.

Lycette, Margaret, and Karen White. 1988. "Acceso de la mujer al crédito en América Latina y el Caribe." In *La mujer en el sector informal, trabajo femenino y microempresa en América Latina,* ed. Marguerite Berger and Mayra Buvinic, 35–66. Caracas, Venezuela: ILDIS-Quito and Editorial Nueva Sociedad.

MacEwen Scott, Alison. 1986a. "Economic Development and Urban Women's Work: The Case of Lima, Perú." In *Sex Inequalities in Urban Employment in the Third World,* ed. Richard Anker and Catherine Hein, 428–451. London: Macmillan.

———. 1986b. "Women and Industrialization: Examining the 'Female Marginalization' Thesis." *Journal of Development Studies* 22:649–680.

———. 1986c. "Women in Latin America: Stereotypes and Social Science." *Bulletin of Latin American Research* 5 (2): 21–27.

———. 1991. "Informal Sector or Female Sector? Gender Bias in Urban Labor Market Models." In *Male Bias in the Development Process,* ed. Diane Elson, 105–132. Manchester: Manchester University Press.

McFarland, Joan. 1987. "The Construction of Women and Development Theory." *Canadian Review of Sociology and Anthropology* 25 (2): 299–308.

Massiah, Joycelin. 1984. *La mujer como jefe de familia en el Caribe: Estructura familiar y condición social de la mujer.* Paris: UNESCO.

Merrick, Thomas W., and Marianne Schmink. 1983. "Households Headed by Women and Urban Poverty in Brazil." In *Women and Poverty in the Third World,* ed. Margaret Lycette and William McGreevey, 244–271. Baltimore: Johns Hopkins University Press.

Mies, Maria. 1983. "Towards a Methodology for Feminist Research." In *Theories of Women's Studies,* ed. Gloria Bowles and Renate Duelli Klein, 117–139. New York: Routledge and Kegan Paul.

Mohanty, Chandra Talpade. 1991. "Under Western Eyes: Feminist Scholarship and Colonial Discourses." In *Third World Women and the Politics of Feminism,* ed. Chandra Talpade Mohanty, Ann Russo, and Lourdes Torres, 51–80. Bloomington: Indiana University Press.

Molyneux, Maxine. 1986. "Mobilization without Emancipation? Women's Interests, State, and Revolution." In *Transition and Development: Problems of Third World Socialism,* ed. Richard R. Fagen, Carmen Diana Deere, and José Luis Coraggio, 280–302. New York: Monthly Review.

Moser, Caroline. 1991. "Gender Planning in the Third World: Meeting Practical and Strategic Needs." In *Gender and International Relations,* ed. Rebecca Grant and Kathleen Newland, 83–121. Bloomington: Indiana University Press.

Nash, June, and M. Patricia Fernández Kelly. 1983. *Women, Men, and the International Divison of Labor.* Albany: State University of New York Press.

Nash, June, and Helen I. Safa. 1980. *Sex and Class in Latin America: Women's Perspectives on Politics, Economics, and the Third World.* South Hadley, Mass.: J. F. Bergin.

———. 1986. *Women and Change in Latin America.* South Hadley, Mass.: Bergin and Garvey.

Nelson, Nici, ed. 1981. *African Women and the Development Process.* London: Frank Cass.

Nicholson, Linda J. 1990. *Feminism/Postmodernism.* New York: Routledge.

Pantojas García, Emilio. 1992. "La economía puertorriqueña ante el reto de la reestructuración de la economía global." Keynote address to the Association of Puerto Rican Economists, San Juan, Puerto Rico, June 5.

Pearson, Ruth. 1986a. "Latin American Women and the New International Division of Labor: A Reassessment." *Bulletin of Latin American Research* 5 (2): 67–79.

———. 1986b. "Female Workers in the First and Third Worlds: The 'Greening' of Women's Labour." In *The Changing Experience of Employment: Restructuring and Recession,* ed. Kate Purcell, Stephen Wood, Alan Waton, and Sheila Allen, 75–94. London: Macmillan.

———. 1991. "Male Bias in Women's Work in Mexico's Border Industries." In *Male Bias in the Development Process,* ed. Diane Elson, 133–163. Manchester: Manchester University Press.

Peña, Devon. 1987. "Tortuosidad: Shop Floor Struggles of Female *Maquiladora* Workers." In *Women on the U.S.-Mexico Border: Responses to Change,* ed. Vicki L. Ruiz and Susan Tiano, 129–154. Boston: Allen and Unwin.

Pieres de Río Caldeira, Teresa. 1990. "Women, Daily Life, and Politics." In *Women and Social Change in Latin America,* ed. Elizabeth Jelin, 47–78. London: Zed.

Pineda, Magaly. 1990. " . . . *la vida mía no es fácil*": La otra cara de la zona franca. Santo Domingo, Dominican Republic: Centro de Investigación para la Acción Femenina.

Presser, Harriet B., and Sunita Kishor. 1991. "Economic Development and Occupational Sex Segregation in Puerto Rico, 1950–80." *Population and Development Review* 17 (1): 53–85.

Redclift, Nanneke. 1985. "The Contested Domain: Gender, Accumulation, and the Labour Process." In *Beyond Employment: Household, Gender, and Subsistence,* ed. Nanneke Redclift and Enzo Mingione, 93–125. London and Oxford: Basil Blackwell.

Reinharz, Shulamit. 1992. *Feminist Methods in Social Research.* New York and Oxford: Oxford University Press.

Rivera, Marcia. 1986. "The Development of Capitalism in Puerto Rico and the Incorporation of Women into the Labor Force." In *The Puerto Rican Woman: Perspectives on Culture, History, and Society,* ed. Edna Acosta-Belén, 30–45. New York: Praeger.

Roldán, Martha. 1988. "Industrial Outworking, Struggles for the Reproduction of Working-Class Families, and Gender Subordination." In *Beyond Employment: Household, Gender, and Subsistence,* ed. Nanneke Redclift and Enzo Mingione, 249–285. London and Oxford: Basil Blackwell.

Rubin, Gayle. 1975. "The Traffic in Women: Notes on the 'Political Economy' of Sex." In *Toward an Anthropology of Women,* ed. Rayna R. Reiter, 157–210. New York: Monthly Review.

Safa, Helen I. 1980. "Class Conciousness among Working-class Women in Latin America: Puerto Rico." In *Sex and Class in Latin America: Women's Perspectives on Politics, Economics, and the Third World,* ed. June Nash and Helen I. Safa, 69–85. South Hadley, Mass.: J. F. Bergin.

———. 1986a. "Runaway Shops and Female Employment: The Search for Cheap Labor." In *Women's Work: Development and the Division of Labor by Gender,* ed. Eleanor B. Leacock and Helen I. Safa, 58–71. South Hadley, Mass.: Bergin and Garvey.

———. 1986b. "Female Employment in the Puerto Rican Working Class." In *Women and Change in Latin America,* ed. June Nash and Helen I. Safa, 84–106. South Hadley, Mass.: Bergin and Garvey.

———. 1990. "Women and Industrialisation in the Caribbean." In *Women, Employment, and the Family in the International Division of Labour,* ed. Sharon Stichter and Jane L. Parpart, 72–97. Philadelphia: Temple University Press.

Saffioti, Heleieth. 1978. *Women in Class Society.* New York: Monthly Review.

———. 1986. "Technological Change in Brazil: Its Effects on Men and Women in Two Firms." In *Women and Change in Latin America,* ed. June Nash and Helen I. Safa, 109–135. South Hadley, Mass.: Bergin and Garvey.

Salazar, Claudia. 1992. "Unruly Women: Deconstructing Development Practices." In *The Knowledge Explosion,* ed. Cheris Kramarae and Dale Spender, 448–458. New York: Teachers College Press.

Schmink, Marianne. 1977. "Dependent Development and the Division of Labor by Sex: Venezuela." *Latin American Perspectives* 4 (1–2): 153–179.

———. 1984. "Household Economic Strategies: Review and Research Agenda." *Latin American Research Review* 19:87–101.

———. 1986. "Women and Urban Industrial Development in Brazil." In *Women and Change in Latin America,* ed. June Nash and Helen I. Safa, 136–165. South Hadley, Mass.: Bergin and Garvey.

Sen, Gita, and Caren Grown. 1987. *Development, Crises, and Alternative Visions.* New York: Monthly Review.

Serrano, Claudia. 1990. "Mujeres de sectores populares urbanos en Santiago de Chile." In *Mujer y crisis,* ed. DAWN/MUDAR, 93–104. Caracas, Venezuela: Editorial Nueva Sociedad.

Souza, Julia Filet-Abreu de. 1979. "Paid Domestic Service in Brazil." *Latin American Perspectives* 1:35–63.

Standing, Guy. 1989. "Global Feminization through Flexible Labor." *World Development* 17 (7): 1077–1095.

Tiano, Susan. 1984. "The Public-Private Dichotomy: Theoretical Perspectives on 'Women in Development.' " *Social Science Journal* 21 (4): 11–28.

————. 1986. "Women and Industrial Development in Latin America." *Latin American Research Review* 21:157–170.

————. 1987a. "Gender, Work, and Capitalism." In *Analyzing Gender: A Handbook of Social Science Research,* ed. Beth B. Hess and Myra Marx Ferree, 216–243. Beverly Hills, Calif.: Sage.

————. 1987b. "*Maquiladoras* in Mexicali: Integration or Exploitation?" In *Women on the U.S.-Mexico Border: Responses to Change,* ed. Vicki L. Ruiz and Susan Tiano, 77–101. Boston: Allen and Unwin.

————. 1990. "*Maquiladora* Women: A New Category of Workers?" In *Women Workers and Global Restructuring,* ed. Kathryn Ward, 193–223. Ithaca, N.Y.: ILR Press.

Truelove, Cynthia. 1990. "Disguised Industrial Proletarians in Rural Latin America: Women's Informal-Sector Factory Work and the Social Reproduction of Coffee Farm Labor in Colombia." In *Women Workers and Global Restructuring,* ed. Kathryn Ward, 48–63. Ithaca, N.Y.: ILR Press.

Vasques de Miranda, Glaura. 1977. "Women's Labor Force Participation in a Developing Society: The Case of Brazil." *Signs: Journal of Women in Culture and Society* 3 (1): 261–274.

Ward, Kathryn. 1984. *Women in the World System: Its Impact on Status and Fertility.* New York: Praeger.

Wellesley Editorial Committee, ed. 1977. "Women and National Development." *Signs: Journal of Women in Culture and Society* 3 (1).

Yudelman, Sally W. 1987a. *Hopeful Openings: A Study of Five Women's Organizations in Latin America and the Caribbean.* West Hartford, Conn.: Kumarian Press.

————. 1987b. "The Integration of Women into Development Projects: Observations on the NGO Experience in General and in Latin America in Particular." *World Development* 15:179–187.

Zabaleta, Marta. 1986. "Research on Latin American Women: In Search of Our Political Independence." *Bulletin of Latin American Research* 5 (2): 97–119.

CHAPTER 4

❋

Recasting Women in the Global Economy

Internationalization and Changing Definitions of Gender

M. PATRICIA FERNÁNDEZ KELLY AND
SASKIA SASSEN

Writings on the world economy underscore the link between the internationalization of investments and the growing incorporation of women into the labor force since the 1960s (Fröbel, Heinrichs, and Kreye 1980; Fernández Kelly 1983; Nash and Fernández Kelly 1983; Ward 1988; Enloe 1990). In the United States and other advanced countries internationalization led to industrial restructuring and a shift from manufacturing to services. That, in turn, resulted in the expansion of technical and professional jobs and the growth of an even larger number of occupations with features generally associated with women's employment, including temporality, comparatively low wages, and reduced union membership (International Labour Organization 1987).[1]

In less developed nations—particularly in Asia and Latin America—integration into the global economy altered development strategies (Chaney 1984; Mohammed and Shepherd 1988; World Bank 1990; Wolf 1992; Moghadam 1993). During the 1950s and 1960s many governments in poorer countries pursued economic growth through import-substitution industrialization. At present the tendency is toward the liberalization of national economies, a concerted response to international market demands, and the expansion of export processing zones. As in the case of advanced countries, these trends have paralleled the unprecedented feminization of the labor force.[2] Why are women playing such a conspicuous role in the reconfiguration of the global economy?

In partial answer to that question, in this chapter we explore two converging processes that are recasting the participation of women in

99

paid employment. The first process entails transformations in the system of production that have led, in advanced countries, to a reorganization of industrial activity and the recomposition of the labor force. The second process encompasses a reconceptualization of women as economic actors, in contrast to preexisting definitions that emphasized their domestic role. During the early stages of industrial capitalism the split between labor market and home widened. This promoted gender definitions that tied women to the private sphere of family and unpaid work and connected men to the public world of remunerated employment. How is economic restructuring transforming economic and social options, and how are those tendencies modifying gender demarcations?

The Context

During the 1970s the rapid loss of manufacturing jobs raised concerns about the future of industry in the United States. Researchers described an emerging international division of labor according to which direct production would drastically diminish in advanced countries at the same time that export-oriented industrialization would expand in developing nations (Fröbel et al. 1980). Theorists foresaw the coming of a postindustrial society, reliant on computer technology and characterized by the proliferation of well-paying professional jobs and the disappearance of class conflict (Bell 1976; Drucker 1990; Teich 1990). Neither of the two visions materialized. The number of high-tech jobs requiring symbolic skills has grown since the 1970s, as predicted by postindustrialists, but even larger has been the growth of menial, low-skill occupations (Newman 1988; Sassen 1993). To be sure, the movement of jobs to overseas locations, in search of cheap labor, slowed down the growth of industry in the United States, as anticipated by students of the new international division of labor, but it did not lead to the disappearance of domestic manufacturing. In fact, manufacturing continued to grow in this country at the same time that investments overseas increased.

A case in point is the electronics industry. Despite major losses in actual and potential employment, electronics production has expanded in the formal and informal sectors (Sassen-Koob 1985; Portes and Sassen-Koob 1987; Portes, Castells, and Benton 1989). Electronics is still the fourth largest industry in the United States and one of the fastest growing sectors. There were 2.35 million people formally employed in electronics production in the United States by May 1992. Formal employment in that sector peaked at 2.5 million in 1984 and then again at 2.6 million in 1989; furthermore, some evidence suggests that informal employment grew during the same period as a result of the overall reconfiguration of the industry.

In the same vein, and contrary to popular portrayals, garment production has expanded over time, especially in Los Angeles County and the New York metropolitan area. This expansion is largely explained by the persistence of subcontracting arrangements linking established firms to unlicensed shops and industrial homeworkers. Nationwide, the garment industry includes approximately twenty-five thousand firms employing more than two million people, with a $15 billion annual direct payroll. In addition, this sector indirectly employs two hundred thousand farmers involved in cotton and wool processing. From that point of view, apparel is a larger employer than the automobile and steel industries combined, and despite the blows endured in the 1970s and 1980s, it continues to expand in the United States. Most garments sold in this country are manufactured domestically, with New York still the leader in apparel production and Los Angeles County second.

The domestic resilience of garment and electronics manufacturing raises a key question: Why do companies continue to produce in the United States, despite large international wage differentials and the advantages derived from overseas investments?

In an attempt to answer that question, we conducted, between 1985 and 1988, a study of Hispanic women in the garment and electronics industries.[3] We selected the two locations with the fastest growing Hispanic populations—New York and southern California—and hypothesized that the incorporation of immigrant and ethnic women into manufacturing activities in the two areas was symptomatic of a broader process of industrial reorganization. In other words, we conjectured that the incorporation of Hispanic women, many of them foreign-born, into labor-intensive operations in the United States was a complementary aspect of the same process that had led to the relocation of operations to places such as Asia and the U.S.-Mexican border. The theoretical significance of this project can be summarized as follows.

a. It conceived industrial restructuring as a multifaceted process entailing parallel, not mutually exclusive, adjustments at the domestic and international levels.
b. It redefined globalization to include international movements of labor, not just capital.
c. It conceptualized changes in the ethnic composition of the electronics and garment labor force as part of the process of industrial restructuring.
d. It placed gender at the center of the process that enabled industries to compete domestically and internationally.

The importance of Hispanics in general, and of Hispanic women in particular, for contemporary industry was suggested by our review of aggregate data. A comparison of the 1970 and 1980 censuses of population showed that Hispanics were the only ethnic group in the United States that had maintained or raised its representation in blue-collar employment. In other words, the same period that had witnessed so-called industrial decline also paralleled the growing incorporation of Hispanics into the manufacturing workforce. In Los Angeles, Orange, and San Diego counties Hispanics account for only 20.5 percent of the labor force but over 30 percent of those employed in the manufacturing sector (Bean, Edmonston, and Passel 1990; Kleiman 1992, 6).[4] These rates are far above those found among other ethnic groups in the United States. In the New York area Hispanics are about 20 percent of the labor force but 35 percent of those in manufacturing. Census data also show that approximately 35 percent of all women involved in direct production nationwide are Hispanic (Bean and Tienda 1987).

Historically, the garment industry has been a provider of entry-level jobs for immigrants and women of all nationalities. In New York early waves of European migration were later replaced by increasing numbers of Asians and more recently Hispanics. In southern California the garment industry has employed mostly Mexican women since the nineteenth century. But it is not only garment work, a notoriously competitive industry, that targets women for employment. Our aggregate and ethnographic data point to the conspicuous presence of women, minorities, and immigrants in the lower echelons of electronics production. For example, in southern California, one of the leading industrial centers in the world, fully 67 percent of the workforce in the large occupational category "operators, fabricators, and laborers" belong to ethnic minority groups. Of those, 51 percent are Hispanic females. Minority women constitute 70 percent of all "machine operators, assemblers, and inspectors." Hispanic women comprise 76 percent of that group. Finally, ethnic minorities make up 71 percent of all "metal and plastic machine operators," a category of special relevance to the electronics industry. Hispanics represent almost 80 percent of that figure.

To understand the relationship of industrial adjustment, immigration, and Hispanic women's employment in garment and electronics, we combined the strengths of survey and ethnographic research and took a comparative approach in our study. We collected information on a random sample of two hundred electronics firms and one hundred fifty garment manufacturers in New York and southern California. In addition to extended interviews with firm owners and managers, we conducted in-depth case studies of a smaller number of companies to identify the junctures at which gender, ethnicity, and migratory background converge with the reorganization of production.

In both industries standardized production requiring low levels of quality control and abundant inputs of manual labor were relocated on a large scale to Asia, Latin America, and the Caribbean Basin in the 1970s. During the 1980s, the period of our research, both industries responded to foreign competition through strategies that combined (a) a shift toward flexibility in production and labor arrangements, (b) a move away from vertically integrated operations and a reduction of plant size, (c) an emphasis on customization and specialization in production, (d) a reliance on various types of subcontracting and the resulting expansion of the informal sector, including the proliferation of small shops outside government regulation and industrial homework (Silver 1989); and (e) the tapping of labor pools formed by increasing numbers of women, particularly those belonging to specific ethnic and immigrant groups.

Women and Electronics Production in New York and Southern California

In 1954, the integrated circuit was perfected in New York City's Bell Laboratories by William Shockley and his associates (Shurkin 1984; Siegel 1984). More distinctly than others, that moment marked the birth of the modern electronics industry, which in the succeeding years evolved into a reality and a metaphor for the age of advanced technology. Despite this significance, the New York electronics industry experienced setbacks beginning in the 1970s. An early clustering of large, vertically integrated corporations in New York City gave way to a multiplicity of small companies in New York's periphery, including the neighboring counties in New Jersey. Relocation within the region paralleled changes within firms, especially regarding the size of operations, the types of products manufactured, and the level of specialization pursued. Reductions in plant size, an emphasis on tailored production, and a reliance on contracted work furnished new competitive advantages. While the number of large companies diminished over time, the number of small firms increased. From slightly more than 300 firms in the area in 1980, electronics production burgeoned to more than 680 firms in 1986; 40 percent of those hired between one and fifty workers.

Throughout the 1980s popular and specialized writings gave attention to smallness in plant proportions, with some celebrating and others deriding downsizing (Piore and Sabel 1984; Waldinger 1994). Supporters pointed to the competitive gains of "lean and mean" operations. Detractors saw small firms as potential sweatshops, an indication of debasement in the terms of production and employment. To some extent both interpretations were accurate. Many firms in New York exemplify the tendency toward "manucrafting," the term used by an owner in our sample of firms to describe his work: a paradoxical combination of advanced technology, customization, and labor-intensive production. Other small firms in our study, including home operations, illustrate the potential for the evasion of labor and tax regulations and for the deterioration of labor conditions.

Table 4-1 summarizes the characteristics of the electronics firms in our New York sample. Two-thirds of the firms were dedicated to the production of communications equipment and electronics components. Most firms were located in Suffolk County and in New Jersey's Bergen and Essex counties, an effect of spatial recomposition that started with the fragmentation or disappearance of larger firms in the center of the metropolitan area and the growth of smaller firms in Manhattan's outer ring. The shuffling across spatial boundaries was also evidenced by the

TABLE 4-1

Profile of a Random Sample of Electronics Firms in the
New York Metropolitan Area (N = 101)

Percentage that produce communications equipment and electronics components (Missing cases: 1)		25.0
Percentage that had been located elsewhere (Missing cases: 1)		72.3
Concentration by county (Missing cases: 1)	Bergen	17.8
	Essex	15.8
	Passaic	10.9
	Suffolk	30.7
	New York City	8.9
Percentage privately owned		78.0
Percentage that contract from others (Missing cases: 4)		65.0
Percentage that contract out (Missing cases: 35)		42.6
Percentage that customize products		90.0
Percentage that subcontract to homeworkers (Missing cases: 22)		25.7
Percentage of workforce female (Missing cases: 7)		56.5
Percentage of workforce Hispanic		5.7

extent to which companies had changed addresses; 70 percent of the firms in our sample had been previously located elsewhere.

The vast majority of firms (78 percent) were privately owned, with a significant proportion started by engineers formerly employed in larger companies. An emphasis on customization, quality control, and flexible production characterized those smaller firms. Contracting arrangements were widespread. Almost two-thirds of the firms in the New York sample took work orders from other companies. Two-thirds, in turn, contracted work out to other firms. Even more striking: fully one-third of our respondents admitted to subcontracting to homeworkers, and that percentage may be an underestimate because, given the dubious legality of industrial homework, many managers were reluctant to make such admissions; 22 percent of our respondents declined to answer questions about homework.

As anticipated, women play an important role. In about half the firms in our sample, 50 percent of the labor force was female. On the average, about one-third of all workers in the firms surveyed were women, although there were variations by location and type of production. On the other hand, Hispanics were sparsely represented in the New York electronics industry; only 5.7 percent of the labor force was Hispanic. That was a major difference by comparison to southern California.

Our firsthand interviews with electronics producers in Los Angeles, San Diego, and Orange counties indicate that, in addition to the proximity to markets and research and development centers, employers perceive benefits derived from the presence of large, affordable labor pools and comparatively low wage and unionization rates. All these advantages are associated with the employment of immigrants, particularly those who have recently arrived in this country and those who are undocumented. A significant number of foreign-born Hispanics are employed in electronics in southern California.

The profile that emerged from the study of our random sample of electronics firms in southern California is condensed in Table 4-2. The typical firm employed 446 workers, and 41.5 percent of its total costs went to labor. Only 3 percent of the companies were fully automated, with 12.6 percent of employees in research and development and 36.7 percent in direct production. Approximately 20 percent of the firms surveyed had fifty employees or fewer; 7 percent had ten employees or fewer.[5]

Thus, contrary to a popular impression, the southern California electronics industry is characterized by comparatively low levels of automation and devotes a considerable percentage of its operation costs to labor-intensive activities. In fact, direct production accounts for the largest proportion of employment in these electronics firms.

TABLE 4-2

Profile of a Random Sample of Electronics Firms in Southern California (N = 100)

Average number of employees	446
Average number of direct production workers	163
(Missing cases: 4)	
Percentage of costs that go to labor	41.5
(Missing cases: 11)	
Percentage of fully automated companies	3.0
Percentage of employees in research and development	12.6
(Missing cases: 3)	
Percentage of workforce in direct production	36.7
Percentage of firms with 1–50 employees	20.0
Percentage of firms with 1–10 employees	7.0
Percentage of semiconductor component–producing firms	71.0
(Missing cases: 9)	
Percentage of direct production workers female	60.0
Percentage of direct production workers Hispanic	44.0
(Missing cases: 2)	
Percentage of direct production workers foreign-born Hispanic	30.0
(Missing cases: 17)	

The assembly of semiconductor components of various kinds represents the predominant type of production in southern California. Percentages varied by size of firm. More than 60 percent of large firms, but
almost 82 percent of small firms (those with fewer than fifty workers),
were dedicated to that kind of manufacture. In contrast, slightly less than
8 percent produce microwave equipment, and only 2.6 percent produce
artificial intelligence. Large firms are more likely to produce highly
advanced electronics equipment.

Large firms have the largest number of employees, the highest percentage of employees in research and development, and the smallest proportion of labor costs as part of total expenditures. By contrast, small firms
have lower sales, a higher percentage of labor costs (almost 50 percent),
and the largest percentage of all employees involved in assembly. Small
firms in southern California thus represent the most vulnerable sector in
electronics production and, theoretically, can be conceived as a locus for
informalization. That explains the propensity of firms in that sector to
appear in the Labor Code violations listings of the Wage and Hour
Division.[6]

Between 1985 and 1987 adjusted hourly wages earned by direct production workers in southern California electronics firms averaged slightly
over $7.00; almost 60 percent of direct production workers were women,
and more than one-third of those were Hispanic. The small and poten-

tially informalized establishments had the largest proportion of Hispanic women involved in direct production (48.6 percent).

A large number of workers engaged in electronics assembly are native- and foreign-born Hispanics. The significance of this finding may be appreciated when the broader demographic composition of the region is considered. Slightly over 23 percent of the southern California popula- tion is Hispanic, but 44.1 percent of direct production workers in our sample, and upward of 57 percent of those employed in small firms cited for Labor Code violations, belong to the same ethnic group. Perhaps more significant, almost 35 percent of direct production workers in small firms are foreign-born Hispanics. There are fewer immigrants in very large firms (30 percent) and a larger proportion in small informalized establishments (43.8 percent). Although Asians represent 5 percent of the southern California population, 20 percent of direct production workers in our sample are Asian. The demographic balance is reversed in the case of African Americans, who represent 12 percent of the southern Califor- nia population and almost half the labor force, but only 3 percent of direct production workers in electronics. In other words, labor-market selectivity does not operate randomly; it expresses preferences and per- ceptions on the part of employers about the suitability of women, immi- grants, and ethnic minorities for certain types of employment.

As in the case of New York, a large number of companies represented in this survey had turned toward tailored production and customization to remain competitive and to shelter themselves from large-scale stan- dardized production. Almost 59 percent of companies in our sample offered products manufactured to specification. Although large firms exhibited an even higher tendency toward customization (70 percent), many of the companies that produced to specification were very small. As few as two or three employees can be found in lucrative companies specializing in the production of highly technical components and ma- chinery. Thus, though smallness can be an indication that a firm occupies a vulnerable position at the lower end of the industrial structure and a particular propensity toward informalization, it can also be a feature of advanced and profitable segments in electronics production.

Electronics firms rely on a complex chain formed by subcontracting arrangements. We found various forms of subcontracting, including licensing agreements, to be the backbone of the southern California electronics industry. More than half of all companies rely heavily on various forms of domestic and international subcontracting. Some firms subcontract to operations in foreign locations *and* to small independent firms in southern California. The trend is toward a combination of strategies rather than full reliance on any particular form of production.

Assembly emerged as the principal type of subcontracted activity in our survey.

Subcontracting has two complementary effects. First, it allows employers to lower production costs by displacing unskilled and semiskilled operations to small, independent firms specializing in individual tasks such as coiling, sorting, counting, and finishing. These firms are also the most likely to hire vulnerable workers, including immigrants and women. Second, subcontracting leads toward the decentralization of production, affording companies greater flexibility in adapting to fluctuating market conditions. Flexibility in production is the primary motivation cited by southern California firms that subcontract. Subcontracting as a means to reduce costs was stressed by less than 11 percent of the firms in our sample. The trend appears to be toward the use of subcontracting mainly to increase flexibility in production and adjust to cyclical market demands.

In addition, electronics companies depend on the intermittent use of homeworkers. Homeworkers are used by 13.2 percent of firms in our sample and by fully 30 percent of small firms. This finding confirms our expectation that producers at the lower end of the industrial structure— many of whom are Hispanic or Southeast Asian entrepreneurs—would be more likely to rely on the services of homeworkers. Thus, electronics may be conceived as a many-layered industry that uses a complex series of strategies to maximize access to markets, flexibility, and responsiveness to the specific needs of customers. Some of those layers encompass manners of production that seem more congruent with older industries such as apparel. That is the case of industrial homeworkers, who tend to be systematically concealed by aggregate figures.

The wide representation of Hispanic women in one of the major centers of the electronics industry is significant for several reasons. Paradoxically, electronics—the epitome of advanced technology—is predominantly an employer of unskilled and semiskilled workers, many of whom are minority women. To a large extent, employment policies in electronics manufacturing mirror national trends. Forecasts anticipate that the largest number of jobs through the end of the century will be created in low-paying occupations in services and in the direct production of nondurable and durable goods. Electronics manufacture alone will require fifty times more custodians than engineers by the end of the century (U.S. Department of Labor 1990). More than 50 percent of all workers in the same industry will be involved in direct production and assembly. A significant, albeit smaller, proportion of the labor force in electronics will be formed by high-skilled technicians, engineers, computer designers, and programmers. Most direct production workers will be women, while, on the average, specialized occupations will be filled by professional men.

Electronics is likely to remain an example of acute stratification on the basis of skill and sex.

The Apparel Industry in New York and Southern California

The garment industry has been described in journalistic and scholarly writings as a declining sector (Grenier et al. 1992). Our research showed, however, that garment production in general, and particularly in Los Angeles County and the New York metropolitan area, has expanded over time.

Garment production has clearly suffered major setbacks in various types of production at the national and regional levels. What has not been sufficiently recognized is the extent of change in the geography and composition of the industry. Massive losses of factories in central New York City went along with growth in new locations within the city and in the outer rim of the larger metropolitan area, which includes points in New Jersey. Our study found that these outlying firms produce, in fact, for New York City firms. But although production has decentralized, fashion and design firms are most likely to be in New York proper. This points to a recomposition and spatial reorganization of the New York garment industry. In the same vein, the impression that restructuring rather than decline characterizes the recent history of the garment industry in southern California is supported by our review of the number of employees hired by various types of firms over time. For example, there was a noticeable increase in the total number of workers in the Los Angeles apparel industry, from 51,719 in 1965 to 83,424 in 1982. The number of firms expanded and shrank at different points during the same period (Waldinger and Lapp 1993).

In Los Angeles the apparent contradiction between a reduced number of companies specializing in certain types of apparel and a growing number of workers in the industry as a whole is explained by the proliferation in the number of small firms since the mid-1970s. Of 2,717 registered apparel and textile manufacturers in Los Angeles in early 1984, 1,695, or 62 percent, employed between one and nineteen workers; the majority of firms within that sector employed between one and four people. By contrast, there has been a striking reduction in the number of plants hiring between one hundred and five hundred workers. Operations with larger workforces have virtually disappeared.

These findings suggest that it is the lower stratum of garment production, characterized by the existence of small licensed and unlicensed garment shops, that is expanding. In these establishments production is relatively unstable, a large number of undocumented immigrant workers are found, and wage and labor code infractions are frequent. Not surprisingly, during the late 1970s and throughout the 1980s alarm grew over the large-scale employment of undocumented women, violations to the Labor Code and Tax Law, and the expansion of homework. Our interviews with government officials in agencies such as the Employment Development Department, the Division of Labor Standards Enforcement, the Department of Industrial Relations, and the Wage and Hour Division of the U.S. Department of Labor further substantiate the impression that homework and other types of unregulated assembly in the garment industry experienced increases between 1982 and 1986.

Other adjustments in the garment industry are documented by our research. First, there has been a reduction in the number of vertically integrated firms and an increase in the decentralization of the labor process. For example, the same firm may subcontract its long-lead-time standardized production to firms located in Asian export processing zones, at the same time using the services of small domestic companies to tap opportunity markets demanding novelty products. According to our direct interviews, subcontracting offers advantages such as the lowering of production costs by diffusing the need to maintain stable labor forces, and the reduction of conflict caused by the demands of unionized workers (Fernández Kelly 1993).

Second, the fragmentation of garment production has created a need for quick adaptation, speed in production, and flexibility on the part of subcontractors. This, in turn, has led to renewed violations of state and federal regulations. Our study of small firms in garment production shows that they generally cannot weather market fluctuations by operating legally, nor can they easily meet the costs of regulation—especially taxes and licensing fees. They tend to hire workers (a large number of whom are undocumented immigrants) at peak seasons and to dismiss them perfunctorily when contracts end or when demand for a particular product wanes. Jobs in these shops offer few benefits and are the lowest paying among all industrial jobs in the United States. A modality of this type of operation is home assembly.

Paradoxically, the expansion of subcontracting has also opened new opportunities for small businesspeople and created new categories of buyers and intermediaries. Start-up costs in garment manufacture have always been comparatively low. Thus, investment in this sector has historically attracted ethnic and immigrant entrepreneurs. The presence of immigrants in the garment industry is not a new phenomenon. On the other hand, economic restructuring has accentuated the demand for immigrant workers, at the same time militating against the consolidation of vertically integrated firms capable of providing stable work to native-born U.S. citizens. Our study documented the presence of brokers in southern California who specialize in the matching of ethnic and immigrant labor pools and garment contractors. Brokers tend to be individuals with experience in the industry. Some are former contractors acquainted with the habits and preferences of manufacturers. Perhaps more significant, they also tend to be members of ethnic minorities. Their bilingualism as well as their practical experience allow them to serve as a link between manufacturers and Hispanic and Asian workers, the majority of whom are foreign-born.

Finally, industrial restructuring has had a peculiar impact on Hispanic women's chances for becoming small independent subcontractors. We have identified two mechanisms as a result of direct interviews with employers and women owning or managing garment operations. First, the trend toward decentralization of the labor process and the attempt to lower production costs have led many employers to encourage women workers to open their own firms. Employers often lease out idle machinery to these women while providing them with some of the orders they obtain from larger manufacturers (Fernández Kelly and García 1992).

Second, women turn to self-employment and business ownership as part of a search for flexibility in time allocations. The rationale behind Hispanic women's decisions to become entrepreneurs is not very different from the one that leads many to become involved in home assembly. In both cases women aim at reconciling home care responsibilities with financial need. But the contradictions stemming from their involvement in unremunerated and wage labor often place them at a disadvantage in terms of competitiveness and leverage vis-à-vis large contractors.

Firsthand interviews with women small business owners indicate that they live on the edge of financial disaster, their profit margins are negligible, their orders widely irregular, and their ability to master administrative skills almost nonexistent. Consequently, they are a favorite target for periodic inspections, citations, and penalties assessed by state officials. In spite of this risk, the measure of autonomy provided by entrepreneurial activity is appreciated by these women. It may be one of the unanticipated consequences of restructuring in the garment industry that spaces are being created for the incorporation of women as small businesspeople.

Women Redefined: The Ideological Issues

Garment and electronics production represent a limited segment of economic activity in the United States. The importance of that segment resides not in size alone, however, but in the extent to which it captures tendencies that, although widespread throughout the economy, assume a sharper profile in the two industries. The search for flexibility in production *and* in terms of employment, the tendency toward subcontracting, and the targeting of strategic labor pools formed by women and immigrants are all features present beyond the confines of garment and electronics production. Historically, the two industries have been at the forefront of internationalization since the 1960s; their structure and adaptations (as described in the previous sections) illustrate the conditions that are recasting men's and women's economic roles.

In our interviews with women employed in southern California firms, we found that the economic underpinnings sustaining the definition of women as specialized homemakers and men as providers is being replaced by an understanding of individuals with an obligation to participate in the labor market *regardless of gender and/or domestic responsibilities*. The words of these women capture central issues.

María Talavera, a twenty-five-year old unwed mother of two, was working as a seamstress and living with her parents in East Los Angeles in 1986.[7] She was a third-generation American whose ancestors had immigrated to the United States from Sonora, Mexico, after the Great Depression. María's interpretation of the changes faced by working women is excerpted here: "I hear a lot about woman's lib and all that but I don't know what it means because . . . see . . . when my mother was young, the rules were clear: men support the family, women raise the kids. Now it's different because the man doesn't want to bear the burden [of a family] anymore; they want someone who can pull her own weight. So I guess the woman has to work [outside the home] all the time but, who's helping her with the kids at home?"

Luisa Nazario, originally from Puebla, Mexico, had lived in San Diego, California, most of her life. She had held several jobs, including one in direct production in a small electronics shop in Kearny Mesa. At the time of our conversation in 1986 she was intermittently doing assembly work at home: "I don't know if things are better now. I guess so because women can work [outside the home] without being hassled. The problem is you can't stay at home just to take care of the family without everyone looking at you like you've gone crazy and your man's a fool!"

At age twenty-nine, Marina Robles was married and living with her husband and six-year-old daughter in Escondido. She too was an American of Mexican descent and worked as a quality control supervisor in a high-tech firm. She told us:

> Things aren't the same, and who knows how it's all going to be for men and women by the time my daughter is old enough to get married. Maybe people won't even get married then. Why bother if you can support yourself? Even now, women are expected to get a job and it's not like it's a

choice. Before, if you worked [outside the home] everybody knew it was to help your husband but it was his obligation [to support the family]. Now it's your obligation; people expect women to work [outside the home] whether they like it or not.

The statements above have three features in common: (a) they acknowledge that expectations about the proper role of men and women have changed, (b) they hint at benefits and disadvantages derived from the perceived changes, and (c) they omit causal explanations for the changes in question. When asked further, the women above, and many others, pointed to shifts in values over time as the main reason for the transformation of gender roles. Change was described in purely personal terms. Of fifty women interviewed, only five saw a connection between the labor market and altered gender roles.[8] Yet the changes to which they alluded cannot be understood outside the context created by economic restructuring at the domestic and international levels.

Beginning in the 1980s scholars have advanced several interpretations about growing female employment. Some observers minimize the novelty of women's paid employment by pointing out that women have always worked inside and outside the home (Kessler Harris 1981). What is new, those observers note, is not the extent to which women have been, and continue to be, economic actors but rather their recognition as workers, a recognition concealed by earlier ideologies that defined them as domestic beings.

Others argue that, although women have always worked, the extent to which they have pursued paid employment since the 1960s merits additional explanation. In this view, changes in consciousness explain the influx of women into the labor force. Propelled by feminist ardor, women are presumed to be seeking personal fulfillment outside the home (Hartmann 1987). A variant of this perspective is found in less developed countries, where even representatives of the private sector see economic liberalization and the shift toward export-oriented industrialization as processes that are opening new opportunities for women and breaking the shackles that subordinated them to men in traditional societies (Ward 1988).

According to our perspective, changes in consciousness are a significant but small aspect of a complex process rooted in the structural requirements of contemporary capitalism. It is true that, either by historical coincidence or as a result of structural connections only half understood, the emergence and diffusion of feminist ideologies has coincided with economic internationalization. Nevertheless, heightened feminist awareness cannot fully explain the rapidity with which women have strived for paid employment in the latter years of the twentieth century. Instead, labor demand factors must be considered. Women in advanced and less developed countries are being targeted by employers because they represent one of the most vulnerable segments of the labor force. Women's subordination to men as wives, mothers, and daughters makes them a particularly attractive source of low-cost labor at a time when investors seek to maintain an edge in fiercely competitive international markets (Fernández Kelly 1990). One of the implications of this perspective is that economic internationalization has not abolished older patriarchal definitions but transformed them instead to meet the requirements of global competition.

The three interpretations sketched above pinpoint distinct features in the relationship between gender and economic change. Each gives priority to aspects of a larger process that entails structural and ideological transformations. But how are gender definitions, first consolidated in the late nineteenth century, being altered by internationalization and industrial restructuring?

Throughout the nineteenth century the separation between wage and domestic labor that followed early attempts to rationalize capitalist production in Europe and in the United States also corresponded to redefinitions of the roles of men and women. Women in agrarian societies, such as those that preceded the onset of industrial capitalism, experienced subordination but not the marked distinction between home and workplace that we associate with modern society. The advent of the factory and the office, while allowing greater output and more efficient organization of labor, made it difficult for women to coordinate wage and domestic work (Tilly and Scott 1987). Gradually, women were pushed out of the labor market and charged with such domestic chores as childcare and the regeneration of human energy. As mechanization advanced, remunerated employment became the prerogative of men even in those areas of production that had been a female domain (Nash and Safa 1980). Women and children became dependent on men for access to resources in an increasingly monetarized marketplace.

The particulars of this development are well documented; although the process has varied according to historical period and geographical area, its effects have been similar. In less developed countries industrialization and the mechanization of agriculture had a profound impact on women. Those belonging to privileged classes benefited to some extent by gaining access to paid employment in industry, government, or education, while leaving domestic work in the hands of servants, most of them also female. Rural women, in contrast, found their conditions of life debased by the same transformations. Investments in commodity crops displaced them from agricultural employment, and their artisanal goods competed at a disadvantage with mass commodity production (Deere 1978, 1990; Benería and Sen 1986).

As servants and assembly workers, women faced new dilemmas. The need to support families led them to become wage earners; caring for families, however, often prevented them from holding permanent jobs. That tension, resulting from a systemic requirement to maintain a devalued reproductive sphere outside the realm of paid employment, was tenuously resolved under capitalism in three complementary ways. First, women clustered in a few niches of the occupational structure where jobs were defined as an extension of their domestic responsibilities. Second, those jobs were assigned low productivity and wages. Finally, the two phenomena were captured in ideological constructions that defined women's paid employment as a supplement to that of men. Wage differentials between men and women may thus be interpreted as an effect of the belief that the former should have higher earnings because they have families to support, whereas the latter merely add to the gains of their husbands or fathers. That idea partly explains why, universally, women earn less than men when employed in jobs requiring similar levels of education, training, and responsibility.

The casting of women as domestic beings over the past two hundred years did not occur in isolation. It was matched by a complementary process that defined men as providers and charged them with the support of women and children. The ideal of a wage that could adequately support an entire family appeared in the United States as early as the 1820s and 1830s. It developed during the late nineteenth and early twentieth centuries and was expressed in the speeches of union leaders, Progressive era reformers, and some employers, including Henry Ford. Those presentations consistently expressed concerns about the threat to family subsistence from cheap female labor, the disintegration of the working-class family, and worker productivity. The struggle for a family wage was an effort to increase the standard of living of the majority of workers who earned only enough to support one person (Spalter-Roth, Hartmann, and Andrews 1990). The struggle, however, was grounded in the belief that it was the male breadwinner who should earn this wage and that paying him adequate wages would limit the participation of women and children in the workforce. A 1909 textbook in economics captured this view: "A man in industry requires a wage sufficient to maintain himself and his family, whereas many women living at home, with little or nothing to do, are willing to go into industry in order to secure spending money, or enough money to guarantee the little necessities and luxuries of life that a young woman naturally desires" (Nearing and Watson 1909, 148).

Thus, from its inception the ideal of the family wage corresponded to an emerging class structure rooted in diverging gender definitions: men should earn wages commensurate with the maintenance of families; women, if they had to work outside the home, should earn a smaller, supplementary wage. The family wage remained only an ideal for the families of minority men, who were, by and large, excluded from higher-paid, union-protected jobs, and for the families of many unskilled workers. The privileges and responsibilities that accompanied the role of provider made it possible for employers to gain tighter control over a predominantly male working class (Ehrenreich 1984). The emergence of the nuclear family as a normative concept and aspiration was thus predicated on polarized gender definitions that corresponded to a separation between the private and public realms.[9] What made the domestic sphere unique, in this new world view, was its presumed lack of economic significance. Economic reality was only made visible, acknowledged, and inscribed in the public sphere of paid employment, money, and productive work.

Two corollaries of these gender constructions are of special interest. First, women's work at home became invisible from an economic standpoint, and their work outside the household—no matter how widespread—was viewed as an exception, that is, in terms significantly different from those accompanying the work of men (Bose 1987). Second, the casting of gender identities did not emerge over time as a secondary contradiction; on the contrary, gender definitions were embedded in class conflict and in the gradual establishment of a tacit pact between employers and workers in the early stages of industrial capitalism.[10] In other words, the stabilization of the tensions between capital and labor in the early twentieth century entailed a validation of the concept of the family wage and other entitlements aimed at bolstering the emerging gender identity of male workers. To be a real man, an individual had first to become a provider; that condition, in turn, was predicated on his ability to secure and maintain a job. In the geometry of class and gender, males were directly subordinated to market demands, while women were subordinated to men in their families and only indirectly to the market.

Beginning in the 1960s, economic globalization transformed this order. Several economic and political factors altered the relationship between capital and labor that had been modeled in consonance with the definition of men as providers and women as housewives. The concentration of industrial production in core countries since the nineteenth century and the associated rise of real wages resulting from successful mobilization by (predominantly male) workers eventually led to a crisis of profitability. That, in turn, provided a stimulus for technological change and the relocation of manufacturing. Relocation to less developed countries allowed employers to tap large wage differentials while eluding rising workers' demands in advanced countries. The same trend permitted investors to sidestep comparatively high wages and unionization rates in advanced nations and to harvest benefits derived from low-cost labor in less developed countries. Host governments in Asia, Latin America, and the Caribbean provided incentives that led to the growth of export processing zones where millions of workers, most of them women, assemble products for the world market. From this standpoint, internationalization entailed large-scale attempts at redisciplining labor (Sassen 1993).

In the United States the transition from basic industry to services was accompanied by complementary subprocesses. There was a reduction or redefinition of blue-collar employment in capital- and labor-intensive sectors, with an increase in automation in some types of manufacture and the growth of subcontracting as a means to decentralize the economic and political risks of production. The rise of services and the decline of manufacturing paralleled growing class and income inequalities, epidemics of plant closings during the 1970s and early 1980s, staggering drops in rates of unionization, and the deterioration of standards of living for many working-class Americans (Harrison and Bluestone 1988). In many sectors these phenomena were linked to the employment of international migrants, many of them undocumented and many of them women. It is in this respect that the adjustments of electronics and garment producers, described in the previous sections, aptly illustrate the larger process.

Changing economic conditions are fueling new gender definitions. To a large extent, the material foundations that held together the notion of males as providers and women as submissive mates are being eroded. The growth in the number of two-earner households is one of the by-products of this development. Two-earner households can be divided into two categories, one formed by comparatively affluent professionals plugged into the most advanced sectors of the economy.[11] Another, larger group is formed by households where women seek employment to maintain or raise comparatively modest standards of living. For example, women's labor force participation increased from 20 percent in 1900 to 55 percent in 1988, with much of the growth among mothers in families with annual earnings below $20,000. By 1988, 67 percent of mothers who were single parents, 65 percent of mothers in dual-parent families, and 53 percent of mothers of children under three years of age were in the labor force (Hartmann 1987).

Despite their growing importance as paid workers, women continue to assume major obligations in the home, especially regarding the care of children. Ironically, the reconstitution of gender definitions occurs at a time when there is no evidence to suggest that men are significantly increasing their share of childcare and other domestic chores. In that respect, patriarchal mores remain largely unaltered. What has changed, nevertheless, is the perception that domestic and reproductive work are women's only responsibilities. Most men and women in the United States now expect women to be at least potentially able to support themselves and make substantial contributions to their households. These perceptions are not only the function of new value systems. They also correspond to transformed arrangements of production that have led to the growing atomization of the labor force in terms of gender. The shift is toward a collective understanding that every individual, whether male or female, should support at least one person: himself or herself.

In the past, work outside the home could be an option for affluent women and was always a necessity for working-class women. In both cases, men and women saw the latter's employment as a departure from the natural order. At present, that perception has been reversed. Specializing in parenthood and nonremunerated domestic work has become an expensive choice that many women would not anticipate and most men would shun.

The contemporary ideal of flexible production as a means to maintain industry's competitive edge in domestic and international markets is matched by the search for flexible labor forces. Workers are exhorted to adjust to the demands of industry by acquiring versatile skills, embracing temporary employment as the norm rather than the exception, and demonstrating autonomy through self-employment, the acceptance of contracted work, and the development of individual entrepreneurship. It is partly for this reason that self-employment has expanded and that women represent the fastest growing group of small business owners in the United States. In this brave new world of increasing fragmentation among workers, self-employment is perceived as one of the few viable alternatives to bridge the gap between domestic responsibilities and the need to work for pay outside the home.

It is undeniable that changes in consciousness have taken place since the 1960s, thanks to the diffusion of feminist thought and the consolidation of women's movements. It is also probable that changes in consciousness may have propelled and rationalized women's growing participation in the labor force. At the same time, there has been a conspiracy of reality against theory in that changes in consciousness have occurred at a time when political and economic forces, larger than ideology, were already creating new demands for women as bearers of comparatively low-cost labor.

For the same reason, the dynamics of gender are critical for appraising new understandings of national development in less developed countries. Earlier in this century Latin American governments attempted to consolidate domestic industrial bases through import-substitution strategies allied to nationalist agendas. The prescriptions put forth by the United Nations Economic Commission for Latin America (1969) carried an implicit affirmation of men as providers and heads of households. By contrast, current modalities of export-oriented industrialization further the atomization of the labor force. Integration into the world economy through the implementation of incentives to attract foreign investment relies heavily on the preservation of pools formed by individuated workers, many of whom are women and few of whom are expected to earn a family wage. The goal is development through direct competition in the world market on the basis of pliant, low-cost labor.

As a result, many government officials in developing nations perceive the debasement of workers' earnings and the curtailment of political demands as requirements for successful economic integration on a world scale. It seems, therefore, that the recasting of women in the global economy is occurring in consonance with shifts in the structure of dependence and domination among nations and among classes within those nations.

Conclusion

Two points are worth noting here. The first concerns our analysis of changing definitions of gender as an embedded aspect of social, political, and economic life. The second, related point is that the study of women cannot be conducted in isolation from an examination of the parallel experience of men. Both conclusions are of interest to the literature on gender and development. Authors in that field have stressed and documented the extent to which women have been placed in a situation of disadvantage vis-à-vis men. What has not been sufficiently emphasized in that literature is the extent to which women's subordination is part and parcel of larger systems of domination entailing class. In the age of internationalization, gender dynamics permeate the reorganization of production within and across borders.

In earlier stages of industrial development in the United States, the casting of women as mothers and wives exacerbated their subordination to and dependency on men. Nevertheless, the same process was associated with the consolidation of workers' organizations and the uplifting of the standards of living for working-class people in general. In some instances, the separation of home and workplace created domains where women could potentially wield power and find autonomy without directly confronting the shocks of competition in the marketplace. This alternative was probably more common among affluent women, but it was available also to working-class women.

On the other hand, atomization of the labor force on the basis of new gender definitions has brought about the promise of independence and personal fulfillment for women, as well as greater equality between the sexes. Paradoxically, the same process is associated with higher levels of class polarization in the United States, the persistence of patriarchal mores, and the continuance of contradictions between reproductive and productive work. Contrary to a popular notion, there has not been a steady trend toward greater emancipation among men and women. The course has been one of halting contestation, negotiation, resistance, and compromise requiring repeated adjustments at the material and ideological levels.

Our illustrative examples focusing on Hispanic women in garment and electronics industries aimed at specifying some of the structural dimensions of industrial reorganization. The push toward flexibility in production and labor arrangements and the reliance on customization, subcontracting, and the recruitment of immigrants and women are among the factors shaping the environment where new definitions of gender are being articulated.

NOTES

1. According to the International Labour Organization (1987), women's share of the workforce in the United States rose from 43.5 percent in 1982 to 44.1 percent in 1985. By 1990 47 percent of employable women in the U.S. were working outside the home, up from 29 percent in 1960.

2. The Latin American labor force will double—from 97 million to 195 million—between 1975 and the year 2000. A major factor is increased participation by women, who now represent almost 30 percent of those working in the formal sector, up from 18 percent in 1950. The female workforce of 40 million is expected to reach 53 million by the year 2000 (Inter-American Development Bank 1990). Moreover, those figures may be underestimates, because up to 50 percent of those working in the informal economy are likely to be women. The visibility of women is even more striking in export-oriented industries, where up to 75 percent of those employed are women.

3. Research in New York was mainly sponsored by the Revson Foundation (grant no. 84016). The major portion of research in southern California was supported by grant 070–1149 from the Ford Foundation.

4. According to the U.S. Bureau of Labor Statistics, there are almost 53 million women in the U.S. civilian labor force. Of those, some 3.6 million are Hispanic. Fifty-three percent of all Hispanic women are employed. Of those, almost 59 percent are of Mexican origin. The number of Hispanic women in the labor force is expected to increase to 5.8 million by the year 2000, with a labor force participation rate of 57 percent.

5. These figures convey a somewhat lopsided image of southern California

electronics firms, given the presence in our sample of a few giant manufacturers. Small firms represent a growing stratum characterized by native-born owners but also by an emerging class of ethnic and immigrant entrepreneurs, mostly Hispanic and Southeast Asian.

6. Our research in southern California included the study of a small purposive sample of firms cited for violations to the Labor Code by the Wage and Hour Division. For further details, see Fernández Kelly and García 1988.

7. The names of individuals in this section are fictitious; their characteristics and statements are not.

8. Over several months in 1986 we interviewed a nonrandom sample of fifty women employed in southern California electronics and garment firms. These interviews were part of an exploratory inquiry about gender perceptions and expectations.

9. For a useful discussion of the conceptual distinction between family and household, refer to Rapp 1982.

10. For a detailed discussion of contextual issues, see Griffin, Wallace, and Rubin 1986.

11. For a discussion of contextual issues, see Ehrenreich 1989 and Sassen 1991.

REFERENCES

Bean, Frank D., Barry Edmonston, and Jeffrey S. Passel. 1990. *Undocumented Migration to the United States: IRCA and the Experience of the 1980s.* Santa Monica, Calif.: Rand Corporation.

Bean, Frank D., and Marta Tienda. 1987. *The Hispanic Population of the United States.* New York: Russell Sage.

Bell, Daniel. 1976. *The Coming of Post-Industrial Society.* New York: Basic Books.

Benería, Lourdes, and Gita Sen. 1986. "Accumulation, Reproduction, and Women's Role in Economic Development: Boserup Revisited." In *Women's Work: Development and the Division of Labor by Gender,* ed. Eleanor B. Leacock and Helen I. Safa, 141–157. South Hadley, Mass.: Bergin and Garvey.

Bose, Christine. 1987. "Dual Spheres." In *Analyzing Gender: A Handbook of Social Science Research,* ed. Beth B. Hess and Myra Marx Ferree, 267–285. Beverly Hills, Calif.: Sage.

Chaney, Elsa M. 1984. "Women of the World: Latin America and the Caribbean." Report prepared for the Office of Women in Development, U.S. Agency for International Development. Washington, D.C.: U.S. Department of Commerce, Bureau of the Census.

Deere, Carmen Diana. 1978. "The Development of Capitalism in Agriculture and the Division of Labor by Sex." Ph.D. dissertation, University of California at Berkeley.

———. 1990. *Household and Class Relations: Peasants and Landlords in Northern Peru.* Berkeley: University of California Press.

Drucker, Peter F. 1990. "New Technology: Predicting Its Impact." In *Technology and the Future*, ed. Albert H. Teich. New York: St. Martin's Press.

Ehrenreich, Barbara. 1984. *The Hearts of Men: American Dreams and the Flight from Commitment*. Garden City, N.Y.: Doubleday.

———. 1989. *Fear of Falling: The Inner Life of the Middle Class*. New York: Pantheon.

Enloe, Cynthia. 1990. *Bananas, Beaches, and Bases: Making Feminist Sense of International Politics*. Berkeley: University of California Press.

Fernández Kelly, M. Patricia. 1983. *For We Are Sold, I and My People: Women and Industry in Mexico's Frontier*. Albany: State University of New York Press.

———. 1990. "International Development and Industrial Restructuring: The Case of Garment and Electronics in Southern California." In *Instability and Change in the World Economy*, ed. William Tabb and Arthur McEwan, 147–165. New York: Monthly Review.

———. 1993. "Labor Force Recomposition and Industrial Restructuring in Electronics: Implications for Free Trade." *Hofstra Labor Law Journal* 10 (Spring): 623–717.

Fernández Kelly, M. Patricia, and Anna M. García. 1988. "Invisible amidst the Glitter: Hispanic Women in the Southern California Electronics Industry." In *The Worth of Women's Work: A Qualitative Synthesis,* ed. Anne Statham, Eleanor Miller, and Hans Mauksch. Albany: State University of New York Press.

———. 1992. "Power Surrendered, Power Restored: The Politics of Work and Family among Hispanic Garment Workers in California and Florida." In *Women, Politics, and Change,* ed. Louise A. Tilly and Patricia Gurin, 130–152. New York: Russell Sage.

Fröbel, Folker, Jürgen Heinrichs, and Otto Kreye. 1980. *The New International Division of Labour*. New York: Cambridge University Press.

Grenier, Guillermo J., Alex Stepick, Debbie Draznin, Aileen LaBorwit, and Steve Morris. 1992. "On Machines and Bureaucracy: Controlling Ethnic Interaction in Miami's Apparel and Construction Industries." In *Structuring Diversity: Ethnographic Perspectives on the New Immigration,* ed. Louise Lamphere, 65–94. Chicago: University of Chicago Press.

Griffin, Larry, Michael Wallace, and Beth A. Rubin. 1986. "Capitalist Resistance to the Organization of Labor before the New Deal: Why? How? Success?" *American Sociological Review* 51:147–167.

Harrison, Bennett, and Barry Bluestone. 1988. *The Great U-Turn: Corporate Restructuring and the Polarizing of America*. New York: Basic Books.

Hartmann, Heidi I. 1987. "Changes in Women's Economic and Family Roles in Post–World War II United States." In *Women, Households, and the Economy,* ed. Lourdes Benería and Catharine R. Stimpson, 33–64. New Brunswick, N.J.: Rutgers University Press.

Inter-American Development Bank. 1990. *Economic and Social Progress in Latin America*. Washington, D.C..

International Labour Organization. 1987. *Yearbook of Labour Statistics*. Geneva.

Kessler Harris, Alice. 1981. *Women Have Always Worked: A Historical Overview*. Old Westbury, N.Y.: McGraw-Hill.

Kleiman, Carol. 1992. "Women at Work." *Chicago Tribune*, February 2, p. 6.

Moghadam, Valentine M. 1993. *Modernizing Women: Gender and Social Change in the Middle East*. Boulder, Colo.: Lynne Rienner.

Mohammed, Patricia, and Catherine Shepherd, eds. 1988. *Gender in Caribbean Development*. Mona, Jamaica: University of the West Indies.

Nash, June, and M. Patricia Fernández Kelly, eds. 1983. *Women, Men, and the International Division of Labor*. Albany: State University of New York Press.

Nash, June, and Helen I. Safa, eds. 1980. *Sex and Class in Latin America: Women's Perspectives on Politics, Economics, and the Third World*. South Hadley, Mass.: J. F. Bergin.

Nearing, Scott, and Frank D. Watson. 1909. *Economics*. New York: Macmillan.

Newman, Katherine S. 1988. *Falling from Grace: The Experience of Downward Mobility in the American Middle Class*. New York: Vintage.

Piore, Michael J., and Charles F. Sabel. 1984. *The Second Industrial Divide*. New York: Basic Books.

Portes, Alejandro, Manuel Castells, and Lauren Benton, eds. 1989. *The Informal Economy: Studies in Advanced and Developing Countries*. Baltimore: Johns Hopkins University Press.

Portes, Alejandro, and Saskia Sassen-Koob. 1987. "Making It Underground." *American Journal of Sociology* 93 (July): 30–61.

Rapp, Rayna. 1982. "Family and Class in Contemporary America: Notes toward the Understanding of Ideology." In *Rethinking the Family: Some Feminist Questions*, ed. Barrie Thorne and Marilyn Yalom, 123–147. New York: Longman.

Sassen, Saskia. 1991. *The Global City: New York, London, Tokyo*. Princeton: Princeton University Press.

———. 1993. "Economic Globalization: A New Geography, Composition, and Institutional Framework." In *Global Visions: Beyond the New World Order*, ed. Jeremy Brecher, John Brown Childs, and Hill Cutler. Boston: South End Press.

Sassen-Koob, Saskia. 1985. "Growth and Informalization at the Core: The Case of New York City." In *The Urban Informal Sector: Recent Trends in Research and Theory*. Baltimore: Department of Sociology, Johns Hopkins University.

Shurkin, Joel. 1984. *Engines of the Mind: A History of the Computer*. New York: W. W. Norton.

Siegel, Leni. 1984. *Delicate Bonds: The Semiconductor Industry*. Mountain View, Calif.: Pacific Studies Center.

Silver, Hilary. 1989. "The Demand for Homework: Evidence from the U.S. Census." In *Homework: Historical and Contemporary Perspectives on Paid Labor at Home*, ed. Eileen Boris and Cynthia R. Daniels, 103–129. Urbana: University of Illinois Press.

Spalter-Roth, Roberta, Heidi I. Hartmann, and Linda M. Andrews. 1990.

"Mothers, Children, and Low-Wage Work: The Ability to Earn a Family Wage." Revised version of a paper presented at the 85th meeting of the American Sociological Association, Washington, D.C., August 11–15. Mimeographed.

Teich, Albert H. 1990. *Technology and the Future*. New York: St. Martin's Press.

Tilly, Louise A., and Joan W. Scott. 1987. *Women, Work, and Family*. New York: Methuen.

United Nations Economic Commission for Latin America. 1969. *Development Problems in Latin America*. Austin: University of Texas Press.

U.S. Department of Labor. 1990. *Labor Market Forecasts*. Washington, D.C.

Waldinger, Roger. 1994. "The Making of an Immigrant Niche." *International Migration Review* 28 (1): 3–30.

Waldinger, Roger, and Michael Lapp. 1993. "Back to the Sweatshop or Ahead to the Informal Sector." *International Journal of Urban and Regional Research* 17 (1): 6–29.

Ward, Kathryn. 1988. "Women and the Global Economy." In *Women and Work Annual Review, vol. 3,* ed. Barbara Gutek, Anne Stromberg, and Laurie Larwood, 17–48. Urbana: University of Illinois Press.

Wolf, Diane L. 1992. *Factory Daughters: Gender, Household Dynamics, and Rural Industrialization in Java*. Berkeley: University of California Press.

World Bank. 1990. *Women in Development: A Progress Report on the World Bank Initiative*. Washington, D.C.

CHAPTER 5

*

Gender, Industrialization, and Development in Puerto Rico

PALMIRA N. RÍOS

All human societies exhibit a gendered division of labor, but the particular configurations assumed by the allocation of tasks vary within and across groupings of people over time. The gender-typing of tasks, although most rigidly expressed in the domestic sphere, plays a determining role in the organization of production relations, and it conditions the participation of men and women in the labor force.[1]

Gendered divisions in the labor market are manifested in the differences between men and women in labor force participation (and nonparticipation) rates, degrees of segregation, wage levels, opportunities for mobility, and other working conditions. The persistence of a gendered labor market—along with racial, age, and national hierarchies, among others—constitutes a major obstacle to the abolition of social and economic inequalities.

Notwithstanding their crucial explanatory power, gender relations were absent from the economic development literature of the 1950s and 1960s. Most modernization and dependency theorists ignored gender relations and the role of women in the processes of change that developing societies were experiencing. Two major modernization studies, Alex Inkeles and David Smith's *Becoming Modern* (1974) and Joseph Kahl's *The Measurement of Modernism* (1968), did not include women among their thousands of respondents. June Nash argued that this action was not an oversight but "a fundamental premise of social change in which men are the measurement of change" (Nash 1980, 5).

The belated recognition of the dynamics of women's roles within development processes, generally attributed to Ester Boserup's (1970) pioneer work, is but a reflection of the increasing militancy of women's groups worldwide and the impact they have had on the academy and policy making. World-system models, particularly the new international division-of-labor perspective, can be credited with highlighting the central role played by women in contemporary development and global restructuring processes.

If analysts of developing countries are partly responsible for the evolution of gender theories, it is because women in those countries are playing a central role in the restructuring of those economies. Manufacturing industries are proliferating in developing nations, and women are being employed by these establishments in unprecedented numbers. This trend is not an aberration or a chance occurrence but an inherent feature of a development strategy that has been part of the post–World War II restructuring of the world economy. Although the hierarchy of the old economic order has survived these transformations, this process of global economic restructuring constitutes a qualitatively different mode of reproducing the most advanced labor processes worldwide and integrating new markets into the global economy (Sanderson 1985).

The restructuring of the world economy consolidated a single international market of capital, labor, and commodities. It also redefined the role of developing nations within the global economy. Several studies have pointed out that a new international division of labor is replacing the traditional function of developing nations as suppliers of raw materials (Trajtenberg 1978; Fröbel, Heinrichs, and Kreye 1980; Vuskovic 1980; Safa 1981; Nash 1983; Sanderson 1985). Underdeveloped nations are rapidly becoming sites of manufacturing activities. While advanced nations are concentrating on research and development, financing, specialized services, and administration, developing nations are increasingly engaged in the manufacturing of goods for the world market (Fernández Kelly 1985; Sassen 1988). The proliferation of offshore export processing zones (or free trade zones) represents a new mode of incorporating developing nations into the world economic system.

The main reason for the expansion of manufacturing activities in developing nations is that, in many cases, they provide a more profitable environment than traditional sites. Labor costs are generally lower and workers are less likely to be organized, thus giving management a greater flexibility and control over the production process. This means not that industrialized nations are no longer profitable but that, in spite of their many shortcomings, for some economic activities, developing nations provide a much better environment.

The relocation of manufacturing establishments was not just the consequence of economic decisions. Technological innovations made possible the coordination of a global system of production by breaking down complex manufacturing activities into simple tasks that could be easily learned even by unskilled workers. Innovations in transportation and communications systems also facilitated the relocation of manufacturing establishments to nontraditional sites. The implementation of export-oriented developmental policies throughout the developing world and liberal tariff codes constituted additional incentives. Hence, the global assembly line was born.

Out of this myriad of processes has emerged a more flexible and mobile capitalist organization of production. Moreover, the new international division of labor represents a global mechanism for the incorporation of new segments of the population into the labor market, consequently creating an international labor market (Barkin 1985). That new worker is often a woman.

Women constitute the principal new source of labor in today's economy, both in highly developed as well as in developing countries. In both cases, the increasing feminization of labor markets is attributed to the growth of "women's jobs." The rapid expansion in manufacturing activities experienced by developing nations beginning in the 1960s generated not just a strong demand for female labor but a decided preference for female workers, thus propelling a rapid process of proletarianization of women.

There are several explanations for the trend of some industries to prefer female to male workers. First, women's wages are usually lower. Female salaries in export processing zones are generally 20 to 50 percent lower than men's (Fröbel et al. 1980). Second, there is a belief among employers that women have "natural" manual dexterity and are, therefore, better suited for assembly line tasks (Elson and Pearson 1981). There is a related notion that women are better than men at tolerating tedious, repetitive, and monotonous tasks. Employers consider women more tractable workers and, therefore, more willing to accept the discipline of the workplace (Lim 1978; Grossman 1979; Elson and Pearson 1981) and less likely to join labor unions (Safa 1980).

Regardless of whether a scientific basis exists for these beliefs, they constitute powerful conditioners of management and labor behaviors. Gender-typing of tasks is an ideological construct that, once crystallized in a particular labor market, plays a central role in the reproduction of the social relations of production. The "ideology of sex-typing," as Ruth Milkman (1987) labeled it, is very hard to change, even when the specific conditions that gave rise to it are no longer present.

Several studies have noted the high proportion of women employed by Puerto Rico's manufacturing establishments (Reynolds and Gregory 1965; History Task Force 1979; U.S. Department of Commerce 1979; Silva Bonilla 1982). Although Puerto Rican women always were present in production activities (Ríos 1990a, chaps. 3 and 4), it was the establishment of U.S.-owned manufacturing enterprises at the turn of this century that created the conditions for the increase in the number of Puerto Rican women who joined the labor force (Azize 1979; Picó-Vidal 1980; Rivera-Quintero 1980). The 1948 implementation of Operation Bootstrap, Puerto Rico's model for economic development, accelerated the proletarianization of Puerto Rican women. In spite of the many changes experienced in manufacturing, it still constitutes a pocket of concentration for women, employing a greater percentage of them than in the Puerto Rican economy as a whole.

The process of industrialization in Puerto Rico did not exclude women from the paid labor force or reduce them to informal activities, as was the case in other developing countries. Rather, the opposite occurred: the expansion of manufacturing activities, a consequence of local development initiatives and the emergence of a new global organization of production activities, generated a strong demand for women workers.

The Puerto Rican experience, which constituted the pioneer of the new international division-of-labor model, illustrates how gender plays a role in the configuration of the manufacturing labor force and in the formulation of development policies. Economic development strategies are not gender neutral in their intentions or in their consequences. This case shows how the gendered organization of the workplace can pit the interests of employers against those of policy makers. The many attempts to privilege male workers through policy mechanisms were sustained by a publicly stated objective of linking economic development to the survival of patriarchal relations. Policy makers clearly indicated that development goals were subordinated to the much broader and central social objective of reproducing a gendered social structure. Therefore, the continuing demand for women workers in Puerto Rico's factories was an unintended, albeit quickly recognized, outcome of the expansion of assembly establishments in the island.

Operation Bootstrap

In 1948 the government of Puerto Rico launched Operation Bootstrap, or Operación Manos a la Obra, a modernization program that aimed to industrialize the economy and improve the welfare of its people. It offered incentives to private investors such as tax exemptions, subsidized factory space, and assistance in recruiting trained personnel and obtaining loans. The government of Puerto Rico also assumed the responsibility for building the infrastructure of the island, which now enjoys modern transportation, energy and communications systems, and major publicly funded education and health systems. The island's other incentives were very seductive to entrepreneurs: a large labor pool, a government willing to accommodate the demands of foreign capital, and the financial and military protection for investments ensured by the island's colonial relationship with the United States.

Since its inception, Operation Bootstrap has been hailed as the model for the economic development of the Third World. Many scholars and policy makers argued that Puerto Rico had several problems in common with other developing nations. In 1953 John Kenneth Galbraith and Carolyn Solo, for instance, identified those shared problems as (1) "a characteristically unsatisfactory relation of people to land," (2) a "tropical location," (3) "an accumulation of social and cultural attitudes that reflect hostility or at least disinterest toward economic change," and (4) "a Malthusian problem of starkly classical form" (Galbraith and Solo 1953, 55–56).

Puerto Rico's colonial relationship with the United States was not a feature shared with other developing nations, but it constituted a major component in the formulation and implementation of Operation Bootstrap. Since 1898, when Spain was forced to surrender its hegemony over the island to the United States, the Puerto Rican economy rapidly has come under U.S. control. The political and economic relations between Puerto Rico and the United States, prescribed by a series of executive orders, congressional acts, and judicial rulings, turned this Caribbean island into a U.S. territorial possession subject to its judicial, monetary, tariff, commercial navigation, environmental, postal, and wage laws. In 1917 Puerto Ricans became U.S. citizens. They are not subject to the federal tax system, however, since they do not have the right to vote in U.S. presidential elections.[2]

Hence, having free access to the U.S. market, enjoying the protection of its monetary, fiscal, and military systems, and being exempted from federal taxes, Puerto Rico would be used as a key political and marketing tool for U.S. interests abroad. It became a showcase of democracy, a tale of a Third World industrial revolution under a democratic system. After 1959, following the establishment of a Communist regime in Cuba, Operation Bootstrap entered into the Cold War rhetoric and this island nation became democracy's answer to communism in the region.

This economic path transformed Puerto Rico into a modern industrial society within a short period of time. The major indicators of economic progress—gross national product, per capita income, gross domestic investments, and the like—improved significantly. The island's economic activities grew in number and diversity. Manufacturing—and more recently, services—surpassed agriculture as the principal source of jobs and income. The quality of life also improved for Puerto Ricans, as manifested by their higher literacy rates, educational attainment, and life expectancy and consumption rates, which are far superior to those of their Caribbean neighbors.

Despite its many successes, Operation Bootstrap failed in several significant areas. It did not generate the numbers and kinds of jobs needed to
reduce unemployment to acceptable levels. The thousands of jobs generated by the new industries were not sufficient to compensate for the many
lost in the declining sectors and at the same time to create opportunities
for newcomers to the labor market. Consequently, poverty rates and
levels of dependency on federal assistance programs are higher than in
any state of the Union. Furthermore, these dislocations generated a
massive emigration movement toward the United States, where one-third
of the island's population lives today.

Since the enactment of Operation Bootstrap in 1950, the labor force
participation rate of workers in Puerto Rico has dropped slightly, explained primarily by a significant decline in the workforce rates of Puerto
Rican men (see Table 5-1). While the male labor force participation rate
shrank by 18.2 percentage points, that of women improved slightly, and
in 1990 it reached the highest level in the post–World War II period.
Moreover, women's share of total employment has increased steadily
since 1950, and by 1990 women represented 38.6 percent of all employed
workers on the island.

Operation Bootstrap's most glaring weakness is its dependency on low
wages and fiscal privileges. As its achievements became well known and
more countries implemented similar development models, the island lost
some of its comparative advantages. The proliferation of free trade zones
throughout the Caribbean Basin and Southeast Asia has seriously eroded
the privileged position enjoyed by the island. The number of countries
that can match Puerto Rico's incentives to investors increased rapidly.
Many of those countries offer much lower wages, no federal regulations,

TABLE 5-1

Puerto Rican Labor Force Participation Rate, by Gender, 1950–1990

| Year | Labor Force Participation Rate (Percentage) | | | Women as Percentage of Total Employment |
	All	Men	Women	
1950	54.6	79.8	30.0	28.2
1960	45.5	71.5	22.1	25.9
1970	48.0	70.8	28.0	31.2
1980	43.3	60.7	27.8	36.1
1990	45.4	61.6	31.4	38.6

Source: Department of Labor and Human Resources 1992.

and few or no environmental codes. Furthermore, the enactment of the Caribbean Basin Initiative (CBI) opened even more of the U.S. market to countries that are competing directly with Puerto Rico in attracting foreign investors. The island's success has become its Achilles' heel. Consequently, the stability of the country's fragile socioeconomic system can be seriously shaken by any budget cut in welfare programs, the enactment of free trade agreements (such as the North American Free Trade Agreement), and/or the closing of federal tax loopholes—all of which are targeted as high priorities in the attempt to rebuild the U.S. economy.

Stages in the Expansion of Manufacturing Activities

The industrial composition of the manufacturing sector has gone through three distinct stages under Operation Bootstrap. During the first stage, from 1950 to 1963, most of the industries that set up operations on the island were labor-intensive factories that required modest levels of capital investment, produced consumer goods highly susceptible to changes in demand, and had little or no relation among themselves (Economic Development Administration 1982, 8).

The second stage of industrialization, that of capital-intensive heavy industries, started around 1963. The centerpiece of this stage was the petrochemical industry. In 1963 the legislature approved the Law of Industrial Incentives, which extended tax exemptions to industries that paid high salaries and generated male jobs. Another goal was to establish on the island a long chain of mutually interdependent manufacturing establishments (Economic Development Administration 1982, 10). In addition, the U.S. Department of the Interior assigned to Puerto Rico a higher quota of foreign oil for the proposed refineries.

By 1977 Puerto Rico entered into its third and current phase of industrialization, that of high-technology manufacturing activities such as electronics and professional and scientific instruments. Increases in the price of crude oil, the economic recession of the mid-1970s, and changes in the world economy forced many petrochemical establishments to close their Puerto Rican operations and the government to redefine its strategy for economic development. The expansion of high-technology industries and the continuing growth of pharmaceutical activities enabled the manufacturing sector to regain many of the jobs lost during the recession.

Throughout these periods the manufacturing sector experienced significant transformations. It became more complex and thus less dominated by a single product as new and diverse establishments set up operations on the island. Of particular interest is the declining significance of apparel as the dominant manufacturing activity in Puerto Rico. Another logical change has been the increase in average (real) wages. Although Puerto Rican wages remain lower than those paid in the United States, they are higher than those paid for comparable activities in other developing nations and are the highest in the Caribbean Basin. This is related to the expansion of capital-intensive and high-technology industries, which have driven up the average earnings of Puerto Rican workers, and to minimum-wage legislation.

Between 1950 and 1990, manufacturing employment increased at a moderate rate and its share of total employment remained stable, between 19 and 16 percent (see Table 5-2). The manufacturing sector generated about 30 percent of all net new jobs created by the Puerto Rican economy between 1950 and 1980. By 1965 it overtook agriculture to become the leading employer on the island. By the mid-1970s, however, manufacturing lost its leading position to the public administration sector, and by the

TABLE 5-2

Employment Distribution of Selected Industrial Groups in Puerto Rico, by Gender, 1950–1990

Year	Total (in thou- sands)	% dist.	Agricul- ture % dist.	Manu- facture % dist.	Com- merce % dist.	Ser- vice % dist.	Public Adminis- tration % dist.
1950	601	100.0	34.9	18.4	15.3	13.4	7.8
Men	431	100.0	46.8	8.8	17.1	7.4	6.0
Women	170	100.0	4.7	42.9	10.5	28.2	12.3
1960	558	100.0	23.4	16.3	17.5	13.9	11.4
Men	414	100.0	30.4	11.3	18.3	9.1	8.2
Women	145	100.0	3.4	30.3	14.4	27.5	20.6
1970	693	100.0	9.5	19.0	18.7	16.0	15.4
Men	477	100.0	13.2	14.6	19.9	12.7	12.1
Women	216	100.0	1.3	28.2	16.2	25.9	22.6
1980	760	100.0	5.3	18.5	18.5	17.8	24.3
Men	487	100.0	8.0	15.6	20.7	15.6	19.3
Women	273	100.0	—a	23.0	14.2	21.9	33.3
1990	971	100.0	3.6	16.9	19.5	21.9	22.4
Men	596	100.0	5.5	15.4	21.6	19.7	17.6
Women	375	100.0	—a	19.7	16.2	25.3	30.1

Source: Department of Labor and Human Resources 1992.

aToo few cases in the sample to make a reliable estimate.

mid-1980s it dropped even further as service industries became the second most important source of employment in Puerto Rico.

Although manufacturing has been an important source of employment in Puerto Rico, women have depended on it to a greater degree than men. Between 1950 and 1970 it was the leading source of employment for women, a role this sector has never played for Puerto Rican men. In 1950 manufacturing industries employed 42.9 percent of all working women in Puerto Rico. By 1990, however, manufacturing had dropped to third place, preceded by public administration and services. That same year, manufacturing was the fourth most important source of employment for men, surpassed by commerce, services, and public administration.

Gender-Typing of Manufacturing Activities

The fact that women constitute a high proportion of Puerto Rico's manufacturing workforce is not a novel finding. Many studies have noted this phenomenon. Furthermore, women's presence in significant numbers in manufacturing activities was evident at the onset of Operation Bootstrap. A survey of Puerto Rican industrial workers conducted during the mid-1950s by Peter Gregory (1958) found that the job opportunities created by the newly established factories were a major factor in women's entry into the labor force. The study established that, although the majority (54 percent) of all Puerto Rican workers had once been employed in agriculture, 79 percent of the women surveyed found their first job in a factory. The survey identified other reasons why women responded so eagerly to employment opportunities in manufacturing: economic need, the desire to escape the boredom of household activities, and the new sense of independence that being employed gave them (Gregory 1958, 455).

Although historically there has been a high level of women in manufacturing, they are not evenly distributed throughout the many industries and activities that make up this sector. Women are concentrated within a few manufacturing industries that in Puerto Rico and elsewhere have become gender-typed. Hence, the presence of women in manufacturing activities in Puerto Rico comes hand in hand with the growth of female-dominated industries and gender-typed manufacturing activities.

Women's share of manufacturing employment has always exceeded their share of jobs.[3] Although in 1990 women constituted 46.7 percent of all manufacturing workers (see Table 5-3), the lowest reported since 1952,[4] they accounted for 38.6 percent of all employed workers in Puerto Rico. Only for a brief period of time during the mid-1950s, shortly after the implementation of Operation Bootstrap, have women represented

TABLE 5-3
Employment in Puerto Rico's Manufacturing Industries and Percentage of Women in

	1952		1955		1960		1965	
	Total	Women (%)	Total	Women (%)	Total	Women (%)	Total	Women (%)
All industries	60,056	49.9	71,691	52.5	81,740	47.2	111,953	47.3
Food and kindred products	14,130	6.5	13,747	9.6	15,883	10.7	19,877	13.5
Tobacco manufacture	10,800	81.9	11,929	80.6	5,628	74.0	8,446	59.9
Textile mill products	3,103	41.7	3,971	56.3	5,018	47.8	5,987	47.7
Apparel and related products	15,176	90.0	18,736	89.7	22,409	88.4	30,809	87.4
Lumber, wood and related products	3,031	4.3	3,139	4.9	3,454	6.6	4,729	6.8
Paper, printing, publishing, and allied products	1,578	11.7	1,962	11.8	2,538	12.6	3,255	13.1
Chemical and allied products	989	15.8	1,630	14.3	1,921	17.0	2,477	19.7
Petroleum, rubber, and related products	N.A.	—	N.A.	—	2,359	18.5	4,072	24.9
Leather and leather products	1,972	75.5	2,272	62.2	3,881	63.1	8,018	64.9
Stone, clay, and glass products	3,035	11.4	3,884	9.6	4,458	7.5	5,856	5.7
Metal products	279	5.3	2,385	10.8	2,670	10.1	4,208	8.4
Machinery, except electrical and transportation equipment	1,082	4.0	N.A.	—	1,049	6.6	1,725	6.7
Electrical machinery, equipment, and supplies	748	55.7	2,087	58.9	4,502	49.6	6,310	52.5
Professional and scientific instruments	525	60.0	1,195	52.4	1,772	67.7	2,383	63.3
Miscellaneous	3,608	60.4	4,754	66.8	4,198	62.8	3,801	63.2

Source: Department of Labor and Human Resources 1953, 1956, 1961–92.

Major Industry Groups, 1952–1980

1970		1975		1980		1985		1990	
Total	Women (%)	Total	Women (%)	Total	Women (%)	Total	Women (%)	Total	Women (%)
136,737	48.5	136,617	49.0	154,643	48.3	148,780	48.4	158,484	46.7
20,580	15.8	22,950	23.6	23,368	24.5	23,204	27.9	23,385	26.8
6,120	59.8	4,980	52.1	2,104	45.8	804	25.4	1,089	32.7
8,904	53.8	4,898	56.8	3,356	52.2	2,787	53.7	3,679	48.7
36,819	86.5	36,075	86.6	33,575	83.9	30,077	84.8	31,238	83.5
5,089	7.7	3,891	11.6	3,573	12.5	3,134	15.8	3,425	17.7
3,950	16.7	3,812	15.6	5,051	18.4	4,680	20.4	5,768	24.8
4,890	22.5	10,615	27.5	15,606	32.8	17,152	35.7	22,659	35.6
6,964	26.0	5,364	21.4	7,726	24.5	6,733	29.7	6,708	26.9
8,309	70.6	5,161	71.2	6,642	68.0	4,848	62.2	6,284	61.4
6,838	5.6	6,169	8.5	4,816	11.9	3,822	14.4	5,136	16.6
6,066	7.6	5,597	7.0	5,349	9.5	4,476	13.4	5,187	14.5
1,937	8.6	3,469	28.1	7,931	39.9	7,587	43.8	5,347	34.1
10,716	54.0	9,919	55.1	18,024	58.0	22,882	52.7	20,567	51.3
5,246	68.7	10,829	65.9	13,607	63.1	13,747	58.5	14,798	55.6
4,309	58.8	2,888	56.9	3,915	47.7	2,847	42.8	3,214	49.2

over 50 percent of the manufacturing workforce. Between 1952 and 1955 more than seven thousand women entered the manufacturing sector, taking 65.9 percent of all net new jobs generated by it.

Between 1950 and 1990 the Puerto Rican manufacturing workforce experienced significant changes in size and composition, and women reflected many of those transformations. In 1952 apparel was undeniably the leading manufacturing industry. It employed one-fourth of all manufacturing workers and 45.5 percent of all women engaged in those same activities. Apparel, food, and tobacco manufacturing establishments employed 66.7 percent of all manufacturing workers. Apparel and tobacco had predominantly female workforces: 90.0 and 81.9 percent, respectively. Ironically, the food manufacturing industry was then, and remains today, a male stronghold, in spite of the fact that the domestic manufacturing of food is primarily a female activity.

Four decades later, despite the emergence of new manufacturing activities, Puerto Rican men and women are found concentrated in different sectors. Apparel and food remain the two most important sources of employment, both playing lesser roles, and along with the new industries—chemicals, electronics, and professional and scientific instruments—they now constitute the top five sources of employment. These five sectors employ 71.0 percent of all manufacturing workers. Three of them—apparel, electronics, and professional and scientific instruments—also have a majority of female employees.

A closer look at Table 5-3 reveals why women have sustained such a strong presence in the manufacturing sector. They are concentrated in the industry with the largest number of jobs (apparel), as well as in some of the fastest growing ones (electronics and professional and scientific instruments). Although it has remained below the average, women's share of jobs in the important chemical industry, particularly pharmaceuticals, has increased steadily.

The data also indicate that women's share of jobs has not kept up with the growth rate of the manufacturing sector and that in some industries women have lost their dominance. Two historically female-dominated industries experienced a gender reversal during the period examined. By 1990 women no longer represented the majority of the workers engaged in tobacco and textile manufacturing. In both cases these gender reversals followed technological innovations in their production processes.

The female workforce also has been affected negatively by the sluggish growth rate of apparel factory employment. This industry has been hurt by the greater internationalization of clothing manufacturing, particularly by competition from lower-wage areas. In order to deter this trend, the Puerto Rican government has promoted the concept of "twin plants." It entails a division of labor in which the most labor-intensive portions of clothing manufacturing take place in nearby islands, leaving the most skilled tasks in Puerto Rico. Hence, in addition to an international division of labor, we are witnessing an emerging regional division of labor.

Gender-typing is also manifested in the different occupational distributions of men and women. This phenomenon can be appreciated at the most detailed levels of occupational classifications. An analysis of the occupational structure of the manufacturing sector reveals the existence of pockets in which men and women are concentrated, even in those industries in which one or the other might be marginally represented. Women in blue-collar jobs are employed primarily as operatives but not as craft workers. They are hired for highly manual tasks such as sewing, assembling, and examining. Very few work as precision machine operators, welders, solderers, flamecutters, and oilers (Ríos 1990a, 246–250).

The second most important occupation in which women are found in the manufacturing sector is clerical work. Women employed in male-typed industries are more likely to be clerical workers than operatives (Ríos 1990a, 250). Likewise, few women are employed as professionals and administrators in manufacturing establishments. These two trends indicate that the presence of women in traditional male bastions does not necessarily represent a breakdown of gender barriers but rather is a consequence of the demand for white-collar workers in the industrial setting (Ríos 1990a, 253).

At this point it is useful to look more closely at the characteristics of female-dominated industries, that is, those industries in which women constitute over 50 percent of the workers. Four industries consistently have employed more women than men since the 1950s: apparel, leather, electronics, and professional and scientific instruments. The textile industry always has had an above-average proportion of female workers, although in 1990 they fell below the 50 percent threshold. Tobacco, historically a female stronghold, is today the opposite, with only 32.7 percent women employees. In 1990 the four female-dominated industries employed 45.9 percent of all manufacturing workers and 65.8 percent of all women hired for these factories.

Female-dominated industries have three main distinguishing features. Their first common denominator is that they are assembly-type operations. The traditional dichotomy that women are located in light, labor-intensive manufacturing while men are engaged in heavy, capital-intensive activities is not supported. Even the sophisticated, capital-intensive operations of producing professional and scientific instruments such as heart pacemakers essentially entail the assembly of very small units.

This feature is related to another characteristic of female-dominated industries: their high proportion of production workers. All these industries have an above-average (80.5 percent) proportion of production workers. More than nine-tenths of the leather workers (94.0 percent) and apparel workers (93.9 percent) are engaged directly in production activities. This phenomenon lends support to the thesis of a new international division of labor: while Puerto Rican workers are engaged in assembling activities, their U.S. counterparts are likely to be working in more advanced tasks, since most of the research and development components of production are not relocated to the island along with the jobs (Department of Labor and Human Resources 1992).

A third feature of female-dominated industries is that they are composed of large establishments. Whereas the average manufacturing establishment employs 83 persons, all four female-dominated industries employed an average of more than 100 workers per establishment, leather (209.4) being the largest (Department of Labor and Human Resources 1992). This means that Puerto Rican women are working in large factories, not in isolated, small, cottage units.

Contrary to expectations, women are not concentrated only in the lowest-paid industries. Though the apparel and leather industries do pay among the lowest average weekly wages, $147.91 and $166.93, respectively—well below the average of $233.24—the electronics and instruments industries ($261.66 and $267.54, respectively) paid the second and third highest average wages in 1990, exceeded only by the chemical industry ($339.62) (Department of Labor and Human Resources 1992).

Although the data are inconclusive and dated, there is strong evidence that female-dominated industries are primarily foreign-owned or subsidiaries of U.S. companies and that their production is geared mostly for export (Ríos 1990a, 262). What is uncontroverted is that Puerto Rican women are not employed by declining manufacturing industries. Rather than being marginalized from the labor force, women have been incorporated into the core industries of the island's export-oriented manufacturing sector. Operation Bootstrap successfully attracted to the island an array of manufacturing establishments that were highly susceptible to international competition. In doing so, this economic policy strengthened Puerto Rico's ties to the world economy. It also integrated Puerto Rican women into the networks of exchange among labor, capital, and commodities in the global economy.

Gender and Development Policies

Economic development policies must attempt to reconcile social needs and values with economic and political imperatives, and as such these policies embody the image of the society policy makers want to build.

Hence, nobody should be surprised by expressions of concern over development policies that seemed to privilege women more than men in a country characterized by a strong patriarchal tradition and a high rate of male joblessness. There were voices of discontent and uneasiness among officials of the Puerto Rican government over a public policy that was apparently ineffective in achieving its main objective, that is, alleviating male unemployment (Reynolds and Gregory 1965; Barton 1966). Some correctly diagnosed the problem as the unavoidable consequence of a gender bias inherent to the types of manufacturing industries relocating to Puerto Rico. The response, however, was to accept the gendered nature of the labor market and redirect the bias to the benefit of men.

Various government documents provide unquestionable evidence that gender considerations played a conscious and deliberate role in the formulation and evaluation of development policies in Puerto Rico. The Commonwealth of Puerto Rico assigned a top priority status to the reduction of unemployment among men and was not concerned with the consequences of female unemployment. For example, in 1960, when women's share of the labor force dropped to its lowest level in the post–World War II period, a report published by the Government Bank for the Development of Puerto Rico interpreted this fact as an indicator of progress. According to that report, the declining proportion of women workers meant that more men were able to find high-paid jobs, which in turn enabled more women to become full-time homemakers (Guzmán and Esteves 1963).

This policy was restated a decade later by the Economic Development Administration (EDA) when it formulated the following argument:

> Another cardinal objective of the industrialization program is to create jobs for men. Undoubtedly, in a society in which a greater part of the jobs are held by women, unless it be a matriarchal society, there will be serious social problems when the woman works and the man is unemployed. Not only does it affect the matrimonial institution of a society in which traditionally the male is the principal breadwinner, but it also affects the development of the family when a mother is unable to give proper attention to her home and children. The problem requires attention on a high priority since projections of the work force for 1975 anticipate a greater growth in the number of males than females. (Economic Development Administration 1975, 20)

A similar argument appeared in the *Twenty-ninth Economic Program (1973–76),* issued by the Planning Board of Puerto Rico. The report stated that "female unemployment is not necessarily associated with poverty nor with great human suffering since, in most cases, it does not fall upon the head of household. Therefore, in the development of a public policy to reduce unemployment, the masculine factor should occupy a top priority" (Comisión de Derechos Civiles 1972, 2). Accordingly, tax incentives were tailored to meet the needs of the men's labor market. In 1963 the Puerto Rican legislature approved the Law of Industrial Incentives, which aimed to promote, among other things, manufacturing establishments that would employ men (Economic Development Administration 1982).

The Petrochemical Complex

Although the story of Puerto Rico's petrochemical complex is well documented, few studies have paid attention to the role that gender concerns played in the formulation of the capital-intensive strategy. The success of Operation Bootstrap was such that by 1963 plants promoted by the EDA employed almost seventy thousand workers. About 60 percent of the new jobs were held by women, however, leaving most of the male unemployment unaffected (Reynolds and Gregory 1965). The belief that Operation Bootstrap was not helping much in reducing the high unemployment rate of Puerto Rican men forced policy makers to review their strategy.

As early as 1957, at the annual meeting of the Puerto Rican Economic Association (a forum in which Teodoro Moscoso, then serving as head of EDA, was a discussant), Hubert Barton, another key officer in the EDA, articulated the rationale for a new course of action in the industrialization program. Heavy industries, Barton argued, would generate a large number of jobs, increase the general level of wages, and decelerate the growth of nonintegral, labor-intensive industries (Barton 1957). Furthermore, heavy industries represented "largely male employment, in contrast to the present situation among Fomento plants which employ two-thirds women" (Barton 1957, 13). Barton recognized that the gender-typing he observed was not a consequence of Puerto Rican habits; it was a common characteristic of those types of industries, both in Puerto Rico and in the United States. He argued that Puerto Rico's manufacturing industries were concentrated in a relatively narrow range of industries that covered only one-third of the spectrum of industries found in the United States and other highly industrialized countries (Barton 1976, 2).[5] In a 1966 report Barton stated the following:

> This concentration in the non-durable goods industry accounts for the high proportion of women in Puerto Rican manufacturing. Nearly half of the factory workers in Puerto Rico are women while in the United States women account for only about a quarter of total factory employment.

Industry by industry, the sex ratios are similar but Puerto Rican employment is concentrated in apparel, especially women's underwear and brassieres, and in the leather goods industry, in electronics, all of which employ a high proportion of women in the United States as well as in Puerto Rico. (Barton 1966, 13–14).

The economic development policy that followed promoted different kinds of industries, those in which men typically worked.

Consequently, by the mid-1960s Puerto Rico had inaugurated a new strategy for economic development. The EDA actively promoted such capital-intensive industries as petrochemicals and pharmaceuticals and sought investors to exploit the island's copper mines. The petrochemical refineries were conceived as a first step in the development of a vast industrial complex based on the manufacturing of petroleum derivatives. The EDA envisioned the establishment of a chain of interdependent plants to produce everything locally, from tires to textiles and plastic products. The strategy included the building of a special dock in Guayanilla where oil tankers could deliver the black gold. Officials estimated that the multiplier effect of the proposed industrial network would generate approximately two hundred thousand new jobs. They also hoped this industrial complex would increase the level of wages and provide greater stability to Puerto Rico's manufacturing sector (Economic Development Administration 1982).

This strategy enjoyed a mixed success. Special quotas granted to Puerto Rico by the U.S. Department of the Interior facilitated the expansion of corporations such as the Caribbean Gulf Refining Company, the Commonwealth Oil Refining Company, Phillips Petroleum, and Sun Oil. Political opposition to the petrochemical complex, however, motivated by environmental and nationalistic concerns, and increases in the price of crude oil dictated by the Organization of Petroleum Exporting Countries slowed the implementation of this policy and led to a crisis in Puerto Rico's petroleum industry. Consequently, government officials set their sights on the high-technology and service industries as an alternative strategy. Ironically, the high-technology industry was yet another sector with a high proportion of female employees.

The attempts to alter the gender composition of manufacturing industries did not constitute an evil conspiracy to drive women out of the labor market. Although it is true that public officials believed in the ideal of women as homemakers, it is also true that their misgivings about the labor-intensive strategy were based on the undeniable fact that most of those women's jobs were unstable and paid low wages. A development strategy based on such traditional female-typed industries would have been precarious at best. Although Barton believed that capital-intensive industries could exert a positive effect on women's wages, the bottom line was that public officials seemed to fear only the political consequences of male joblessness.

Conclusion

Although Puerto Rico represents just one case within a complex global economy, its experience can help us understand the processes and contradictions that underlie the transformations being experienced by many nations today. This island nation served as a testing ground for many policies that were implemented later by other countries.

In spite of the existence of a growing literature on the new international division of labor, Puerto Rico's role as the pioneer of this historical phenomenon has been ignored. Most studies date its origins to the mid-1960s, when Fairchild opened his first offshore electronics plant in Hong Kong (Nash 1983; Snow 1983; Fernández Kelly 1985). I argue that Operation Bootstrap paved the way for the new international division of labor and that its basic components were tested in Puerto Rico before being exported to other developing nations. Operation Bootstrap proved, a decade before Fairchild started operations in Hong Kong, that developing nations could be feasible and profitable sites for modern manufacturing.[6]

Puerto Rico represented a relatively safe testing ground. The Commonwealth of Puerto Rico established a free trade relationship with the United States, and its constitution reaffirmed the island's subordination to U.S. tariff, monetary, fiscal, and commercial navigation regulations. As a U.S. territory, it offered U.S. and other foreign investors a financial and military security that no other country could match at that time. Furthermore, U.S. manufacturers were familiar with the island and its workers because they, particularly those in the garment industry, had been operating in Puerto Rico since the early twentieth century.

The success of Operation Bootstrap in demonstrating that workers in developing nations could adjust to the modern factory was well publicized throughout the world by Puerto Rican and U.S. government agencies and by academics. Puerto Rico was portrayed as a model for developing nations. Many of the architects of Operation Bootstrap played an important role in the formulation and implementation of similar programs in developing nations. Puerto Rican governor Luis Muñoz Marín became an international advocate for the program. Teodoro Moscoso—who headed the Economic Development Administration between 1942 and 1961 and served as U.S. ambassador to Venezuela (1961–62) and U.S. coordinator of the Alliance for Progress (1962–64)—was a consultant to various governments implementing Operation Bootstrap–like programs. Hubert Barton also served as an adviser to several Caribbean nations implementing this export-oriented strategy.

Consequently, variations on the Puerto Rican model are functioning today in the Caribbean Basin, Ireland, and Southeast Asia. M. Patricia Fernández Kelly estimated that there are two hundred export processing zones that employ approximately three million workers. Although most are engaged in garment, textile, and electronics manufacturing, new industries are joining the international trend. The latest advent is the data-processing industry, which is relocating its data-entry activities to countries such as Barbados, the Dominican Republic, and Ireland. Even former president Ronald Reagan's proposed enterprise zones constitute an urban twist on this model.

As in Puerto Rico, the spread of export processing activities throughout the developing world played an important role in the incorporation of women into the labor force. There is extensive evidence of the feminization of export processing labor markets (Lim 1978; Elson and Pearson 1981; Safa 1981; Fernández Kelly 1985). Women, mostly young and single, represent between 85 and 90 percent of the export processing workforce (Fernández Kelly 1985). The list of countries is quite long: Mexico (Bustamante 1983; Fernández Kelly 1985), the Dominican Republic (Cortén and Duarte 1981), Haiti (Garrity 1981; LeBell and Lewis 1983), Barbados (Gill 1984), Jamaica (Bolles 1983), Curaçao (Abraham-Van Der Mark 1983), St. Lucia (Kelly 1987), Morocco (Elson and Pearson 1981), Hong Kong (Salaff 1981), Malaysia (Lim 1978; Grossman 1979), Singapore (Deyo and Chen 1976; Lim 1978; Wong 1981), and Taiwan, Indonesia, and the Philippines (Grossman 1979).

The Puerto Rican case provides additional evidence in support of the thesis that the incorporation of women into the labor market is associated with the expansion of female-typed industries and occupations. The massive entry of women into the world of wage employment has not taken place at the expense of men; male and female workers remain relatively noncompetitive. Moreover, the feminization of the labor market is not limited to developing nations. Valerie Oppenheimer (1977, 187) documented increases in the participation of U.S. women in the labor force related to the growth of industries and occupations that generally employ women.

The creation and reproduction of a gender ideology, often sustained by policies within the public and private sectors, condition the manner of incorporation as well as the terms of female participation in the labor market. Hence, it should not suffice to study women's presence (or nonpresence) in the labor market. We also must analyze the socially constructed relations through which men and women are incorporated into production processes. Both are included in some activities and excluded from others on the basis of gender.

Finally, the Puerto Rican experience highlights in several ways the intersection between gender and public policy. If policies are to be effective, they must incorporate gender as a central variable. To neglect it is to ignore the fact that policies are never gender-blind, since their consequences for men and women are different. A government's ability to intervene effectively is conditioned by a society's gender relations. Moreover, if a gender perspective is absent from policy making, we will miss the opportunity to implement a proactive gender-based public policy to redress social inequalities.

Puerto Rico's Operation Bootstrap demonstrates that public policies, even development policies, satisfy goals other than utility and efficiency. Export-oriented economic strategies, as public policies, sustain and encourage gender hierarchies and women's subordination. This model was clearly and consciously subordinated to the social goal of reproducing a patriarchal structure. Hence, in the analysis of economic development public policy we cannot overlook the fact that these kinds of decisions are conditioned by social and ideological imperatives as much as by economic determinants.

NOTES

1. An earlier version of this chapter appeared in *Gender & Society* (Ríos 1990b). For a detailed analysis of these issues, see my doctoral dissertation, "Women and Industrialization in Puerto Rico" (Ríos 1990a).

2. The right to participate in national elections is abridged only for Puerto Ricans who reside on the island. Those living in any of the fifty states and the District of Columbia can vote for the president of the United States and elect their representatives to the U.S. Congress. As of 1994 there are three Puerto Ricans serving in the House of Representatives, in addition to a commissioner with limited membership rights who is elected by the residents of the island.

3. There are no reliable estimates of the numbers of foreign workers in Puerto Rican manufacturing industries. Given the large and growing immigration of workers from the Dominican Republic, it is very likely that some are working in these establishments.

4. The Census of Manufacturing Industries of Puerto Rico, the main source of data on manufacturing activities on the island, was first conducted by the Department of Labor (now the Department of Labor and Human Resources) in 1946, but only after 1952 was it conducted on a regular yearly basis. Although it uses the Standard Industrial Classification Manual of the U.S. Bureau of the Census, its data are not strictly comparable with those of the U.S. Census.

5. A comparison of U.S. and Puerto Rican manufacturing establishments found that between 1960 and 1980 the island's establishments did not represent a

cross-section of those in the mainland. Those in Puerto Rico specialized more in nondurable products. In 1980 nondurable industries employed 62.5 percent of Puerto Rican manufacturing workers; their U.S. counterparts employed only 39.2 percent of U.S. manufacturing workers. Puerto Rican industries also employed a greater proportion of production workers. The U.S. Department of Commerce (1979) stated that the basic difference was that manufacturing establishments on the island are production units rather than complete corporations. Consequently, highly skilled white-collar jobs remained in the U.S. or the investing country (Ríos 1990a, 267–276).

6. A look at the early modernization studies of the Puerto Rican model indicates a concern with the possibility of successfully setting up modern manufacturing operations in Third World settings. Studies such as Reynolds and Gregory 1965 proved that it was a feasible proposition.

REFERENCES

Abraham-Van Der Mark, Eve E. 1983. "The Impact of Industrialization on Women: A Caribbean Case." In *Women, Men, and the International Division of Labor,* ed. June Nash and M. Patricia Fernández Kelly, 374–386. Albany: State University of New York Press.

Azize, Yamila. 1979. *Luchas de la mujer en Puerto Rico, 1898–1919.* San Juan, Puerto Rico: Graficor.

Barkin, David. 1985. "Proletarianization." In *The Americas in the New International Division of Labor,* ed. Steven E. Sanderson, 26–45. New York: Holmes and Meir.

Barton, Hubert. 1957. "Puerto Rico's Industrial Future." Paper presented at the Sixth Annual Meeting of the Puerto Rico Economic Association, San Juan, February 2.

———. 1966. "Distinctive Characteristics of the Puerto Rican Economy." Unpublished document.

———. 1976. *An Appraisal of Industrial Incentives in Puerto Rico.* Report prepared for the Economic Development Administration. San Juan: Puerto Rico Development Group.

Bolles, Lynn. 1983. "Kitchens Hit by Priorities: Employed Working-Class Jamaican Women Confront the IMF." In *Women, Men, and the International Division of Labor,* ed. June Nash and M. Patricia Fernández Kelly, 138–160. Albany: State University of New York Press.

Boserup, Ester. 1970. *Women's Role in Economic Development.* New York: St. Martin's Press.

Bustamante, Jorge. 1983. "*Maquiladoras:* A New Face of the International Capitalism on Mexico's Northern Frontier." In *Women, Men, and the International Division of Labor,* ed. June Nash and M. Patricia Fernández Kelly, 224–256. Albany: State University of New York Press.

Comisión de Derechos Civiles (P.R.). 1972. *Resumen de conclusiones y recomendaciones del Informe de la Comisión de Derechos Civiles sobre la igualdad de derechos y oportunidades de la mujer puertorriqueña.* Río Piedras: Departamento de Ciencias Políticas, Universidad de Puerto Rico.

Cortén, Andre, and Isis Duarte. 1981. "Proceso de proletarianización de mujeres: Las trabajadoras de industrias de ensamblaje en la República Dominicana." *Revista de Ciencias Sociales* 23 (3–4): 529–567.

Department of Labor and Human Resources (P.R.). 1953. *Census of Employment in Manufacturing Industries, 1952.* San Juan: Bureau of Labor Statistics.

———. 1956. *Manufacturing in Puerto Rico: Employment, Hours, and Earnings, 1955.* San Juan: Bureau of Labor Statistics.

———. 1961–92. *Census of Manufacturing Industries, 1960, 1965, 1970, 1975, 1980, 1985, 1990.* San Juan: Bureau of Labor Statistics.

———. 1992. *Serie histórica del empleo, desempleo y grupo trabajador en Puerto Rico, 1947–1991.* San Juan: Negociado de Estadísticas.

Deyo, Frederick, and Peter Chen. 1976. *Female Labour Force Participation and Earnings in Singapore.* Bangkok: Clearinghouse for Social Development in Asia.

Economic Development Administration (P.R.). 1971. *Economic Development in Puerto Rico during the Last Twenty Years.* San Juan: Report of the Office of Economic Research.

———. 1982. *Resumen del desarrollo económico de Puerto Rico.* San Juan: Imprenta del Gobierno.

Elson, Diane, and Ruth Pearson. 1981. "Nimble Fingers Make Cheap Workers: An Analysis of Women's Employment in Third World Export Manufacturing." *Feminist Review* (Spring): 87–107.

Fernández Kelly, María Patricia. 1985. "Contemporary Production and the New International Division of Labor." In *The Americas in the New International Division of Labor,* ed. Steven Sanderson, 206–225. New York: Holmes and Meir.

Fröbel, Folker, Jürgen Heinrichs, and Otto Kreye. 1980. *The New International Division of Labor.* Cambridge: Cambridge University Press.

Galbraith, John K., and Carolyn Solo. 1953. "Puerto Rican Lessons in Economic Development." *Annals of the American Academy of Social Sciences* 285:55–59.

Garrity, Monique P. 1981. "The Assembly Industries in Haiti: Causes and Effects." *Journal of Caribbean Studies* 2:25–35.

Gill, Margaret. 1984. "Women, Work, and Development." In *Women, Work, and Development,* ed. Joycelin Massiah, 1–40. Cave Hill, Barbados: Institute for Social and Economic Research, University of the West Indies.

Gregory, Peter. 1958. "El desarrollo de la fuerza obrera industrial en Puerto Rico." *Revista de Ciencias Sociales* 2 (4): 447–467.

Grossman, Rachel. 1979. "Women's Place in the Integrated Circuit." *Southeast Asia Chronicle* 66:2–17.

Guzmán, Vicente, and Vernon Esteves. 1963. *El problema del desempleo en Puerto Rico.* San Juan: Banco Gubernamental de Fomento para Puerto Rico.

History Task Force of the Center for Puerto Rican Studies. 1979. *Labor Migration under Capitalism: The Puerto Rican Experience.* New York: Monthly Review.

Inkeles, Alex, and David Smith. 1974. *Becoming Modern.* Cambridge, Mass.: Harvard University Press.

Kahl, Joseph. 1968. *The Measurement of Modernism.* Austin: University of Texas Press.

Kelly, Deirdre. 1987. *Hard Work, Hard Choices: A Survey of Women in St. Lucia's Export-Oriented Electronic Factories.* Cave Hill, Barbados: Institute for Social and Economic Studies, University of the West Indies.

LeBel, Allen, and Faith Lewis. 1983. *Report on Haitian Factory Women.* Washington, D.C.: Agency for International Development.

Lim, Linda Y. E. 1978. *Women Workers in Multinational Corporations: The Case of the Electronic Industry in Malaysia and Singapore.* University of Michigan Occasional Paper no. 9. Ann Arbor: University of Michigan Women's Studies Program.

Milkman, Ruth. 1987. *Gender at Work: The Dynamics of Job Segregation by Sex during World War II.* Urbana and Chicago: University of Illinois Press.

Nash, June. 1980. "A Critique of Social Science Roles in Latin America." In *Sex and Class in Latin America: Women's Perspectives on Politics, Economics, and the Third World,* ed. June Nash and Helen I. Safa, 1–21. South Hadley, Mass.: J. F. Bergin.

———. 1983. "The Impact of the Changing International Division of Labor on Different Sectors of the Labor Force." In *Women, Men, and the International Division of Labor,* ed. June Nash and M. Patricia Fernández Kelly, 3–39. Albany: State University of New York Press.

Oppenheimer, Valerie. 1977. *The Female Labor Force in the United States.* Westport, Conn.: Greenwood.

Picó-Vidal, Isabel. 1980. "The History of Women's Struggle for Equality in Puerto Rico." In *Sex and Class in Latin America: Women's Perspectives on Politics, Economics, and the Third World,* ed. June Nash and Helen I. Safa, 202–213. South Hadley, Mass.: J. F. Bergin.

Reynolds, Lloyd, and Peter Gregory. 1965. *Wages, Productivity, and Industrialization in Puerto Rico.* Homewood, Ill.: Richard Irwin.

Ríos, Palmira N. 1990a. "Women and Industrialization in Puerto Rico: Gender Division of Labor and the Demand for Female Labor in the Manufacturing Sector, 1950–1980." Ph.D. dissertation, Yale University, New Haven.

———. 1990b. "Export-Oriented Industrialization and the Demand for Female Labor: Puerto Rican Women in the Manufacturing Sector, 1952–1980." *Gender & Society* 4 (3): 321–337.

Rivera-Quintero, Marcia. 1980. "Incorporación de las mujeres al mercado de trabajo en el desarrollo del capitalismo." In *La mujer en la sociedad puertorriqueña,* ed. Edna Acosta-Belén, 41–66. Río Piedras, Puerto Rico: Ediciones Huracán.

Safa, Helen I. 1980. "Conciencia de clase entre las trabajadoras, en Latinoamérica: Un estudio de casos en Puerto Rico." In *La mujer en la sociedad puertorriqueña,* ed. Edna Acosta-Belén, 157–182. Río Piedras, Puerto Rico: Ediciones Huracán.

———. 1981. "Runaway Shops and Female Employment: The Search for Cheap Labor." *Signs: Journal of Women in Culture and Society* 7 (2): 418–433.

Salaff, J. 1981. *Working Daughters of Hong Kong.* New York: Cambridge University Press.

Sanderson, Steven. 1985. "A Critical Approach to the Americas in the New International Division of Labor." In *The Americas in the New International Division of Labor,* ed. Steven Sanderson, 2–25. New York: Holmes and Meir.

Sassen, Saskia. 1988. *The Mobility of Labor and Capital: A Study in International Investment and Labor Flow.* Cambridge: Cambridge University Press.

Silva-Bonilla, Ruth. 1982. "Amas de casa en la fuerza de trabajo asalariado en Puerto Rico: Un estudio del lenguaje como mediación ideológica en la reificación de la conciencia femenina." Ph.D. dissertation, Union for Experimental Colleges and Universities, Midwest Division.

Snow, Robert. 1983. "The New International Division of Labor and the U.S. Work Force: The Case of the Electronics Industry." In *Women, Men and the International Division of Labor,* ed. June Nash and M. Patricia Fernández Kelly, 39–69. Albany: State University of New York Press.

Trajtenberg, Raúl. 1978. *Transnacionales y fuerza de trabajo en la periferia: Tendencias recientes en la internacionalización de la producción.* Mexico City: Instituto Latinoamericano de Estudios Transnacionales.

U.S. Department of Commerce. 1979. *Economic Study of Puerto Rico.* 2 vols. Washington, D.C.: Government Printing Office.

Vuskovic, Pedro. 1980. "Latin America and the Changing World Economy." *NACLA* 14:12–15.

Wong, Aline. 1981. "Planned Development, Social Stratification, and the Sexual Division of Labor in Singapore." *Signs: Journal of Women in Culture and Society* 7 (2): 434–452.

PART II

✳

*Empowering Women:
Individual, Household,
and Collective Strategies*

CHAPTER 6

✳

Latin American Women in the World Capitalist Crisis

JUNE NASH

Women and children are the principal losers in the shrinking welfare budgets and reduced production for internal consumption that mark the current crisis of capitalism. This fact, dramatically conveyed in international data bases,[1] is a correlate of the present trends in global exchanges, as the last frontiers of the subsistence economies are responding to capitalist penetration. International financial agencies are extracting capital surpluses from the periphery to pay for onerous debt services on loans made when interest rates were lower and currency exchanges more favorable. The conditions for further loans impose restrictions on production for domestic consumption and reorientation of industry to exports along with contraction of welfare services. The restructuring of economies in industrialized countries eliminates jobs in production that provided a "family wage" covering the costs of social reproduction. At a time when they are most needed, welfare budgets are reduced as increasing numbers of women join the paid workforce. Since women and children are the principal producers in domestic consumption enterprises and the predominant recipients of benefits, they have become the disinherited in this period of retraction.

This chapter addresses the issues raised in a gender perspective that is ignored by most current theories of the crisis of capitalism. Yet the theoretical basis for an approach that emphasizes social reproduction has been available since the first half of the nineteenth century. Before Marx and Engels wrote the *Communist Manifesto*, Flora Tristan, a divorced woman who rejected the petit bourgeois society of her family, published *L'union ouvrier* ([1837] 1983), calling for an organization of the employed wage slaves with the unemployed and (in Marx's terms) unemployable lumpen proletariat of the world—the prostitutes, thieves, beggars, and jailed populations of the London and Paris underworld. She ends her book with the ringing phrase, "Workers of the world unite!" If this sounds like only half a sentence, it is because we have been mesmerized by a vision of the revolutionary class uniquely defined as the wage worker in capitalist enterprises.[2] Fixation on the employed workforce as the bearers of the historic mission to transform society caused theorists to overlook other candidates.

The relationship of subsistence production and what we now call the "informal" sector to the accumulation of capital was central to Rosa Luxemburg's (1951, 1972) thesis concerning the necessary coexistence of a noncapitalist subsistence sector with the advance of capitalism. She encountered opposition from Marxists of her day who objected to her thesis that the "third market" of subsistence producers in the "feudal" or household economy was a vital element in the process of accumulation, competing with or even overshadowing the surplus value rendered in the workplace.

Contemporary feminist scholars have revived Rosa Luxemburg's thesis that the production of use-values is essential for the accumulation of capitalism and explains the status of women in subsistence and extended production. Mariarosa Dalla Costa (1972) transformed the view of women's unpaid domestic labor from privatized oppression to extraction of surplus value by emphasizing how it contributed to lowering labor costs. This analysis made it acceptable to a Marxist view of exploitation as the unique form of working-class struggle.

Women's activities ensuring domestic production are becoming the central arenas for the development of consciousness and action for revolutionary change in the present crisis of capitalism. The issues feminist theorists raise question the legitimacy of systems that force increasing numbers of people into an underclass of the underemployed or marginally employed. The failure of capitalist enterprises throughout the world to incorporate the majority of the populations of highly industrialized and less industrialized countries within the wage-earning workforce thrusts the class struggle onto the streets or into the communities of the underclass. Those who are employed in secure jobs in the formal sector are cut off from the issues of survival faced by the unemployed or self-employed in the informal economy and may even feel threatened by them.

The commitments of most women to families and communities rather than to wage employment means that their struggle is phrased in terms of moral issues often ignored by Marxists, who focus on the arena of proletarian movements. Housewives, as the principal contributors to the subsistence sector in core industrialized countries, women who are heads of families in urban *barriadas* of countries that have become peripheral economies to that core, and petty commodity producers in small-plot cultivation and artisan production in the rural areas of the periphery raise the moral issue of the right to survival rather than the exploitation in the labor market as their basic political message.

Dimensions of the Capitalist Crisis

Marxist theory of the world capitalist crisis focuses on the declining returns to capital owners as increasing costs for technological innovation and a consequent diminishing workforce limit the surplus value rendered by labor. The resulting imbalance between wages that are the basis for consumer demand and rising capital costs leads to stagnation and decline (Marx 1906; Castells 1980). Expansion overseas in the search for new markets and investment possibilities (Lenin 1934; Marx 1963) fails to resolve the basic contradiction; rather, expansion enhances the crisis by extending the scope of capital penetration (Wallerstein 1974, 1979; Amin 1977; Frank 1978–79).

Most of the controversy among Marxists in the 1970s–90s concerns whether emphasis should be given to production, exchange (Laclau 1971), or the relative share of labor versus fixed capital in producing surplus value (Castells 1980). The relation of these spheres to the domestic economy and reproduction is only recently coming into focus, drawing inspiration from the work of nineteenth- and twentieth-century women scholars who intertwined production and reproduction in a holistic approach that revealed the dialectic of private expropriation of surplus value and social accumulation of capital in a more comprehensive view of the class struggle.

Veronika Bennholdt-Thomsen (1981) challenged the paradigm of crisis limited to the workplace with her notion of extended production, equating the housework of women in core economies with the subsistence activities of peasant producers. Once the role of women in paid and unpaid work contributing to social reproduction is taken into consideration, the theory of crises of accumulation in capitalism can be deepened to capture the reality of revolutionary change. Women have been participants in the class struggle whether or not they worked for wages in capitalist enterprises. Subsistence economies laid the basis for industrial development in the eighteenth and nineteenth centuries and continue to provide surpluses that sustain poorly paid industrial workers in the frontiers of industrialization in Latin America (de Janvry and Deere 1978; Nash 1982), Africa (Wolpe 1972), and Asia (Mather 1982). In the current decline the very survival of urban populations unemployed because of plant shutdowns depends on survival mechanisms devised by poor women (Benería 1989).

Cyclical changes in the market economy can be roughly assessed by international comparisons of gross national product (GNP). The International Monetary Fund (IMF) showed an increase in the GNP of 1,846,788 million in 1970 to a peak of 2,145,192 million in 1981 for all countries. The decline to 1,982,384 million in 1985 (International Monetary Fund 1987) marks the onset of stagnation and decline that has resulted in terminal breakdown of the economies of some countries.

The reaction of women to these changes has been mobilization at work and at home to overcome the failure of capitalist enterprises and the state to respond to human needs.

Trends in Latin America

In Latin America, as a result of twenty years of net capital inflows from both public and private sources abroad and expansion in production, investment, consumption, and trade, the gross domestic product (GDP) grew by more than 4 percent each year from 1960 to 1980. Since then the entire region has experienced a serious recession, with little or no growth, lower standards of living, high unemployment, depressed levels of investment, and shrinking foreign trade (American Development Bank 1987). Per capita GDP was at least 10 percent lower in 1986 than in 1980. Seven countries had a loss of more than 15 percent, and four had more than a 20 percent loss. Nineteen of twenty-three countries show negative rates of change in the sixteen-year period from 1970 to 1986 (American Development Bank 1987). A declining rate of growth in the developed economies means that little help can be expected from external sources. Since 1982 the payment of profits and interest to foreign capital has risen by 32 percent, so that the net transfer of funds became negative for the first time (American Development Bank 1987).

The deterioration in the terms of trade, which the American Development Bank (1987) estimates as 22 percent below the 1979–80 averages, means that efforts to increase the export of basic commodities have failed to overcome the indebtedness incurred in the preceding decade. The expansion of agroindustrial enterprises has reduced the land and labor devoted to subsistence agriculture. The international financial agencies, such as the World Bank and the IMF, require that the indebted nations restrict imports, intensify exports, and deflate national currencies in relation to the dollar, and at the same time restrict the money supply, hold down wages, and cut government expenditures on social welfare. Inflation is reduced, with disastrous consequences for national industries and their workforces. The net effect is that wages have fallen more than the per capita net product, aggravating an already large disparity between rich and poor and threatening the balance between production potential and consumption. Women are working harder for less income as men are forced out of stable jobs in the industrial sectors (Barbieri and de Oliveira 1987). Research in five countries in Latin America—Uruguay, Mexico, Chile, Peru, and Bolivia—has documented the response of women to the negative consequences of these trends.

Uruguay

Uruguay's export-oriented growth in the 1970s was followed by an 11 percent decline in the 1980s that had negative consequences for women. Their responses were outlined at a conference sponsored by the collective Development Alternatives with Women for a New Era (DAWN). According to Suzana Prates (1987), initial growth of industries up to the end of the 1950s was followed by a period of prolonged stagnation from 1955 to 1973, when the annual growth of only 0.5 percent brought about high emigration and class polarization. An urban guerrilla movement tried to maintain decent levels of living for the working class, but it was defeated by a military coup in 1973. The military junta forged closer ties with the international financial system, and in the following decade the economy showed a 5.0 percent annual growth. The introduction of export processing zones produced booms in that sector but slowed down national enterprises dependent on intensive labor. The result was unemployment and deterioration of wages for workers in the internal economy, where pay levels dropped to 80 percent of the 1970 median manufacturing wage. Military repression limited the scope of political movements that tried to restore the standard of living of the masses of wage earners.

The participation of women in the workforce rose from 38.7 percent in 1981 to 44.2 percent in 1984 as the lack of employment for men forced more women to enter gender-segregated jobs. The jobs paid only one-half to two-thirds of men's wages in a stagnating economy. Despite these increases in active participation of women in the labor force, the unemployment rates of both men and women doubled in the same period, rising from 5.1 to 10.5 percent for men and 9.0 to 18.9 percent for women.

Women responded to the crisis by transforming the domestic scene into political space (Prates 1987). They organized collective meals for the unemployed as well as for those working. They ran health cooperatives, providing care where it had never existed. This collective action strengthened existing networks of kin and community alliances and enabled them to aid political prisoners. Prates concludes that women's incorporation in public action in this period of crisis is beginning to redefine feminine identity as women find empowerment within their own political base.

Mexico

Mexico's phenomenal growth of 40 percent GDP in the 1960s and 1970s was often referred to as a miracle. Its industrialization program is wider and deeper than that of Uruguay but follows a similar course. Beginning in 1955 the opening of the country to foreign capital led to the expansion of transnational enterprises. These firms competed for the same resources, including capital and labor, as small national firms, resulting in a weakened internal economy (Alonso n.d.). The country experienced a dramatic economic crisis in 1981, when the prices for oil, on which much of Mexico's growth had come to depend, dropped, and interest rates rose. The government announced that it was unable to pay its debts to international financial institutions in 1982, and since then the economy has been subject to the austerity conditions of the IMF, whose principal requirement is privatization.

The denationalization of industry in which the bulk of stable, well-paying jobs were located, the suppression of wages, and the restriction of social services have shifted the burden for paying the debt to workers (Alonso n.d.; Keren 1986). Those industries that have survived the crisis subject workers to periodic layoffs, limited job mobility, and speedups. The threat of layoffs and plant shutdowns is an effective means of ensuring compliance in the tight job market (Keren 1986). Formal employment in industries under state control and regulation has given way to labor-intensive processing plants and underground shops.

Work that used to be done in small factories is now done by women in their own homes on machines that they purchase (Alonso n.d.). Despite the fact that these women shoulder all the risks of entrepreneurs, they receive very little compensation, since the major profits go to the jobbers. Women have also sought jobs in services, some hiring out as maids, and others have tried to create their own work in the informal economy, such as street selling. Within the home they have expanded the processing of goods for family use. Part of their daily work is to maintain networks to obtain public services (de Oliviera 1987). This additional work, though uncompensated, has the unplanned consequence of politicizing women's domestic responsibilities in the collective settings in which it is carried out in a way that challenges the power structure.

Chile

Chile experienced a modest growth when the United States poured in capital to sustain the economy after the Pinochet coup in 1973. The influence of U.S. advisers, particularly those from Milton Friedman's University of Chicago monetarization school, has resulted in the dismantling of the nationalized enterprises created by the Allende government and the elimination of social security provisions for workers.

The failure of the monetarist policies can be read in the 31 percent unemployment rate and the 17 percent drop in the GNP in the fifteen years since the coup. Urban neighborhoods are devastated, and two-thirds of the families consume less than the daily nutritional requirements (Serrano 1987). State programs for emergency employment and family subsidies are insufficient. M. Claudia Serrano (1987) concludes that this impoverishment is permanent.

Just as in Uruguay and Mexico, women in Chile have become the central actors in the drama of daily survival. According to Serrano (1987), they are able to stretch scarce resources through exchanges of goods and services among kin and neighborhoods. Women sew, wash, and clean houses for others, sell cigarettes, or make handicrafts and toys for an international market. The *arpilleras*, hand-sewn dioramas depicting these activities, have become a synecdoche for these survival strategies, of which they are an important part.

The Programa de Economía del Trabajo (Program of the Economy of Work) includes 1,383 organizations in the metropolitan region that in 1986 provided a basis for emerging social politics. As members worked together, they discussed their shared problems and reinforced the demands they present to government agencies and political parties. Women have organized 364 workshops producing textiles, clothing, wool toys, weavings, embroidery, and shoes. They also provide services, such as barbershops and beauty salons. Through this network of enterprises women have seized local initiatives in productive enterprises and erased the distinction between public and private (Serrano 1987).

Peru

The American Popular Revolutionary Alliance (APRA) party in Peru has had success in co-opting the organizations of low-income women. The government provided employment projects and welfare benefits in response to women's organized demonstrations for land and housing from 1985 to 1987 (Radcliffe 1988). Despite this support by major parties, women's organizations maintained their autonomy. Women candidates have been successful in local and national elections, mobilizing poor women around issues of family income and local conditions related to the supply of drinking water, housing, and sanitary conditions.

This increasingly significant role of low-income women, many of whom are illiterate, represents a distinct break with the past. The few predominantly women's occupations, such as laboratory and pharmaceutical work, relied on male union leaders. In contrast, domestic workers, organized in the Sindicato de Trabajadores del Hogar (Union of Domestic Workers), are led by women who served as maids. Their goal is to bring domestic servants into the ambit of labor legislation, which would provide at least the minimum benefits associated with the status of workers. Legislation regulating hours of work and securing social security for servants was introduced in 1970 (Bunster, Chaney, and Young 1985) but never enacted. The domestic workers' movement has been increasingly supported by middle-class women in the teachers' union, many of whom teach these women in night schools.

The primary basis for mobilization is the neighborhood, where women join with men in fighting for water, health clinics, wood, kerosene, and schools. Mothers' clubs and communal dining areas are sites for women's collective action (Blondet 1988). Whereas older women who arrived in the city as immigrants fought to establish an identity as *pobladores* (shanty dwellers), their children have a higher level of education and different expectations. They seek wage employment or higher-education degrees. Credit associations link groups that span generations of women as they engage in collective action with outreach agencies of the church and government. In the process, recent migrants introduce a new dynamism into the efforts of earlier migrants to uphold their standard of living in the present crisis in which *they* are emerging as leaders.

Bolivia

Bolivia experienced a precipitous decline in the 1980s, culminating in a 27 percent loss in GDP in 1986, when the mining economy was destroyed. The resulting crisis has brought about a more profound restructuring of the economy than in any other Latin American country. Although the country's debt of $5 billion may seem insignificant in comparison with that of Brazil and Mexico, where it surpasses $100 billion, it requires 60 percent of dwindling exports annually to service the interest and amortization. In a country where the average annual income is $288, the debt, if distributed per capita, amounts to $552 (Strengers 1985). In 1981 Bolivia was the first Latin American nation to fail to pay the servicing of its debt. Renegotiation of the debt during General García Meza's term of office from July 1980 to August 1981 set disastrous interest rates and terms for repayment. The public recognition of the failure to meet the debt service in 1984 carried with it the loss of international credit and the complete collapse of Bolivian currency.

After the election of President Victor Paz Estenssoro in 1985 inflation was brought under control by the devaluation of the national currency and the cutting of expenditures in national institutions. The "dollarization of the economy," a process in which all exchanges were calculated in terms of their equivalent value in U.S. currency, undermined the internal economy during Hernán Siles Zuazo's term of office from October 1982 to July 1985. The nationalized mines, which had been operating at a loss, were transferred to private enterprise or closed down, with no plans for relocating thousands of miners.

In the growing crisis of the 1980s each of the major economic regions of Bolivia—the mining centers, the agricultural valley of Cochabamba, and the tropical lowland agricultural area—developed distinct strategies. Many women traveled to the rural areas in Cochabamba to work in the harvest, returning with corn, vegetables, and oil instead of cash. When the shutdown came in 1986, women and children were abandoned in the mining centers as men traveled to the lowlands in the southeast to work in agroindustrial enterprises or to the cocaine production centers of Beni, Chapari, and the Yungas. Some emigrated to the neighboring countries of Brazil and Argentina.

In Cochabamba during the growing crisis of the 1980s, households expanded the scope of strategies to which they had traditionally resorted: out-migration of men who went to work in Argentina or Brazil, diversification of crops and productive activities, and intensification of petty vending. As Jorge Dandler and Carmen Madeiros (1985) have shown, the retention of strong family ties makes all these strategies a household phenomenon. The family remained the principal unit economically, ceremonially, and communally as it strived to survive.

The mobilization of the family depends on resources that are typically supplied by women. Women and children are the ties that keep male migrants to other regions of the country or to Argentina and Brazil returning to their home base. The remittances that the men send enable women to capitalize their ventures in petty vending and to make improvements on homes and commercial establishments (Dandler and Madeiros 1985).

In contrast to the smallholder agricultural areas of Cochabamba, the agroindustrial region of Santa Cruz grew enormously in population and production in the 1970s. The wealth of the cocaine traffic is even more evident here than in Cochabamba, where "dish" antennas and Mercedes Benzes indicate the homes of the traffickers. In Santa Cruz whole neighborhoods of luxurious homes are patrolled by private police forces carrying machine guns. This wealth coexists with the miserable impoverishment of agricultural workers who are cut off from the domestic networks that make life possible in Cochabamba. Frontier communities extend far out into the formerly forested area as colonizers are dispossessed of the lands they clear and penetrate farther into the hinterland.

The daily wage for field hands was the equivalent of 50 cents in U.S. currency in 1985. Even skilled masons make less than a dollar. Although commercial crop cultivation of cotton and sugarcane are organized by unions, the large landowners hire children as young as seven. They are trucked in from Potosí and work just for their daily food. The government workers in charge of labor report that the seventy thousand workers who migrated to Santa Cruz on the promise of land and tools received no help from the government. Inflation wiped out their savings, and they lacked transportation to take their crops to market (Nash 1988).

The desperation reached a peak in July 1986 when people from the mining communities organized a March for Peace and Bread. More than ten thousand men, women, and children joined the march to La Paz in the hope that they could persuade the president to keep the mines open until they could find other sources of employment. They were met by the army twenty miles short of their goal. Some returned to the mining communities to join a hunger strike in a last attempt to change the course of Paz Estenssoro's government (Nash 1988).

In Bolivia, as in the other Latin American countries, the collapse of the productive base of the country has transformed the political mobilization of the class struggle into a struggle for life and bread involving broad sectors of the population. In this changing struggle the role of women in the reproduction of society has become critical to political action.

Women in Core Industrial Countries

These extreme levels of impoverishment are not experienced to the same degree in the core industrial countries. Nonetheless, there is a growing threat to the survival of families as unemployment, homelessness, and malnutrition spread from urban center to small towns and rural areas. According to Goran Therborn (1987), struggles of advanced capitalism are now being fought out on a terrain largely shaped by the welfare state with the primary emphasis on new social forces. In Europe the trend toward welfare-state provisions for income maintenance and for child-care, medical, and educational facilities gives public recognition to the failure of private enterprise to attend to such issues. It has fundamentally changed the nature of class relations and the thrust of class struggle. Social welfare programs threaten the power structure by undermining patriarchy and religious forms of social control, at the same time diminishing the dependence of the propertyless on the labor market.

Despite the socially recognized need for comprehensive welfare provisions, capitalist economies did not adequately respond to increased demands during the 1980s. In England young workers entering the labor market could not find work. As they went from compensation to pension stipends, funds were exhausted. The weakening and dismantling of protective wage mechanisms, such as the Fair Wages Resolution and the Wages Councils, led to an increase in the number of families requiring income supplements. Prime Minister Margaret Thatcher addressed the problem by abandoning the annual official calculation of families earning below the poverty level after 1983, when the numbers had increased dramatically (Pond and Burghes 1986). The tax burden on the poor doubled in the period 1978–79 to 1986–87, when the taxes of high-income families were cut by 13 percent (Pond and Burghes 1986).

In contrast, in the United States, where only education is free (and underfunded), the number of persons below the poverty line, defined in 1961 as three times the cost of obtaining a minimally adequate diet (Cutright and Smith 1986), was 32.4 million, for a poverty rate of 13.6 percent of the population by the mid-1980s. These figures represented a decline from the peak levels of 1983, when there were 35.3 million individuals below the poverty line, for a poverty rate of 15.2 percent, but greater than the 1973 poverty rate of 11.1 percent. When we break down those rates by gender and race, we find more dramatic contrasts: 57 percent of black families in 1983 with two and more children were below the poverty line, as were 65 percent of white families with three and more children (Cutright and Smith 1986). The United States clearly does not set a high value on social reproduction.

Women's special burden is related to an outmoded patriarchy that no longer sustains the ideology with a material base. The rising number of families with women heads (66.2 percent of black women in 1984) is a major factor in the rising number of poor people. The failure of income tax assessments to keep up with the realities of these costs can be seen in the allowable deductions. Given the rise in the cost of living, the allowance for dependents (always an underestimated cost) should be $5,600 instead of $1,600, according to Cutright and Smith 1986. The dilemma women face in politicizing their claims is that of losing their rights defined in relation to dependent roles in the household while seeking autonomy as wage workers or as claimants for public assistance.

Frances Fox Piven (1987) puts the political implications of this shift in historical perspective: women are losing their old rights in the family and have not found new ones in the marketplace. As the main beneficiaries of Aid to Families with Dependent Children, food stamps, Medicaid, Medicare, and Social Security, they are the most threatened by the attrition in these programs.

In contrast to the struggles of women in Latin America, the politicizing of women's demands in this new context faces many obstacles. Bureaucratization fragments class issues, and when professionals manage the lives of welfare families, the class issues are further atomized (Morgan 1981; Susser 1982).

The rising gap between wages and the cost of living creates the potential for cross-class alliances that could become the new agenda for a feminist movement. In core industrial countries the struggle to gain equity in the occupational sphere must overcome the antipathy to state intervention in what is construed as privacy of the domestic domain. In contrast, women in Latin America and other peripheral areas have already passed that barrier, as their collective struggle for survival has overcome the privatized domestic role that laid the basis for their oppression. Women in the core industrial countries can learn from the experiences of women in peripheral regions.

Conclusion

The incorporation of women throughout the world in the paid workforce has only increased the burden they bear in the reproduction of families and society. For the vast majority of women, their lower wage rates cannot cover the minimal costs of survival in either core or peripheral economies. The loss of their labor in the subsistence economy reduces the insulation this sector provided from fluctuations in the business cycle.

In the current crisis of accumulation certain commonalities between core and periphery emerge as capitalist class relations threaten the spheres of biological and social reproduction. In core countries this threat takes the form of privatizing reproduction, forcing the family to assume the costs for dependents that had formerly been borne by governments (Brenner 1984). In peripheral countries it is found in the breakdown of the subsistence sector. In both core and peripheral countries the rising rates of marital instability, often caused by unemployment or the forced migration of men to find new sources of work, puts even greater responsibility on women for the care and welfare of dependents. The relative cheapness of women's labor is everywhere more intensively exploited, in the service industries of core capitalist countries and in the export processing zones of the periphery. As opportunities for employment in the formal sector diminish, women are resorting to self-created jobs in the informal economy, engaging in homework, street sales, or vending as they strive to meet the needs of their families. In the more extreme situations of Third World countries the daily struggle of women involves them increasingly in collective action to ensure survival.

Rosa Luxemburg's thesis concerning the importance of the noncapitalist sector in the accumulation of capital can be expanded to show its impact on the class struggle. In Marxist analysis the central dynamic is the contradiction of capitalism between the social ownership of wealth and the private expropriation of surplus value from workers, leading to the consciousness of class and the struggle to overcome exploitation. When we include the noncapitalist subsistence producers as an integral part of the analysis, we can begin to appreciate the broader basis for social movements throughout the world. In this enlarged sector the presence of women changes the class struggle from one limited to the arena of production to a struggle for reproduction, where moral persuasion based on the right to survive rather than the threat of withdrawing labor becomes the imperative.

NOTES

1. See, for example, National Committee on Working Women n.d.; Ward 1984; International Monetary Fund 1986, 1987; World Bank 1986, 1987; American Development Bank 1987; Smith et al. 1988.

2. Marx and Engels ended the *Communist Manifesto* with the phrase "Workers of the world unite! You have nothing to lose but your chains." Since Flora Tristan visited them after the publication of her book in 1837, they surely had knowledge of her work.

REFERENCES

Alonso, José Antonio. n.d. "Sismos, crisis económica y costura doméstica: Un estudio de caso en Ciudad Nezahualcoyotl" (Earthquakes, economic crisis, and domestic seamstresses: A case study in Nezahualcoyotl City). Unpublished manuscript.

American Development Bank. 1987. *Economic and Social Progress Report.* Washington, D.C.

Amin, Samir. 1977. *Imperialism and Unequal Development.* New York: Monthly Review.

Barbieri, Teresita de, and Orlandina de Oliveira. 1987. "La presencia de las mujeres en América Latina en una década de crisis" (The presence of women in Latin America in a decade of crisis). Paper presented at the meeting of Development Alternatives with Women for a New Era, La Paz, December.

Benería, Lourdes. 1989. "The Mexican Debt Crisis: Restructuring the Economy and the Household." Paper presented at the Conference on Women in Development, Albany, SUNY, March 3–4.

Bennholdt-Thomsen, Veronika. 1981. "Subsistence Production and Extended Reproduction." In *Of Marriage and the Market: Women's Subordination Internationally and Its Lessons,* ed. Kate Young, Carol Walkowitz, and Roslyn McCullagh, 16–29. London: Routledge and Kegan Paul.

Blondet, Cecilia. 1988. "Pobladoras, dirigentas y ciudadanas: El caso de las mujeres populares de Lima." Paper presented at the meeting of the Latin American Studies Association, New Orleans, March.

Brenner, Johanna. 1984. "Rethinking Women's Oppression." *New Left Review* 143:33–71.

Bunster, Ximena, Elsa M. Chaney, and Ellan Young. 1985. *Sellers and Servants: Working Women in Lima, Peru.* New York: Praeger.

Castells, Manuel. 1980. *The Economic Crisis and American Society.* Princeton: Princeton University Press.

Cutright, Phillips, and Herbert L. Smith. 1986. "Declining Family Size and the Number of Children in Poor Families in the United States: 1964–1983." *Social Science Research* 15:256–268.

Dalla Costa, Mariarosa. 1972. *Women and the Subversion of Community.* Bristol, England: Falling Wall Press.

Dandler, Jorge, and Carmen Madeiros. 1985. "La migración temporal de Cochabamba, Bolivia, a la Argentina: Trayectorias e impacto en el lugar de origen." Centro de Estudios de la Realidad Económica y Social. Mimeographed.

de Janvry, Alain, and Carmen Diana Deere. 1978. *A Theoretical Framework for the Empirical Analysis of Peasants.* Working Paper no. 66, Giannini Foundation. Berkeley: University of California.

de Oliviera, Cresencia. 1987. "Empleo feminino en México en tiempo de expansión y recesión económica: Tendencias recientes" (Women's employment in Mexico in time of expansion and recession: Recent tendencies). Paper presented at the meeting of Development Alternatives with Women for a New Era, La Paz, December.

Frank, Andre Gunder. 1978–79. *Dependent Accumulation and Undevelopment.* New York: Monthly Review.

International Monetary Fund. 1986. *World Economic Outlook.* Washington, D.C.

———. 1987. *International Financial Statistics Yearbook.* Washington, D.C.

Keren, Donna J. 1986. "Working through the Debt Crisis: Factories and Labor in Querétaro, Mexico." Paper presented at the meeting of the Latin American Studies Association, Boston, October.

Laclau, Ernesto. 1971. "Feudalism and Capitalism in Latin America." *New Left Review* 67:19–38.

Lenin, V. I. 1934. *Imperialism: The Highest Stage of Capitalism.* New York: International.

Luxemburg, Rosa. 1951. *The Accumulation of Capital.* London: Routledge and Kegan Paul.

———. 1972. *The Accumulation of Capital: An Anti-critique.* New York: Monthly Review.

Marx, Karl. 1906. *Capital,* vol. 1. Trans. Samuel Moore and Edward Aveling, ed. Frederick Engels. Chicago: Charles H. Kerr.

———. 1963. *Precapitalist Economic Formation.* Trans. Jack Cohen, intro. Eric J. Hobsbawm. New York: International.

Mather, Celia. 1982. *Industrialization in the Tangerang Regency of West Java: Women Workers and the Islamic Patriarchy.* Working Paper no. 17, Center for Sociology and Anthropology. Amsterdam: University of Amsterdam.

Morgan, Patricia. 1981. "From Battered Wife to Program Client: The State Shaping of Social Problems." *Kapitalistat: Working Papers of the Capitalist State* 9:17–39.

Nash, June. 1982. "Implications of Technological Change for Household Level and Rural Development." In *Technological Change and Rural Development,* ed. P. M. Weil and J. Eltereich, 429–476. Newark: University of Delaware Press.

———. 1988. "The Mobilization of Women in the Bolivian Debt Crisis." In *Women and Work,* ed. Laurie Larwood, Barbara A. Gutek, and Ann H. Stromberg. Newbury Park, Calif.: Sage.

National Committee on Working Women. n.d. *Pay Equity: A Fact Sheet.* Washington, D.C.

Piven, Frances Fox. 1987. "Women and the State: Ideology, Power, and the Welfare State." In *Families and Work,* ed. Naomi Gerstel and Harriet Engel Gross, 512–519. Philadelphia: Temple University Press.

Pond, Chris, and Louie Burghes. 1986. "The Rising Tide of Deprivation." *New Society* 76 (18): 8–10.

Prates, Suzana. 1987. "Participación laboral femenina en el proceso de la crisis" (Women's labor participation in the process of the crisis). Paper presented at the meeting of Development Alternatives with Women for a New Era, La Paz, December.

Radcliffe, Sara A. 1988. " 'Así es una mujer del pueblo': Los nuevos grupos de mujeres y el gobierno de APRA, Perú, 1985–1987" ("That's how a woman of the pueblo is": New groups of women and the government of APRA). Paper presented at the meeting of the Latin American Studies Association, New Orleans, March.

Sen, Gita, and Caren Grown. 1987. *Development, Crises, and Alternative Visions.* New York: Monthly Review.

Serrano, M. Claudia. 1987. "Crisis económica y mujeres de sectores populares urbanos en Santiago de Chile" (Economic crisis and women of popular urban sectors in Santiago de Chile). Paper presented at the meeting of Development Alternatives with Women for a New Era, La Paz, December.

Smith, Joan, Jane Collins, Terence K. Hopkins, and Akbar Muhammad, eds. 1988. *Racism, Sexism, and the World-System: Studies of the Political Economy of the World-System.* Westport, Conn.: Greenwood.

Strengers, Jeroen. 1985. "La pesada carga de la deuda" (The heavy burden of the debt). La Paz: El Centro de Documentación e Información.

Susser, Ida. 1982. *Norman Street: Poverty and Politics in an Urban Neighborhood.* New York: Oxford University Press.

Therborn, Goran. 1987. "The Prospects of Labour and the Transformation of Advanced Capitalism." *New Left Review* 8:143–148.

Tristan, Flora. [1837] 1983. *The Workers' Union.* Trans. Beverly Livingston. Urbana: University of Illinois Press.

Wallerstein, Immanuel. 1974. "The Rise and Future Demise of the World Capitalist System: Concepts for Comparative Analysis." *Comparative Studies in Society and History* 16 (4): 387–415.

———. 1979. *The Capitalist World Economy.* Cambridge: Cambridge University Press.

Ward, Kathryn B. 1984. *Women in the World System: Its Impact on Status and Fertility.* New York: Praeger.

Wolpe, Harold. 1972. "Capitalism and Cheap Labour Power in South Africa." *Economy and Society* 1 (4): 425–456.

World Bank. 1986. *World Development Report.* New York: Oxford University Press.

————. 1987. *World Debt Tables: External Debt of Developing Countries.* Washington, D.C.

CHAPTER 7

✳

Gender and Multiple Income Strategies in Rural Mexico

A Twenty-Year Perspective

FRANCES ABRAHAMER ROTHSTEIN

Increasing attention by social scientists to working-class women and men in Mexico has led to a rich and detailed analysis of the intersection of kinship and income strategies. Several important patterns have surfaced in this analysis. The reliance on multiple wage workers and a variety of income-generating activities, often coupled with subsistence cultivation, is one such pattern. A related pattern is women's increased and more diverse participation in the capitalist industrial economy. This chapter, based on anthropological fieldwork carried out between 1971 and 1989, describes and analyzes multiple income strategies and women's increased labor force participation in San Cosme Mazatecochco, an industrializing community in rural Mexico. As San Cosme changed from a peasant community, to one that was heavily dependent on the wages of men, and most recently to a community dependent on a variety of income-earning strategies, gender patterns have also changed. I suggest that who does what in contemporary multiple income strategies is influenced by local gender definitions and kin patterns affecting the gendered distribution of resources and labor within and among households. The new multiple income strategies found in San Cosme, and by generalization elsewhere, are a consequence of both external conditions and internal family dynamics.

Although the chapter focuses on Mexico, it is important to stress that much of what has been occurring there is part of broader changes in the global economic system. Everywhere global restructuring and vertical disintegration are increasing (see Fernández Kelly 1983; Blim 1991; Fernández Kelly and Sassen 1991). This means more people than before are selling their labor and doing so in a variety of different ways and contexts.

In the Third World multiple income strategies include greater dependence on wages to supplement or replace peasant strategies. In the First
World multiple wages are replacing the single breadwinner strategy.[1] In
rural Kentucky, for example, a single household (sometimes the same
individual at different points in his or her lifetime or even at the same
time) may rely on the wages of a worker in a Toyota factory, the cash
brought in by a household member who grows tobacco, and the profit
that comes from employing tobacco workers (who may be undocumented
workers from rural Mexico whose own families rely on a combination of
remittances, subsistence cultivation, and local wage work) (Kingsolver
1991). Increasingly, everywhere, men and women, parents and children
are pursuing a variety of economic routes to provide for their families.

Although family strategies that pooled labor and wages also characterized peasant economies, the new multiple income strategies differ from
peasant strategies in that there is greater dependence on the market
(especially the market for labor) than on family production. Formerly,
participation in the "modern" economy, especially wage labor, was
primarily male.[2] As we are all aware, women have become more involved
in wage labor and various commercial activities. The growth in women's
paid employment has been especially marked and commented on in
advanced capitalist economies. Although it has received less attention and
is quantitatively much smaller, women's participation in modern wage
and commercial economic activities in the developing world has also
grown.[3]

The pattern of diverse income sources that increasingly characterizes
rural and urban dwellers in both the First and Third Worlds in the 1980s
and 1990s has led some commentators to suggest that today's workers
are not the "classic" workers of social science models of the past. Bryan
Roberts (1989a) notes that the pattern today is one of "uncommitted" or
"flexible" labor, that is, a labor force for which the workplace, work, and
occupation are not the determining forces they were for classic proletarians. Similarly, Ray Pahl (1976, cited in 1984, 6) writes that "the typical
image of the factory worker attending meetings of his union at the
workplace is increasingly outdated." The questions and issues raised by
these scholars are like those of writers such as Colin Leys (1971), Luisa
Paré (1977), Julian Laite (1981), and others who in the 1970s and early
1980s stressed the partial or semiproletarianization of workers in dependent capitalist countries.

The new view differs, however, in important ways. In the 1970s
semiproletarianization was seen as a stage in which Third World workers
were stuck because dependent capitalist countries could not fully develop.
In the contemporary approach Pahl, Roberts, Manuel Castells and Ale-

jandro Portes (1989), and M. Patricia Fernández Kelly and Saskia Sassen (1991) all suggest that partial or semiproletarianization is the beginning of a new stage throughout global capitalism. In this new stage, characterized by unprecedented mobility of capital and labor, a heterogeneous working class (Roberts's term) is created by a new global capitalism in which privileges, including a family wage, once won by some workers in this class, are continually eroded by the incorporation of new workers anywhere and everywhere into an international labor force.[4]

Families and the Heterogeneous Working Class

An important characteristic of the new working class that has received too little attention is that it is *not* made up of the full-time male breadwinners of the Euro-American model of the "classic" proletariat. Although that classic white male worker always existed more in ideology than in reality,[5] the male breadwinner ideology discouraged some women from entering or staying in the labor force; by defining those who entered the labor force as deviant (Davis 1976; Mullings 1986) or temporary workers, the ideology justified paying women lower wages (Sokoloff 1980). The ideology of the male breadwinner and the housewifization (Mies 1986) or domestication (Rothstein 1982) of women was brought to Third World countries along with other Western imports, including the practice of not hiring women in the modern sector (see Boserup 1970; Mies 1986; van Halsema 1991). Whereas in the First World that ideology was perpetuated in part by a relatively long period during which at least some workers were able to win a family wage, under the dependent capitalism of the Third World, few workers earned a family wage and, if they did, it was for only a short period. In Mexico, for example, wages increased for some during the 1970s when the country experienced its "miraculous" growth, but wages have been declining ever since (Mertens and Richards 1987). Unable to rely on the wages of a single breadwinner, Mexicans, like many people elsewhere, now depend on pooling the results of a variety of means of income generation.

This pooling means that groups, rather than individuals, are the important economic units; therefore, our analyses must be based on groups. Pahl (1984), among others, suggests households. But households may not always be the appropriate units either.[6] It may be misleading to look only at relations within households and ignore relations between and among members of different households. Rather than assuming that any particular units, such as households or individuals, are significant, perhaps, as Sylvia Yanagasakio (1979) has argued, we should first identify the exchange transactions in a particular society and then ask what kinds of units engage in these activities.

Suggesting that individuals are embedded in family and/or household units and networks does not mean, however, that the networks or groups make collective decisions in the interests of all. When we look at households and/or families, it is important to examine relations both of conflict and of cooperation. Most studies of households have tended to see either all unity or all conflict.[7] Furthermore, among those who stress conflict, there is sometimes a tendency to see all rural or "traditional" households as strongly and equally patriarchal. In fact, however, although some traditional households are strongly patriarchal, others are not.[8] As Carole Turbin suggests for nineteenth-century Troy, New York, "while hierarchy is fundamental to male-female relations . . . men were not all powerful. And they were not powerful in the same way in all aspects of daily life" (1989, 6).

A related tendency, particularly in the literature on women and employment, is to see only the ways households or families constrain women's choices and limit their opportunities.[9] Both the view that sees a uniform and equally patriarchal "traditional" family and the view that sees only the constraints traditional families impose on women suffer from several misconceptions about rural families. First, few situations, including that of so-called traditional patriarchal families, are as static as is often implied. Although families do resist change, including the proletarianization of their women, and fight incursions by external conditions, they are not immune to these conditions. Often, in fact, their resistance requires change. Nor is it true that, because they respond to external conditions, families are the dependent units of neoclassical economics in which household decisions are nothing but responses to external conditions (Stichter 1990, 33). Families, including more and less patriarchal ones, like other cultural institutions, change in some ways and remain the same in others. Examination of particular historical contexts is necessary for an understanding of when and how they change.

A second misconception that underlies the focus on constraints experienced by women in their families is an erroneous view of women as passive victims. Rural women, like people elsewhere, do not merely accept the constraints imposed on them in even the most patriarchal context. There are numerous indications that women not only are the victims of their families but also are, through their own efforts as well as the efforts especially of their mothers and other women, the beneficiaries of family resources, contacts, and labor. Kin networks and groups, in response to both external and internal factors, broaden the economic opportunities of some women by providing resources, labor, and/or schooling.

From Peasant to Proletarian to Heterogeneous Working Class in San Cosme

Until the 1940s San Cosme was a relatively homogeneous peasant community. Even by 1950, according to the national census, 90 percent of the population walked barefoot, 85 percent spoke Nahuatl, and 56 percent were illiterate. Except for a few families that supplemented small-scale agriculture with a mill or general store and a handful of factory workers, the people of San Cosme relied primarily on subsistence agriculture.

As a result of the national textile boom during the Second World War and the lack of dynamic in peasant agriculture, during the 1940s men from San Cosme began working in textile factories in Mexico City, about sixty miles away, or Puebla, ten miles away. Initially, only a few men went to work in factories, but as the value of agricultural production declined and land pressure mounted, the number of factory workers grew. By 1980 almost half the males twelve years and older were *obreros,* or factory workers, and less than one of every four households relied primarily on what they themselves produced.[10]

The consequences of factory work were enormous. In addition to many material changes, such as improved roads, drainage, electricity, cement or brick houses, radios, televisions, and gas stoves, the structure of the community and social relations changed (see Rothstein 1982 for a fuller description). One of the most important changes was that as the wages of male factory workers became the main sources of cash, these workers increasingly dominated their households, and the community. Their cash enabled them to dominate their households and their cash and political contacts, usually through their unions, enabled them also to dominate local-level politics and community decision making.

It is important to note, however, that male dominance because of wage work was simply the direction many workers and their families were headed in the 1970s. Most families still had land and cultivated it. More egalitarian relations between men and women and respect for women's work still existed in peasant households and were at least within memory for others. Although nuclearization was occurring among many proletarian families, people in San Cosme still had important kin relations beyond the household. It was not unusual, for example, to find hundreds of relatives at a wedding or saint's day celebration. People also continued to rely heavily on kin for jobs, political support, and labor.

In the 1980s San Cosme, like Mexico in general, experienced an economic crisis that brought high inflation, unemployment, and declining real wages. San Cosmeros dealt with the crisis in part with the kind of multiple income strategies that Pahl (1984), Roberts (1989a, 1989b,

TABLE 7-1

Occupations for Males Aged 12 and Older, San Cosme, 1980 and 1989

	1980		1989	
	No.	%	No.	%
Peasant	75	23	91	28
Student	63	19	57	17
Factory worker	159	48	124	38
Other (merchant, mechanic, clerical worker, musician, domestic worker)	32	10	55	17
Total	329	100	327	100
Paid work (factory and other)	191	58	179	55

Source: Author's survey, 1980 and 1989.

1989c), Rhoda Halperin (1990), Ann Kingsolver (1991) and others have described for other regions. This is apparent in the fact that although the proportion of men engaged in paid work stayed about the same between 1980 and 1989 (58 percent in 1980 compared to 53 percent in 1989; see Table 7-1), the number of earners per household increased from 1.2 in 1980 to 1.3 in 1989 (see Table 7-2). On the surface, men's economic activities did not change much during the 1980s. Some diversification had begun, so that men were more likely to be self-employed or selling their labor in different contexts rather than just factories. But the significance of a particular man's income for the household changed. In the late 1970s and early 1980s, although most households in San Cosme still usually

TABLE 7-2

Number of Household Members Engaged in Income Generation in San Cosme, 1980 and 1989

Income generators per household	1980		1989	
	No.	%	No.	%
0	43	20	35	26
1	104	51	45	34
2	36	18	36	27
3	18	9	12	9
4	4	2	3	2
5	0	—	2	2
Total	205	100	133	100
Mean		1.20		1.32

Source: Author's survey, 1980 and 1989.

TABLE 7-3
Households' Paid Workers, by Relation to Head, San Cosme, 1989

	No.	%
Female head only	2	2
Male head only	17	18
Head and other(s)	33	35
Others (other than head)	41	44
Total households with some paid workers	93	99
Households with woman (women) working	31	33

Source: Author's Survey, 1989.

Note: Paid work refers to wage work and self-employment (not including unpaid agricultural work on one's own farm or as exchange labor).

supplemented wages with subsistence production, before the economic crisis the wages of one male could be the main basis of a family's support. By the late 1980s, with the loss of jobs, the decline in wages, and high inflation, the wages of a single male earner were less likely to support a family. As indicated in Table 7-3, of the households where income is generated by paid work, the male head is the sole paid income generator in fewer than one out of five households. In most households with any wage workers or self-employed members, more than one person is generating income.

Residents of San Cosme have increased the number of income generators per household partly by living together. As indicated in Table 7-4, there has been a fairly large increase in the proportion of extended family households and a decline in the percentage of nuclear family units.[11] The former tend to have more income generators; extended families have an

TABLE 7-4
Household Composition in San Cosme, 1971, 1980, 1984, 1989

	1971		1980		1984		1989	
	No.[a]	%	No.[a]	%	No.[a]	%	No.[a]	%
Nuclear family	93	60	132	66	28	60	58	44
Extended family	45	29	25	12	16	34	58	44
Other	17	11	43	22	3	6	17	13
Total	155	100	200	100	47	100	133	101[b]

Source: Author's survey, 1971, 1980, 1984, 1989.

[a]Refers to number of households.

[b]Discrepancy is due to rounding.

TABLE 7-5
Occupations of Women and Men Aged 12 and Older, San Cosme, 1980 and 1989

	1980				1989			
Occupation	Men		Women		Men		Women	
	No.	%	No.	%	No.	%	No.	%
Factory worker	159	48	13	4	124	38	16	5
Workshop worker	0	—	0	—	2	1	6	2
Other	32	10	13	4	53	16	36	10
Peasant	75	23	19	7	92	28	33	10
Student	63	19	39	13	57	17	36	10
Homemaker	0	—	207	71	0	—	213	63
Total	329	100	291	99[a]	328	100	340	100

Source: Author's survey, 1980 and 1989.
[a]Discrepancy is due to rounding.

average of 1.6 income generators per household whereas nuclear families average only 1.2. Another way that San Cosmeros have dealt with the crisis and increased the number of wage earners and self-employees has been to increase the labor force participation and self-employment of women. In 1980 8 percent of the women twelve and over were reported participating in the labor force or in commercial activities; by 1989 the proportion had almost doubled, to 17 percent (see Table 7-5). One out of three households with income generators had one or more women engaged in market activity (see Table 7-3).

Like other working-class communities that are increasingly relying on multiple income pooling strategies, households in San Cosme also now require that more of their members engage in paid work. Although this pattern, as well as the increase in women's employment, has been noted elsewhere, there has been little analysis of its effect on gender relations within or beyond the household or of the effect of gender on earning strategies. It is to gender, therefore, that I now turn.

The Gendered Distribution of Wages and Resources in San Cosme

Gender can play a role in multiple income strategies in at least two related ways. First, gender can directly influence the distribution of wages and other family resources, and second, gender can affect what economic choices are open to various household members. This effect can be direct, as when women are expected to do domestic work and discouraged or prohibited from doing other work, or indirect, as when an individual is given family support to facilitate her or his economic activity.

Men in San Cosme earn more because more men earn wages and tend to be in higher-paying jobs or more lucrative commercial activities. But, as indicated above, few men are the sole earners in their households or alone control a household's income. Not only do few men earn all or most of a household's cash, but often sons and daughters give their contributions (in cash or gifts) to their mothers.

In addition to there not being a single breadwinner who bears the main responsibility for supporting the household, all the households in San Cosme produce some of their own corn, beans, squash, other vegetables, meat, or fruit. In a survey in 1989 most people (78 percent) said they produce enough corn at least for their own consumption.

Although the multiple wages and other income that a household relies on are not likely to come from a single male individual, how a household's resources are distributed, particularly after necessities have been met, is influenced by gender. Men are likely to have more capital for investment because their earnings are often the largest source of cash. The best-paying local factory, which employs men almost exclusively, gives large bonuses at the end of the year. One worker was able to use this bonus to set up a *taller* (workshop) that makes children's clothes.

Men's greater access to cash, however, does not mean that families do not use their cash or other resources to help women establish businesses. Land is divided among all children, male and female, so women inherit land that can be used for crops or a housesite or can be sold. Women may also be given other resources. For example, one woman has a large herd of sheep and goats that was started with a contribution of animals from her mother from her own herd. Another woman successfully runs a butcher shop. Her family (parents and brother) provided her with the space necessary to begin the enterprise. She had learned butchering from her former husband before he left her.

Some businesses that were started largely with the cash from a husband's earnings are run by the husband and wife. They include several sewing workshops (one is the *taller* mentioned above), a restaurant, a chicken store, and several clothing stores. In each one the husband usually has another job or business and the wife supervises the running of the enterprise. The man who has the chicken store, for example, is a veterinarian. It is too soon to say whether these joint efforts will benefit women and men equally. Men usually take on those aspects of the business that involve external affairs, such as buying the food for the restaurant or making arrangements with the chicken distributors. Maria Mies (1983) has argued that in small lacemaking enterprises in India, men control the more powerful and rewarding external activities and the wives are simply an unpaid labor force. I do not think this will be the case in San Cosme, because women's choices are not as limited as they appear to be in the village Mies studied. As indicated above, women are not confined to work at home; they have access to some resources of their own through their natal families, and they have some access to paid employment outside the home.[12]

Gender and Kin Support in San Cosme

I have argued elsewhere (Rothstein 1982) that relations between the sexes among peasants in San Cosme are relatively egalitarian and that the gender inequalities that I observed in the 1970s among proletarians were recent. Additionally, I suggested above that the male breadwinner model on which those inequalities had been developing has not persisted. In other words, the culture of San Cosme was not one of male domination or patriarchy. Although gender inequality was increasing as San Cosme became proletarianized, the crisis of the 1980s and the fact that patriarchy had not established itself, combined with an opening up of some job opportunities for women (including the growth of female employment on the global assemblyline and the Mexican government's increasing attention to women for political reasons), has produced a more favorable context for women than is the case in many other working-class communities, including San Cosme in the 1970s.

Although some local notions suggest that remunerative work is not seen in the same way for women as for men, women in San Cosme are not usually prohibited from engaging in paid work or commercial activities and such work is not seen as deviant or not women's place. Only one woman, a former nurse married to a factory worker, said that her husband does not want her to work because she would then have money and leave him. Interestingly, she is the daughter of a woman who came originally from another, more proletarianized community and who said that, years before, she had stopped going to Puebla (the city about ten miles away) to study to be a practical nurse because her husband objected. Another woman said that if a woman worked, her husband might not, but other than that, she had no objections to women's paid work. People sometimes also talked about women who appeared to be successful and suggested that their success was because of sexual relations with male bosses. It should be noted, however, that men who appeared to be successful were also talked about, their success often being attributed to trade in drugs or women.

TABLE 7-6

Education of 15- to 19-Year-Olds, San Cosme, 1989

Years of Schooling	Women		Men	
	No.	%	No.	%
Fewer than 6	4	7	2	4
6	19	32	14	25
7–9	24	41	32	57
10 and more	12	20	8	14
Total	59	100	56	100

Source: Author's survey, 1989.

In addition to giving daughters land, animals, or money, a major way that families influence their daughters' choices, which is indirectly an indication of their ideas about daughters' future employment, is through their encouragement or discouragement of schooling. During the period when men were becoming proletarians, that is, the late 1960s and 1970s especially, San Cosmeros devoted a great deal of effort to getting more schools and better education for their children (Rothstein 1982). Because more education had become a requirement for their jobs, males benefited much more than females from the stress on education. In the 1980s, however, the gap in education between women and men (see Table 7-6) appeared to be decreasing. As indicated in Table 7-7, women in all age groups have less education than men. But among older women (i.e., before wage work was a significant part of life in San Cosme) and among those under twenty, the differences are much smaller. The greatest gap between men and women is among the twenty- to twenty-nine-year-olds,

TABLE 7-7

Gender, Age, and Education in San Cosme, 1989: Mean Years of Schooling

Age	N	Women	Men	Difference
Under 15	154	2.817	2.915	−0.098
15–19	114	7.949	8.196	−0.247
20–29	189	6.842	8.189	−1.347
30–39	111	5.667	6.588	−0.921
40–49	61	3.625	4.636	−1.011
50–59	59	2.563	2.800	−0.237
60 and over	45	2.429	2.667	−0.238

Source: Author's census, 1989.

Note: Differences are not statistically significantly different.

TABLE 7-8

Occupations by Sex, for 15- to 19-Year-Olds, San Cosme, 1989

Occupation	Women		Men	
	No.	%	No.	%
Factory worker	2	4	16	39
Workshop worker	2	4	0	—
Other	4	8	2	5
Peasant	0	—	5	12
Homemaker	29	59	0	—
Student	12	25	18	44
Total	49	100	41	100

Source: Author's survey, 1989.

that is, among those who were being educated when the breadwinner model was at its peak.

In order to send their daughters to school, parents must not only pay additional costs, such as those for school fees, tuition (if the school is private), transportation, and uniforms; they must also forgo the daughters' labor. Since most daughters do not work for wages, however, it is unpaid domestic labor that is forgone; for sons, it is more likely wage labor that is given up (see Table 7-8). This may be why a household's economic level (as measured by agricultural production) has a clearer effect on the level of education of sons than on the level of education of daughters. As indicated in Table 7-9, sons' education increases with agricultural production, whereas daughters' education varies somewhat inversely. The fact that education affects choices is suggested by the difference it makes in employment. Women with seven years or more education are much more likely to be employed (see Table 7-10) than those with less schooling. As indicated in Table 7-11, employed women average 8.5 years of education versus 5 years for others, and those with the most education are likely to be employed in professional jobs such as nursing or teaching.

The literature on male workers in Mexico has stressed how kin play an important role not only in helping educate workers but also in helping people get jobs and in taking over the tasks that would otherwise be performed by the men who take jobs. Women in San Cosme have always played a critical part in the job network because they, more than men, are involved with kin on a daily basis and thus are more likely to be in a position to hear about a job or to communicate the need for a job. In the past women sought jobs not usually for themselves but rather for their

TABLE 7-9
Agricultural Production in San Cosme, by Sons' and Daughters' Education, 1989

| | Sons' Education (Years) | | | | | |
| | 6 or fewer | | 7–9 | | 10 and more | |
Agricultural Production	No.	%	No.	%	No.	%
Do not produce enough for the household	18	58	11	35	2	6
Produce enough to feed the household	32	41	33	42	14	18
Produce enough to feed the household and to sell	20	44	13	29	12	27
	Daughters' Education (Years)					
	6 or fewer		7–9		10 and more	
Agricultural Production	No.	%	No.	%	No.	%
Do not produce enough for the household	6	40	9	60	0	—
Produce enough to feed the household	32	60	10	19	11	21
Produce enough to feed the household and to sell	14	52	8	30	5	18

Source: Author's survey, 1989.

husbands or sons. Today, however, like the men, they rely on female and male kin and neighbors to get their jobs.

Women, like men, rely also on kin and friends to perform the domestic tasks that are necessary for the reproduction of labor. At least within the remembered past, San Cosmeros have always relied on labor exchange among residential kin, nonresidential kin, *compadres* (ritual kin), and neighbors to perform domestic and extradomestic tasks. The bilateral kindred has been particularly important in the exchange of labor. The range of the kindred, three generations through both males and females, and their participation at weddings, baptisms, and funerals are culturally prescribed. Unless prevented by distance or a family quarrel, members of the kindred are obligated to participate in one another's baptisms, weddings, and funerals (Rothstein 1986b).

With regard to other kin relationships, however, as is characteristic of bilateral descent and kindreds elsewhere, individuals exercise a great deal of choice. A person can select relatives from his or her kindred to help in a variety of ways, but no particular genealogical relationship is associated with particular obligations. The ritual kin system is similar.

TABLE 7-10

Employment of Women in San Cosme, by Marriage and Education (Aged 15 and Older), 1989

Less Educated Women (6 years or fewer of schooling)

	Employed		Not Employed		Total
Marital Status	No.	%	No.	%	No.
Married	22	10	177	89	199
Single	5	19	22	81	27

More Educated Women (7 years or more of schooling)

	Employed		Not Employed		Total
Marital Status	No.	%	No.	%	No.
Married	14	39	22	61	36
Single	11	37	19	63	30

Source: Author's survey, 1989.

Note: Employment includes wage work and self-employment.

Except for some rules, such as the obligation to greet *compadres* formally and the prohibition on marrying ritual kin, relations between *compadres* are variable and optional. Some *compadres* have frequent contacts with one another and continually give food, labor, and other services. In other cases, the relations among ritual kin are minimal (Rothstein 1986b).

In both the bilateral kinship system and the ritual kinship system, cultural rules surround the individual with a number of people. The rules specify that for certain major events of the life cycle (birth, marriage, and death), these people will help by providing goods and/or services. These are the events that are certain or very likely to occur for all individuals. The cultural rules and expectations thus provide for the universal needs of the community. They also provide each person with a large, ego-centered network from which individuals or groups may be selected for more intensive interaction. The system thus also supplies additional support without unnecessary constraint. Not only can various kinship ties be activated or not, but among those that are activated, some may be characterized by balanced reciprocity and others by generalized reciprocity. The type of exchange, balanced or generalized, varies not with genealogical relationship (except within the nuclear family) but rather with interests and needs (Rothstein 1986b).

Given the flexibility of this system of optional reliance on bilateral kin

TABLE 7-11

Current Occupations in San Cosme, by Education, for Men and Women Aged 15 and Older, 1989

	Men		Women	
Occupation	N	Mean Years Schooling	N	Mean Years Schooling
Factory worker	121	6.1	16	7.3
Peasant	76	4.0	22	2.8
Workshop worker	2	9.0	6	6.5
Homemaker	0	—	187	4.8
Student	27	11.1	15	10.5
Teacher	2	9.5	8	12.9
Nurse	0	—	1	13.0
Driver	4	6.5	0	—
Merchant	10	7.3	12	6.4
Waitress	0	—	1	9.0
Mechanic	2	10.5	0	—
Miscellaneous	31	8.2	10	9.5
Total paid workers	172	6.7	57	8.5
Total nonpaid workers	103	5.8	223	5.0

Source: Author's survey, 1989.

and *compadres,* it is not surprising that the economic, political, and social changes related to proletarianization that San Cosme experienced, especially in the late 1960s and 1970s, led to some modifications but not a decline in labor exchange among kin. Many of the modifications had to do with the new needs created by male wage work (see Rothstein 1986b). For example, workers obtained jobs through their kindreds, and union and other political leaders received political support through their kindreds. As indicated above, women now also get jobs through their kin networks or kindreds.

Even more important, however, is women's reliance on their kindreds for reproductive labor. It is necessary to stress that it is the kindred—the flexible, ego-centered network—and not necessarily the coresidential family that is important. Although kin living in the same household often do cooperate, people need not reside together to share food, other items, or labor. This (along with the absence of any ideology saying married women should not work) may be why, among more educated women, marriage does not prevent women from engaging in paid labor or commercial activities (see Table 7-10) and why, contrary to expectations, women in nuclear family residential units are more likely than those in extended family units to be employed (see Table 7-12).

TABLE 7-12

Women's Employment in San Cosme, by Household Type (Women Aged 15 and Older), 1989

Household Type	Employed		Not Employed		Total No.
	No.	%	No.	%	
Extended	15	12	108	88	123
Nuclear	16	20	66	80	82
Other	3	21	11	79	14

Source: Author's survey, 1989.

Note: Employment includes wage work and self-employment.

Childcare and food preparation are among the services that are often exchanged not only between members of a household but between people in different households. A child may go to live with kin, especially grandparents, or may spend varying periods of time visiting. For example, a young woman and her two children, who lived about one hundred miles away, came to stay with her parents for several summers so that she, an elementary school teacher, could get additional training to become a secondary school teacher. Not only did the various members of her parents' household (including brothers, sisters, nieces, and nephews, as well as her mother and father and a visiting anthropologist) help take care of her two children, but they performed most of the domestic work so she was relieved of cooking, cleaning, and shopping. As children get older, they too are expected to contribute labor to the household in which they are living or visiting.

The extent to which some women may be relieved of domestic work was suggested by one woman who described her daughter, who lived with her husband, husband's mother and grandmother, and two children, as being "like a man." The daughter, like her husband, went out to work every day, and the two older women did all the domestic work.[13] Although women, especially older women, do most of the childcare and other reproductive work, it is not confined to women. Males, including grandfathers, brothers, uncles, and cousins, also take care of children, run errands, and shop. Sometimes the labor of kin is supplemented by hiring someone, usually a younger or an older woman, to do some of the reproductive work. The paid worker usually functions within the context of the kin group, and kin are the overseers or managers; the paid workers are often assigned the heaviest tasks, such as laundry.

The practice among San Cosmeros of extensive food sharing also facilitates women's participation in productive work. If someone in the household attends a fiesta, for example, she or he frequently returns with *mole* (the traditional dish served at weddings, baptisms, birthdays, and community festivals). Often portions are brought also to a mother or a sister who lives elsewhere. One summer, when I was living with a family in San Cosme, most of our meat came from the *mole* that someone, in the house or in another household, had brought from a fiesta. Food sharing is not confined to fiestas. When people have corn that is ready to eat boiled or roasted (before it is dry for the major harvesting for tortillas), they may bring uncooked corn or *chilatole* (a prepared dish of corn and pepper) to a sister, mother, or neighbor. Nonhousehold members also frequently or regularly go to a relative's house for meals.

External Constraints on Women's Participation in Paid Work

Given the support that women have available and the increasing participation of San Cosmeros in paid work, one may ask, why do not more women engage in paid labor or commerce?[14] It is here that one must look not only at household, family, and community organization but also at external factors.

The local context supports women's productive work as well as women's reproductive work. By this I mean that neither work outside the home nor work in the home is discouraged, devalued, or considered supplementary or less important. In addition, though the crisis has forced more and more San Cosmeros into wage work and commercial activity, for most San Cosmeros, in part because of their continued reliance on subsistence production, cooperation among kin, and some political success, the situation is not so desperate that they have to take anything at all or proletarianize no matter what.[15] Thus, although the local structure of family, kinship, and culture in San Cosme supports women's labor force participation and commercial activities, it does not force most women into paid activity.

Furthermore, given the limited opportunities of a gender-segregated labor market, women and their families resist women's entering or remaining in the workforce. Among eleven women who reported having left a previous job, for example, only four said they left for family reasons (they got married or wanted to be with their children). Two left to go back to school, three left because the pay was too low, and one left because her shoulders hurt; the remaining three were fired or their contracts were not renewed.

Until the 1980s there were few wage work opportunities for women. The jobs that were available for men in the 1950s, 1960s, and 1970s were not open to women. Except for a few unusually well educated women and a few who acquired special skills or who used family resources to become seamstresses, practical nurses, or *comerciantes*, the main alternatives were paid domestic work or agricultural labor. Only women and/or families that had no alternative or who saw their work as temporary—for example, working as a domestic to further their education—seem to have selected this option.

Today, although there are more job alternatives for women than in the past, work opportunities are still very limited. Formal sector factory jobs, even those on temporary contracts, usually require at least a sixth-grade education and often more. Despite women's greater schooling, a significant portion (43 percent) of women in San Cosme do not have a sixth-grade education and only 20 percent have the nine years that are increasingly being demanded. Men too are experiencing credentialism, but it should be noted that, even though men in San Cosme have more education than women, male factory workers have a lower level of education than female factory workers (see Table 7-11).

Not only can less-educated men get factory jobs, but men with more education have better opportunities than women with comparable schooling. Men with nine or more years of schooling are eligible for the "best" jobs, such as those at the petrochemical plant nearby which people said paid 300,000 to 350,000 pesos (US$120-$140)[16] a week in 1989 and gives large annual bonuses. The "best" factory jobs for women were then paying about 125,000 pesos (US$50) a week. Furthermore, although there is a shortage of factory jobs for men, there is even more of a shortage of factory jobs for women. Although several factories are "women's factories" (the local way of describing factories that employ primarily women), most of the factories in the region (Tlaxcala, Puebla, and the Federal District) employ mainly men.

Talleres represent an opportunity that seems to be expanding for women. These are the small workshops mentioned above that employ almost exclusively women, do not demand higher educational levels, give no benefits, and pay very poorly (between 45,000 and 85,000 pesos [US$18–32] a week in 1989).[17] Although some women own these workshops, usually with their husbands or other males, most women in workshops are workers. Some women work there temporarily while they are in school or until they can find a better job. Some women, however, especially those with less schooling and whose families have little land or other resources, may find they have few choices other than working in a *taller*.

More educated women, although they have more options, tend to be concentrated in women's professions such as teaching and nursing, which are among the lowest-paid professions in Mexico, as elsewhere. In 1989 teachers, for example, earned 100,000 pesos a week (US$40).

Whether San Cosmeros, women and men, will continue to be able to avoid working in *talleres* and other low-paying jobs depends on their continued access to at least some formal sector jobs and some resources. Three factors affect women and their households. First, men are experiencing greater difficulties finding jobs that pay even minimum wages. Second, because of continued high inflation, the need for still more wage earners continues. Third, there appears to be an increase in the abandonment of women and children.

It is impossible to measure unemployment in San Cosme, because people rarely say they are unemployed. Nevertheless, it seems that unemployment has grown. There has been an increase in the proportion of *campesinos* (peasants) and a decrease in factory workers among men since 1980 (see Table 7-1); among *campesinos* who were formerly factory workers, almost half (10 out of 23) said they had lost their jobs because their factory closed or there was a readjustment in the number of workers.

At the same time that men are losing their jobs, inflation, although reduced, continues. After inflation rates of over 100 percent throughout much of the 1980s, in part because of wage controls, rates dropped, but they were still 20 percent in 1989 (Inter-American Development Bank 1990, 151). An increase in husbands leaving their wives and a rise in female-headed (meaning no male head present) households is suggested by case material. In 1980 only 8.5 percent of the households in San Cosme were female-headed (Rothstein 1982, table 3); in 1989 the figure was 14 percent (19 out of 133 households).

In addition, if one counts what Florence Peña Saint Martin (1991) refers to as "hidden female-headed households," that is, where a woman-headed unit exists within another unit, another ten households have eleven women-headed units within them. Thus, 29 out of 133, or 22 percent of the households, have one or more women with children and no spouse present. Some of these women-headed units represent an increasing resistance on the part of women to marriage, made possible by family support and access to jobs or commercial activities; however, the close association between male unemployment and female-headed households found elsewhere (see, for example, Stack 1974; Susser 1982; Garcia and Oliveira 1991) and the fact that male unemployment has increased in San Cosme cannot be ignored. As more women have no choice but to enter the labor market or to participate in commercial activity, either because they are in women-headed units with no or fewer male wage earners or because male wages are inadequate (too few male workers and/or too low wages), how and where they enter depends on the interaction between their access to resources, labor, and education and the structure of jobs and commerce.

Conclusion

Women in San Cosme are increasingly entering the labor force and/or engaging in commercial activities. This is part of a growing general pattern of multiple income strategies in which household members pool wages, cash, subsistence products, and unpaid labor. Such a pattern was noted many years ago by Carol Stack (1974) for urban black Americans. Subsequent studies by Larissa Lomnitz (1977) in Mexico, Ida Susser (1982) in New York, Roger Sanjek (1982) in Ghana, and Adrian Peace (1975) in Nigeria, among others, further documented the importance of sharing among coresident and nonresident kin in other urban areas. More recently, similar patterns have been noted for other working-class populations, and some writers, such as Pahl (1984) and Roberts (1989a, 1989b, 1989c), suggest that multiple income strategies are replacing the single male breadwinner model of the classic Euro-American proletariat of the past. Little attention has been paid, however, to the ways in which multiple livelihoods and gender patterns interact.

In San Cosme local gender definitions and kinship patterns are encouraging some women to participate in multiple income strategies in ways similar to men. Through kinship some women, as well as men, are given access to land and other family resources, education, and domestic labor, making their entry into the labor force or commercial sector less vulnerable than it is for women who enter with fewer resources or skills. This is not to suggest that families in San Cosme do not also constrain and limit women's opportunities or that they do not limit women's opportunities more than men's. More pressure to earn wages or cash through continued inflation, male unemployment, and abandonment may alter the terms on which women from San Cosme enter income-generating activities. Inflation and limited land resources mean also that fewer families will be able to provide women or men with capital, schooling, or domestic labor. It is important to stress, however, that multiple income pooling strategies not only help families stretch their limited resources but, in communities such as San Cosme, where women's income-generating activities are supported, may have other consequences as well.

In a comparison of women workers in the United States in the 1930s and the 1980s, Ruth Milkman (1987) notes that the most important difference between these two periods was that by the 1980s the "family wage" ideal had eroded and there was a shift in the legitimacy of female employment. The data from San Cosme suggest that there has been a similar and, perhaps because the family wage ideal was much less entrenched, even stronger shift. As a consequence, not only is it legitimate for women to be employed but there is kin support for their efforts. Milkman goes on to say that "politically, this shift offers an enlarged potential for alliances between workers across gender lines" (1987, 127).

Despite a heavily state-controlled union movement, women in Mexico are increasingly organizing to improve their work conditions (Carrillo 1990; Ong 1990; Burns 1991, 5). For the Mexican situation, however, and elsewhere where multiple income strategies involve many members of a household in diverse wage and income-generating activities, I believe there is still more enlarged potential for political alliances. Not only may women's employment affect the political ties between women and men in the workplace, but the heterogeneous nature of the contemporary working class may affect the political ties of women and men away from the workplace.

Ironically, however, at precisely the time when proletarianization is greater and when we might expect an enlarged potential for political alliances among workers (and when the literature on social movements suggests that there are such alliances), there is also a growing body of literature that argues that the heterogeneous working class is not politically organized. Pahl (1984), for example, anticipates more individualism rather than collective activity among the heterogeneous proletariat. Roberts (1989a, 1989b, 1989c) similarly sees the heterogeneous working class as fragmented and disorganized and argues that the class basis for popular organizing is weak.

In a discussion of resistance among women workers in Mexico and Asia, Aihwa Ong (1990, 301) notes that although there are "scattered acts of resistance" in the workplace, they are often individual and even covert. She goes on, therefore, to suggest that rather than focusing on class and class struggle, we should examine cultural struggle and solidarity based on kinship and gender. Although I agree with Ong that we must look at solidarity (and conflict) based on kinship and gender, and I agree with Roberts, Pahl, and others that workplace organization is becoming less significant, we must supplement, not replace, class analysis (or class solidarity) with cultural analysis. As Sacks (1989, 546, citing Acklesberg) has suggested in an analysis of gender, race, and class, instead of rejecting all sources of community other than class and seeing nonclass ties as a drag on radical consciousness, as has been customary in Marxist class analysis, we should view class collectively as a relation of communities to the capitalist state more than of employees to employers. Such an approach would allow us not only to incorporate the local actions and histories that Ong rightly stresses but to go beyond local histories and perhaps also beyond local solidarities.

NOTES

Acknowledgments: This chapter is based on a total of two years of fieldwork in San Cosme Mazatecochco, Tlaxcala, between 1971 and 1989. I am grateful to Towson State University and the Wenner-Gren Foundation for Anthropological Research for supporting various phases of the research. In addition, I thank Dakota Sutor for her research assistance and Nancy Breen, Christine Bose, Myra Marx Ferree, Barbara Leons, and Natalie Sokoloff for their many excellent suggestions. Earlier versions of this chapter were presented at the annual meeting of the American Anthropological Association, Chicago, 1991, and the research conference, "Changing Perspectives on Women in Latin America and the Caribbean" held at New York University, April 24, 1992.

1. This increasing resemblance between the First and Third Worlds has led one observer to suggest that "cores may be turning into peripheries" (Roberts 1989a, 355).

2. I include in *modern economy* all the economic activity that is linked to the national and international capitalist economy. See Benería and Roldán 1987 for an excellent discussion showing how homework (and the informal sector) is linked to the formal capitalist economy.

3. Before 1960 there were large increases in labor force activity for men and negligible growth rates or declines for women. Between 1960 and 1970, when the economic activity rates for both men and women in the developing countries decreased, women's activity rate decreased less than men's. Then, between 1970 and 1980, although the rate for men declined, women's labor force participation increased (United Nations 1989, 52). In the 1980s women's labor force participation continued to increase, although at a slower rate than men's (United Nations 1989, 214). Much of the research on women's employment in the Third World has focused on women and the global assembly line (see, for example, Fernández Kelly 1983; Ong 1987; Tiano 1987; Wolf 1990). It is important to stress, however, that most women do not work on the global assembly line and that although assembly line employment accounts for some of the increase in female labor force participation, it is a relatively minor source of employment. Even in Mexico, for example, where *maquila* growth has been spectacular (Cornelius and Craig 1984), most workers are not on the global assembly line.

4. See Ross and Trachte 1990 and Rothstein and Blim 1991 for discussions of capitalists and workers in this new global capitalism. Although Roberts (1989a, 1989b, 1989c) stresses the heterogeneity of the new working class, he does not develop the link between it and global capitalism.

5. The full-time breadwinner was never as widespread as the ideology implied. Pahl (1984) cites a study of nineteenth-century workers in which J. C. Holley found that among skilled workers with good pay, the head's income was 57 percent of family income for woolen workers and 44 percent of family income for paper workers. Among unskilled workers the head's income was an even lower proportion of family income. Karen Sacks (1984) similarly notes that in the United States in the nineteenth century, children's wages, along with various informal activities of married women, made an important contribution. Carole

Turbin (1989) also shows variations in providers and their relations among workers in Troy, New York, in the nineteenth century. For an analysis of the conditions under which wives, as opposed to other household members, were employed, see Bose 1984.

6. For examples of this variation, see Guyer 1981 on Africa; Carol Stack (1974) also shows the importance of examining nonresident as well as coresident kin relations among African Americans in the United States. For a useful analysis of variation suggesting that there has been a tendency in Western feminist texts to underestimate diversity and treat Third World women as a singular monolithic subject with a singular pattern of patriarchy and powerlessness, see Mohanty 1991.

7. For an excellent discussion of the family as a "locus of struggle" as Heidi Hartmann (1987) characterized it, see Ferree 1990.

8. See, for example, Bossen 1984, Ong 1990, and Wolf 1990.

9. A similar approach is to look only at the negative impact of women's employment and ignore the positive effects. See, for example, Roberts 1989c.

10. Unless otherwise specified, the statistical data are taken from my surveys in 1971, 1980, 1984, or 1989.

11. Coresidence does not necessarily mean that income is shared among all the residents. In some households the component units maintain separate budgets. Even among those who have a common budget, the amount of individual earnings that is contributed to the common fund varies.

12. See also Wilson 1990 and Stephen 1991 for cases in Mexico in which women entrepreneurs used that activity to their advantage.

13. Isis Duarte (1989), writing about the Dominican Republic, and Georgina Jaffee (1991), writing about South Africa, similarly note that factory work may exempt some women from domestic chores.

14. Given the difficulty of measuring women's work, especially the part-time and/or informal work that many women engage in, it is very likely that women's participation in paid work is higher than my survey showed. In some cases, a person's part-time or short-term work was overlooked. Sometimes in those cases, the individual generated very little income. For example, some women sell embroidered capes (for Carnival) or tablecloths but usually only one cape or a few tablecloths a year. In another case, however, a laundress, who provided a household's major source of cash, was not mentioned.

15. Anyone who was in such a desperate situation, that is, someone who had no kin and/or land on which to rely, probably could not stay in San Cosme. For a discussion of San Cosmeros' relative success, as compared to that of urban dwellers, in getting jobs and community services, see Rothstein 1988.

16. In 1989 the exchange rate was 2,461 pesos per US dollar (Inter-American Development Bank 1990, 147).

17. In 1989 the workshops in San Cosme were owned by San Cosmeros and operated independently of large firms. I suspect that some of the workshops in the surrounding area are similarly independent and some are closely tied to larger firms (for fuller discussions of this growing pattern in Mexico of small workshops, see Benería and Roldán 1987 and Wilson 1990.

REFERENCES

Arizpe, Lourdes, and Josefina Aranda. 1986. "Women Workers in the Straw-berry Agribusiness in Mexico." In *Women's Work: Development and the Division of Labor by Gender,* ed. Eleanor B. Leacock and Helen I. Safa, 174–193. South Hadley, Mass.: Bergin and Garvey.

Benería, Lourdes, and Martha Roldán. 1987. *The Crossroads of Class and Gender: Industrial Homework, Subcontracting, and Household Dynamics in Mexico City.* Chicago: University of Chicago Press.

Blim, Michael. 1991. "Introduction." In *Anthropology and the Global Factory: Studies of the New Industrialization in the Late Twentieth Century,* ed. Frances Rothstein and Michael Blim, 1–30. South Hadley, Mass.: Bergin and Garvey.

Bose, Christine. 1984. "Household Resources and U.S. Women's Work: Factors Affecting Gainful Employment at the Turn of the Century." *American Sociological Review* 49:474–490.

Boserup, Ester. 1970. *Women's Role in Economic Development.* New York: St. Martin's Press.

Bossen, Laurel. 1984. *The Redivision of Labor.* Albany: State University of New York Press.

Burns, Elaine. 1991. "Female Work Force in Tijuana." *Voices of Mexico* 16 (January–March): 3–7.

Carrillo, Teresa. 1990. "Women and Independent Unionism in the Garment Industry." In *Popular Movements and Political Change in Mexico,* ed. Joe Foweraker and Ann L. Craig, 213–233. Boulder, Colo.: Lynne Rienner.

Castells, Manuel, and Alejandro Portes. 1989. "World Underneath: The Origins, Dynamics, and Effects of the Informal Economy." In *The Informal Economy: Studies in Advanced and Less Developed Countries,* ed. Alejandro Portes, Manuel Castells, and Lauren Benton, 11–37. Baltimore: Johns Hopkins University Press.

Cornelius, Wayne, and Ann L. Craig. 1984. *Politics in Mexico: An Introduction and Overview.* Reprint Series, 1. San Diego: Center for U.S.–Mexican Studies, University of California.

Davis, Angela. 1976. *Women, Race, and Class.* New York: Random House.

Duarte, Isis. 1989. "Household Workers in the Dominican Republic: A Question for the Feminist Movement." In *Muchachas No More: Household Workers in Latin America and the Caribbean,* ed. Elsa M. Chaney and Mary Garcia Castro, 197–219. Philadelphia: Temple University Press.

Fernández Kelly, M. Patricia. 1983. *For We Are Sold, I and My People: Women and Industry in Mexico's Frontier.* Albany: State University of New York Press.

Fernández Kelly, M. Patricia, and Saskia Sassen. 1991. *A Collaborative Study of Hispanic Women in Garment and Electronics Industries.* Final report presented to the Ford, Revson, and Tinker Foundations.

Ferree, Myra Marx. 1990. "Beyond Separate Spheres: Feminism and Family Research." *Journal of Marriage and the Family* 52:866–884.

Garcia, Brigida, and Orlandina de Oliveira. 1991. "Economic Recession and

Changing Determinants of Women's Work." Paper presented at the annual meeting of the Latin American Studies Association, Washington, D.C., April.

Guyer, Jane. 1981. "Household and Community in African Studies." *African Studies Review* 24:87–137.

Halperin, Rhoda. 1990. *Family and Livelihood in Kentucky*. Austin: University of Texas Press.

Hartmann, Heidi. 1987. "The Family as the Locus of Gender, Class, and Political Struggle." In *Feminism and Methodology,* ed. Sandra Harding, 109–134. Bloomington: Indiana University Press.

Inter-American Development Bank. 1990. *Economic and Social Progress in Latin America*. Baltimore: Johns Hopkins University Press.

Jaffee, Georgina. 1991. "Industrial Decentralization and Women's Employment in South Africa." In *Anthropology and the Global Factory,* ed. Frances Rothstein and Michael Blim, 161–176. South Hadley, Mass.: Bergin and Garvey.

Kingsolver, Ann. 1991. "Tobacco, Textiles, and Toyota: Working for Multinational Corporations in Rural Kentucky." In *Anthropology and the Global Factory,* ed. Frances Rothstein and Michael Blim, 191–205. South Hadley, Mass.: Bergin and Garvey.

Laite, Julian. 1981. *Industrial Development and Migrant Labor*. Austin: University of Texas Press.

Leys, Colin. 1971. "Politics in Kenya: The Development of Peasant Society." *British Journal of Political Science* 1 (3): 307–337.

Lomnitz, Larissa. 1977. *Networks and Marginality*. New York: Academic Press.

Mertens, L., and P. J. Richards. 1987. "Recession and Employment in Mexico." *International Labour Review* 128 (2): 229–243.

Mies, Maria. 1983. *The Lacemakers of Narsapur*. London: Zed.

———. 1986. *Patriarchy and Accumulation on a World Scale: Women in the International Division of Labour*. London: Zed.

Milkman, Ruth. 1987. "Women Workers and the Labor Movement in Hard Times: Comparing the 1930s with the 1980s." In *Women, Households, and the Economy,* ed. Lourdes Benería and Catharine R. Stimpson, 111–131. New Brunswick, N.J.: Rutgers University Press.

Mohanty, Chandra. 1991. "Under Western Eyes: Feminist Scholarship and Colonial Discourses." In *Third World Women and the Politics of Feminism,* ed. Chandra Mohanty, Ann Russo, and Lourdes Torres, 51–80. Bloomington: Indiana University Press.

Mullings, Leith. 1986. "Uneven Development: Class, Race, and Gender in the United States before 1900." In *Women's Work: Development and the Division of Labor by Gender,* ed. Eleanor B. Leacock and Helen I. Safa, 41–57. South Hadley, Mass.: Bergin and Garvey.

Ong, Aihwa. 1987. *Spirits of Resistance and Capitalist Discipline: Factory Women in Malaysia*. Albany: State University of New York Press.

———. 1990. "The Gender and Labor Politics of Postmodernity." *Annual Review of Anthropology* 30:279–309.

Pahl, Ray. 1984. *Divisions of Labor*. Oxford: Basil Blackwell.

Paré, Luisa. 1977. *El proletariado agrícola en México: Campesinos sin tierra o proletarios agrícolas?* Mexico City: Siglo XXI.

Peace, Adrian. 1975. "The Lagos Proletariat: Labour Aristocrats or Populist Militants?" In *The Development of an African Working Class: Studies in Class Formation and Action,* ed. Richard Sandbrook and Robin Cohen, 281–302. Toronto: University of Toronto Press.

Peña Saint Martin, Florence. 1991. "Beyond the Extended Household: A Portrait of Garment Workers' Households in Mérida, Yucatán (Mexico)." Paper presented at the annual meeting of the Latin American Studies Association, Washington, D.C., April.

Roberts, Bryan. 1989a. "The Other Working Class: Uncommitted Labor in Britain, Spain, and Mexico." In *Cross-National Research in Sociology,* ed. M. Kohn, 352–372. Newbury Park, Calif.: Sage.

———. 1989b. "Peasants and Proletarians." *Annual Review of Sociology* 16:353–378.

———. 1989c. "Urbanization, Migration, and Development." *Sociological Forum* 4 (4): 665–691.

Ross, Robert, and Kent Trachte. 1990. *Global Capitalism: The New Leviathan.* Albany: State University of New York Press.

Rothstein, Frances. 1982. *Three Different Worlds: Women, Men, and Children in an Industrializing Community.* Westport, Conn.: Greenwood.

———. 1986a. "La crisis y los obreros en un municipio de Tlaxcala: San Cosme Mazatecochco, 1940–1984." In *Historia y sociedad en Tlaxcala,* 166–170. Tlaxcala, México: Gobierno del Estado de Tlaxcala.

———. 1986b. "The New Proletarians: Third World Reality and First World Categories." *Comparative Studies in Society and History* 28:217–238.

———. 1988. "Global Views and Human Action in a Rural Community in Mexico." *Urban Anthropology* 17:363–378.

Rothstein, Frances, and Michael Blim. 1991. *Anthropology and the Global Factory: Studies of the New Industrialization in the Late Twentieth Century.* South Hadley, Mass.: Bergin and Garvey.

Sacks, Karen. 1984. "Generations of Working-Class Families." In *My Troubles Are Going to Have Trouble with Me,* ed. Karen Sacks and Dorothy Remy. New Brunswick, N.J.: Rutgers University Press.

———. 1989. "Toward a Unified Theory of Class, Race, and Gender." *American Ethnologist* 16:534–550.

Sanjek, Roger. 1982. "The Organization of Households in Adabraka: Toward a Wider Comparative Perspective." *Comparative Studies in Society and History* 24:57–103.

Sokoloff, Natalie. 1980. *Between Money and Love.* New York: Praeger.

Stack, Carol. 1974. *All Our Kin.* New York: Harper and Row.

Stephen, Lynne. 1991. *Zapotec Women.* Austin: University of Texas Press.

Stichter, Sharon. 1990. "Women, Employment, and the Family: Current Debates." In *Women, Employment, and the Family in the International Division of Labour,* ed. Sharon Stichter and Jane L. Parpart, 11–71. Philadelphia: Temple University Press.

Susser, Ida. 1982. *Norman Street.* New York: Oxford University Press.

Tiano, Susan. 1987. "*Maquiladoras* in Mexicali: Integration or Exploitation?" In *Women on the U.S.–Mexico Border: Responses to Change,* ed. Vicki L. Ruiz and Susan Tiano, 77–101. Boston: Allen and Unwin.

Turbin, Carole. 1989. "Beyond Dichotomies: Interdependence in Mid-Nineteenth Century Working Class Families." *Gender and History* 1 (Autumn): 293–329.

United Nations. 1989. *World Survey on the Role of Women in Development.* New York.

———. 1991. *The World's Women, 1970–1990, Trends and Statistics.* New York.

van Halsema, Ineke. 1991. *Housewives in the Field.* Amsterdam: CEDLA.

Wilson, Fiona. 1990. *De la casa al taller.* Michoacán, Mexico: Coedición de El Colegio de Michoacán y el Gobierno del Estado de Michoacán.

Wolf, Diane. 1990. "Linking Women's Labor with the Global Economy." In *Women Workers and Global Restructuring,* ed. Kathryn Ward, 25–47. Ithaca, N.Y.: ILR Press.

Yanagisako, Sylvia. 1979. "Family and Household: The Analysis of Domestic Groups." *Annual Review of Anthropology* 8:161–205.

CHAPTER 8

✳

Gender, Microenterprise, Performance, and Power

Case Studies from the Dominican Republic, Ecuador, Guatemala, and Swaziland

RAE LESSER BLUMBERG

The urban informal sector has been with us for a long time, surely as long as there have been cities. But its magnitude, dynamism, and rate of explosive growth became widely known to the development community only in the 1980s. This was the "lost decade of development" in Latin America and Africa: the debt crisis almost sank Argentina, Brazil, Mexico, and Venezuela, and many other Latin American countries were also awash in a sea of red ink. In Africa the debt crisis, the worsening food crisis, and the accelerating rate of population growth meant that the GNP shrank as much in the 1980s as it had grown in the 1960s (World Bank 1989; O'Brien 1991).

The remedy prescribed by the International Monetary Fund, the World Bank, and the Reagan-Bush administrations was "structural adjustment." Most of Latin America and the Caribbean and over thirty-five African countries were pushed into such programs' cold and unknown economic waters. They were urged to abandon the import-substitution model of development that had been promoted for three decades by some of the same international donor agencies. Suddenly, in a paraphrase of Peter Evans, the state was a villain and the market the hero. Structural adjustment called for privatization of parastatals, cutting government bureaucracies and services—especially the "social ministries," including health, education, and the odd women-in-development entity—floating of currencies, "getting the prices right," and, above all, promoting exports.

It was recognized that the poor would suffer, at least in the short run (the World Bank analogy was "crossing the desert"). But the urban poor, who were widely acknowledged as taking the brunt of structural adjustment, which ended the distorted factor prices that had subsidized the cost of food for most Third World urban masses within protesting distance of government palaces, were discovered to be engaged in creating their own livelihoods in the face of disaster. Since they had no safety net of welfare, they intensified their activities in the urban informal sector. Indeed, this sector was found to be the fastest growing in country after country. In some nations, such as Peru, many previously formal sector enterprises slid quietly into informality as economic conditions worsened (see, e.g., articles in Rakowski 1995 for details).

Aiding the petty entrepreneurs of the urban informal sector became an increasingly popular form of development assistance. The right was delighted that money was going to the private sector. The left and center soon recognized that many microenterprise credit projects actually reached poor people, a not particularly common outcome of development aid. These projects not only helped the microentrepreneurs survive but also created jobs for even poorer people who had no chance of being absorbed into the formal sector.

Case studies gradually brought home the fact that in much of the Third World, especially Latin America, the Caribbean, Africa, and Southeast Asia, the lower end of the urban informal sector had a female majority (see, e.g., Berger and Buvinic 1988). Women in almost all Third World countries have less access to better-paid formal sector jobs than their male counterparts. With increasing rates of female-headed households (Folbre 1991a, 1991b; Bruce and Lloyd 1992; Blumberg 1993) and, in general, increasing immiserization in the 1980s, more and more women poured into the urban informal sector, as both microentrepreneurs and employees.

The case studies of microentrepreneurs (hereinafter MEs) and the urban informal sectors also can be used to underline the undercounting of women's activities. They further show that women MEs tend to be gender-segregated in a limited number of economic activities, such as garment and food production and, even more frequently, commerce and services.

Unfortunately, as the international donors discovered both the urban informal sector and microenterprise credit projects and provided more and more funds, they began to build up stereotypes and adopt procedures that reduced women's access to benefits.

Women are viewed as less successful and serious, less productive and entrepreneurial than their male counterparts. Increasingly, the donor community decides to promote growth and job creation over "mere subsistence" and hence to support only microentrepreneurs "with the potential to grow" or only those engaged in "production." The Inter-

American Development Bank's Ecuador loan, for example, adopted regulations prohibiting loans to "commerce," which has a disproportionate share of women (Blumberg 1990a). This was done even though many microenterprises are not pure types engaged in production, commerce, or services, but rather shifting mixtures of whatever it takes at a given moment to stay in business and stay alive (Blumberg 1990a). Or the donors may decide to go for the top of the "microenterprise pyramid," where there are fewer women, in the often mistaken belief that the somewhat better off are more likely to repay loans. Or, distrusting poor people, they decide to impose co-signer or collateral requirements that women are much less likely to be able to meet than their male counterparts.

It is ironic, therefore, that the case study data indicate that women clients of microenterprise credit projects have a payback record as good as or better than men. In fact, women have generally lower rates of delinquency and default, from Bangladesh (Timberg 1988; Helmore 1989) to the Dominican Republic (Blumberg 1989a, 1989c) and from Guatemala (Blumberg and Reibel 1988; Blumberg and Revere 1989) to Indonesia (Timberg 1988).

In this chapter I draw on my case studies of gender and microenterprise in four countries: the Dominican Republic, where in 1985 I twice studied the well-known and generally successful program run by ADEMI (the Association for the Development of Microenterprise, Inc.); Ecuador, where I conducted research on gender and microenterprise in Quito and five secondary cities in 1990; Guatemala, where I studied the much less successful SIMME program (Urban Microenterprise Multiplier System) in 1988 and again in 1989; and Swaziland, where I looked at gender and small enterprise in 1991. The case studies use Rapid Rural Appraisal (RRA) methodology.[1] Almost without exception, these countries were in the midst of hard times (ranging from difficult to disastrous) during my research. Without exception, the women coped successfully with adversity.

Just how empowering and beneficial is the income generated by women microentrepreneurs of the informal sector? Since so many of their activities are home-based and/or extensions of women's traditional reproductive activities, involve hard and low-return labor, and provide no fringe benefits, are these women better off? The data indicate that women gain microlevel power—and their children gain in well-being—regardless of the source of their income.

Given this outcome, and the evidence of the positive performance of women as microenterprise credit risks and as entrepreneurs, what are the characteristics of microenterprise credit projects that do *not* erect barriers to poor women? As we shall see, the variables associated with not excluding women are related to successful microenterprise credit projects. Furthermore, as the women-in-development literature often has found, dealing women into development activities (even if one disapproves of the development model) *that generate income under the women's control* provides what I term a "synergy bonus." Results include more successful projects, more empowered women, and more food, clothing, schooling, and health care for their children.

The Case Studies: Tales from the Edge

The ADEMI Project in the Dominican Republic, 1985

The first case study I undertook of a microenterprise credit project, the Association for the Development of Microenterprise, Inc., (ADEMI) can be summed up with the opening line of *A Tale of Two Cities:* "It was the best of times; it was the worst of times."

The "best" referred to the fact that I had come across one of the early success stories of microenterprise credit (along with the more famous Grameen Development Bank of Bangladesh and Indonesia's BKK). ADEMI drew a steady stream of international visitors, eager to see how it had achieved a payback record approaching 100 percent, and a multiplier effect of almost twelve dollars for every dollar loaned, in business expansion and job creation.[2] Much of the secret lay in its use of what I consider the best extant model of "minimalist" credit, the one developed by Jeffrey Ashe and Steve Gross for Acción Internacional (AITEC). This model is described in detail below, but basically it involves giving short-term working capital loans at market rates of interest to informal sector microentrepreneurs.

The "worst" referred to the fact that both the people of the Dominican Republic and, as it happened, 77 percent of the female clients of ADEMI had fallen victim to the debt and financial crises of the early 1980s shortly before my arrival. A precipitous decline in GDP growth had led the government to turn to the International Monetary Fund (IMF) for financial assistance. The government failed to meet the structural adjustment targets the IMF imposed in return for the aid, including cuts in the government deficit, gradual devaluation of the peso, and other belt-tightening measures. Consequently, the IMF suspended the program in early 1984. Desperate, the government devalued the peso and ended most food subsidies in April 1984. Overnight the price of many necessities tripled. Food riots erupted, and more than sixty people were killed by government security forces.

The president of ADEMI, deeply worried that the poorest clients would be unable to pay back their loans because of the economic crisis, and mindful of the international reputation the project already had developed since its creation in February 1983, began cutting back on the larger of ADEMI's two loan components. These were group loans made to Solidarity Groups (SGs), which were divided equally among each group's four to eight members (typically, five), who knew and trusted each other and mutually guaranteed the debt. The 215 SGs in existence at the time of the riots encompassed 1,150 members, in comparison to the roughly 800 recipients of individual loans, the second and smaller ADEMI loan program. Solidarity Group loans began to be delayed, frozen, or cut— even to groups that had never been late with a single payment. Finally, in September–October 1984, the SG component was formally suspended "for an indefinite period."

As it happened, 43 percent of the Solidarity Group members were women, almost five hundred individuals. In contrast, in May 1985 I found that only about 17 percent of the individual loan recipients were female, 150 out of a total of 874. In short, by suspending the Solidarity Group component, ADEMI had eliminated about 77 percent of its women beneficiaries.

The inclusion of women as clients of this mainstream development project had been inadvertent. The Acción model involved cutting out almost all the lengthy delays and bureaucratic red tape (up-front, or "transaction," costs) and the collateral requirements that generally freeze poor people out of most Third World credit projects.[3] The Acción/ADEMI program targeted the poor (individual clients) and very poor (SG clients) microentrepreneurs of the urban informal sector, and this group includes a high proportion of women. Therefore, the removal of the barriers meant that significant numbers of women were able to get credit.

For most ADEMI clients, these market rates of interest were a bargain: they never before had access to credit below usurious moneylender rates. They took their ADEMI loans very seriously, since the Acción model stipulates that if a loan is paid back on time, the recipient(s) will get another, slightly larger loan within a day or two. Members of some of the Solidarity Group "super groups"—those that had never been even one day late with a payment over an average of seven to nine loans per group—told me of risking bullets during the riots as they attempted to get a payment to the ADEMI offices in the old colonial downtown.

Another element of the successful Acción/ADEMI formula was its use of streetwise promoters (asesores), night school university students majoring in economics, accounting/business, or industrial engineering. They were mostly geographically based and within a brief period learned who the local microentrepreneurs were and what their neighbors thought of their prospects, probity, and payback proclivities. They soon identified with their clients and became persuasive partisans of the virtues of lending money to poor MEs. They told me that the Solidarity Groups had been dropped unfairly.

Just as ADEMI had not consciously attempted to integrate women, it did not intend to eliminate more than three-quarters of them. I decided to investigate whether the Solidarity Groups merited their fate, along with how well the women clients had done both as borrowers and as entrepreneurs.

In a nutshell, I learned that the arguments used to suspend the SG program were contradicted by the data I gathered. The women clients had at least as good a payback record as the men, and the women individual loan clients proved better than their male counterparts at job creation—a primary goal of the project. This was particularly true of women in the clothing/textile sector. Nearly half the microentrepreneurs in this sector, which accounted for the largest number of loans (150 out of 874), were women and their businesses grew faster than those of their male counterparts on five of six standard business parameters.

WHY THE SOLIDARITY GROUPS WERE SUSPENDED. The only reasons given for the freeze, in interviews with project management and in ADEMI documents, were vague: the economy was deteriorating, and those on the bottom would be most hurt, making future loans risky; some clients may have encouraged the migration of "country cousins" to join their SGs and share the ADEMI bonanza; other recipients might abandon the city to return to the country if the economic situation worsened. Space precludes presenting the data, but I found that neither the "country cousin" nor the "fleeing the city" allegation had any empirical foundation. I discovered not a single case of a new migrant added to a Solidarity Group, and no SG member interviewed had any intention of abandoning his or her children's future—the city's better education, health care, and job prospects—for rural life.

Two other anti–Solidarity Group allegations were made: that delinquencies seemed to be increasing, and that SGs did not create jobs. The preliminary data of another consultant who overlapped with my first visit failed to find that Solidarity Groups' delinquencies were outpacing those of individual clients. Moreover, the notion that SGs did not create jobs was an *assumption:* to my knowledge, no study had been carried out concerning whether or not SGs stabilized existing jobs or created new ones. One of the criteria for getting an individual (vs. SG) loan was that an entrepreneur had to have from one to six employees. In contrast, Solidarity Group members were from the bottom of the microenterprise hierarchy—street sellers, recyclers, homebased miniworkshop ventures, and so forth. It is unlikely that many of them had more than sporadic employees

TABLE 8-1
ADEMI Activity in the Dominican Republic to March 31, 1985

Measure	Individual Microenterprises	Solidarity Groups (*N* = 215)	Total
People Benefited			
No. of businesses financed	847	1,150	1,997
Persons benefited			
Directly	5,521	1,150	6,671
Indirectly[a]	27,605	5,750	33,355
New jobs created	1,150	—	1,150
Loan Activity			
No. of loans granted	4,408	1,805	6,213
Total amount loaned (US$)	1,544,882	392,375	1,937,257
Average amount per loan (US$)	350	237	312
Loan portfolio (current) RD$	606,563[b]		
US$	189,551		

Source: ADEMI data, 1985.

[a]Based on the assumption of 5 people per household of each direct beneficiary.

[b]In this table US$1.00 = RD$3.20.

at the start of the program, but it is not clear that none of them had created any employment by the time they had had the benefit of eight or nine successive ADEMI loans. Yet Table 8-1, which ADEMI used proudly to summarize its first two years of operation, credits the Solidarity Groups with zero job creation. That may be the real rationale behind their untimely, otherwise puzzling, demise.

SIZE, GENDER AND REPAYMENT. The consultant who overlapped with my first visit was from Acción and was paid by the Inter-American Development Bank. He found that those with small businesses or small loans were no more likely to be delinquent than their larger-scale counterparts. He did not disaggregate by gender but had the impression that women were overrepresented among the smaller businesses and smaller loans. My own calculations on gender and the repayment record indicated that women had a lower rate of late payments as individual clients and that in Solidarity Groups the women's record was comparable to the men's.

GENDER, JOB CREATION, AND ENTREPRENEURIAL PERFORMANCE. One of the things I was able to accomplish was to persuade the Peace Corps volunteer working with the project and his ADEMI counterpart to disaggregate their computerized data by sex. Although it proved to be technically simple, it had never been done before and provided the material on the 874 individual loan clients presented in Table 8-2, which shows the relative performance of men and women MEs. All told, women proved to hold 150 of the 874 loans, and over 80 percent of them were found in only three economic sectors: clothing (accounting for half of all women), food, and ceramics. This level of gender segregation by economic sector is typical in most countries, not just of women in ADEMI or other microenterprise credit projects.

Overall, women microentrepreneurs created an average of 1.5 new jobs each versus 1.3 for men. This provides one empirical counter to the increasingly common charge—now that ME credit projects are becoming fashionable in development circles—that women microentrepreneurs are merely subsistence-oriented. The relative success of women in the clothing/textile sector is even greater. They created an average of 1.4 jobs versus only 0.64 for men in the sector. Moreover, women's ventures grew faster than men's on sales, profits, savings, salaries, and employees' mean salaries. On a sixth parameter, fixed assets, women initially had more than the men, who appeared to be in the process of catching up.

The human dimension of aggregate data is revealed in vignettes of two women from among the sixteen individual loan clients I interviewed in depth (ten women and six men).

The best-educated woman proved to be the thirty-two-year-old wife of a top executive (he administers two hundred employees). She was trained, but not happy, as a certified public accountant. Some five years before I interviewed her, she began to move into the dressmaking business on a small and often fluctuating scale. After only seven months with ADEMI the exaccountant already was on her fourth loan for her women's clothing manufacturing business. Her loans have increased from DR$400 to DR$1,300. She has added one employee and stabilized and increased the working hours of her other four employees. She feels her business is now organized; soon she hopes to make it grow by adding men's shirts and retail sales to her women's wear line. She feels more self-confident and secure, and because she now feels better organized, she says, "I have more control" in economic decisions in the home.

One of the least-educated women was the fifty-five-year-old household head with fourth-grade schooling and six dependent children. Although she was trained as a dressmaker, she finds she earns more running a backyard factory to make cement blocks—a highly nontraditional business for a female. In eighteen months with ADEMI she has had seven loans, increasing from DR$200 to DR$2,000. She

TABLE 8-2
Men- and Women-Owned Microenterprises in the Dominican Republic, in the Clothing Sector and in General, 1985

Measure Clothing Sector	Men (N = 77)					Women (N = 73)				
	Initial Status		Current Status		Percent	Initial Status		Current Status		Percent
	Total	Mean	Total	Mean	Increase	Total	Mean	Total	Mean	Increase
Fixed assets (US$)	335,780	4,361	487,530	6,332	45	552,779	7,572	625,399	8,567	13
Sales (US$)	269,535	3,500	352,538	4,578	31	178,690	2,448	281,217	3,852	57
Profits (US$)	50,231	652	89,323	1,160	78	38,951	534	92,153	1,262	137
Savings (US$)	6,976	91	19,489	253	179	4,938	68	16,262	223	229
Salaries (US$)	57,440	746	72,796	945	27	44,772	613	69,550	953	55
Employees	299	3.9	348	4.5	16	289	4.0	391	5.4	35
Mean salary (US$)	192		209			155		178		
Jobs Added			49	0.64				102	1.4	

Measure All Sectors	Men (N = 724)					Women (N = 150)				
	Initial Status		Current Status		Percent	Initial Status		Current Status		Percent
	Total	Mean	Total	Mean	Increase	Total	Mean	Total	Mean	Increase
Fixed assets (US$)	3,247,168	4,485	4,317,524	5,963	33	1,055,095	7,034	1,130,869	7,539	7
Sales (US$)	2,617,590	3,615	4,026,125	5,561	54	402,415	2,683	590,822	3,939	47
Profits (US$)	479,983	663	1,060,299	1,464	121	85,073	567	180,167	1,201	112
Savings (US$)	36,118	50	223,687	309	519	6,706	45	22,739	152	239
Salaries (US$)	549,238	759	871,028	1,203	59	85,289	569	126,924	846	49
Employees	3,102	4.3	4,074	5.6	31	583	3.9	804	5.4	38
Mean salary (US$)	177		214			146		158		
Jobs Added			972	1.3				221	1.5	

has added two employees, and as is common, especially among female MEs, most of her children also help when they are not in school. Her volume has increased from one to three truckloads of sand delivered per week. "Sometimes I never even close; sometimes I'm up wetting the blocks at 6:00 A.M., but it doesn't bother me." She is proud of and pleased with her business's growth, and she now wants to buy more land to expand the business. Any small savings go for the children, "so that they can study," and for the house. And her modest home shows it: it contains a set of encyclopedias, a new refrigerator, and the children's stereo.

In addition, it must be remembered that in many informal sector endeavors working capital comes from moneylenders, at usurious rates of interest, with one's capital assets (or person) pledged as collateral. ADEMI's loans at market rates of interest are a great deal cheaper. One woman cried, "ADEMI has freed me from debt slavery to the moneylender!"

GENDER AND "SUPER PERFORMERS" AMONG THE SOLIDARITY GROUPS. Of the 215 SGs, 46 were never late with a payment. There are no gender differences in the composition of the "super groups": all-female, all-male, and mixed groups are represented in the same proportions among the 46 as in the full 215 (Table 8-3).

I interviewed twenty Solidarity Group members (ten men, ten women) from eleven groups, including both "super performers" and the remainder. One of the group meetings was a marathon session (with ten men and two women) in a dilapidated shack perched over a frequently flooded, rutted track along the Ozama River. These people were dirt poor, ragged, and already losing teeth by their thirties, but they were highly intelligent and articulate. I do not think I have ever had a stronger sense of "there, but for the accident of birth, go I" in more than twenty-five years of

TABLE 8-3
Data on 46 Top Solidarity Groups vs. All 215 SGs

| Groups | 46 "Super Performers" | | | All 215 SGs |
	Percent	Mean No. of Loans	Average Group Size	Percent
All-female	3	9.0	5.0	4
All-male	33	7.7	5.6	33
Mixed	63	7.4	5.7	64
50%+ female	24			25
Woman coordinator	26			28

working with Third World poor (since my Peace Corps days) in more than twenty countries. They did not deserve to be cut off.

One of the most persistent findings of development research is that benefits "trickle up." When the target group is poor, female, and/or an ethnic minority, it tends not to retain benefits, especially if these are valuable: the fears of project staff combine with the greater clout of the better off.[4]

I ended my research with a sense that with the appropriate model (e.g., Acción's)—and greater commitment to keeping benefits flowing to the poor—microenterprise credit projects can work. I concluded my first writeups of ADEMI (Blumberg 1985, 1989c) with Jeffrey Ashe's striking phrase that an Acción model (of individual plus Solidarity Group short-term loans, offered to poor people at market rates of interest, with no red tape, a guaranteed-larger next loan as the reward for on-time payment, and the guidance of enthusiastic promoters and committed professionals) could be the "McDonald's of Third World credit projects to help the poor" (Blumberg 1989c, 82). Fast, profitable, efficient, low-cost, and capable of reaching large numbers of people, this new type of "Mc-Donald's," Ashe envisioned, would even generate its own competitors.

Gender and Microenterprise in Ecuador, 1990

By the time I studied microentrepreneurs in Quito and five other cities of Ecuador, I had twice researched the much less successful SIMME project in Guatemala, in 1988 and 1989 (see below), and surveyed the burgeoning worldwide literature on microenterprise credit projects. My perspective could be described as both more cynical and more sophisticated. But I was surprised at how many donors and ME credit organizations were reinventing the (wrong) wheel.

First, in their desire to increase employment, many of them were following the lead of the Inter-American Development Bank's then extant policy of restricting loans to those engaged in "transformative activities" (mainly production).[5] This is part of an accelerating trend to confine ME credit to "serious" entrepreneurs who have the right attitudes and potential to grow. This approach explicitly excludes commerce, where the largest proportion of Ecuadorian MEs in general and women MEs in particular are to be found: 49.1 percent of all people in the informal sector are engaged in commerce (Baca Carbo 1989, 13), and women microentrepreneurs are most concentrated in commercial activities (Blumberg 1990a).

In my opinion, the emphasis on employment, "seriousness," and growth is a recipe for "trickle up." It means that projects define beneficiary groups in ways that reduce the numbers of both women and poorer microentrepreneurs, even though there is evidence that they tend to be better at paying back loans (Blumberg and Reibel 1988; Blumberg 1989a; Blumberg and Revere 1989). This emphasis also gives short shrift to two other goals of ME credit projects: enhancement of incomes and productivity. One of the aims in my Ecuador research was to explore ME employment, income, and productivity, as well as "seriousness," by gender.

Fortunately, I was one of eleven people carrying out a large-scale assessment of the informal sector so there was a great deal of data to draw on. In addition to my Rapid Rural Appraisal methodology, in which I interviewed thirty-one women and twenty men microentrepreneurs in Quito, Cuenca, Santo Domingo, and Manta, and conducted key informant interviews in six cities, I could call for any analysis I chose on our team's own survey of 430 MEs assisted by foundations (65 percent men, 35 percent women) and a control group of 101 MEs who were not foundation clients (66 percent men, 34 percent women). I also commissioned gender-disaggregated analyses of two other surveys. The first (UNEPROM) involved a beneficiary group of 673 (47 percent men, 53 percent women) and a nonbeneficiary group of 134 (55 percent men, 45 percent women). The second (CARE) comprised 447 beneficiaries (62 percent men, 38 percent women) but only 15 nonbeneficiaries (53 percent men, 47 percent women).

The data did not indicate that women consistently lagged behind in job creation, income, productivity, or various measures of "seriousness" as entrepreneurs. (It should be noted that both the CARE and the UNE-PROM studies involved subsamples. Where the specific subsample is relevant, it is identified.)

EMPLOYMENT. In the case of employment the evidence is mixed. In the CARE survey subsample of those who received training (with or without credit), women were just under one-third of the respondents but created fully two-thirds of all new jobs (Hagen and Tiffany 1990). In two of the three subsamples of the UNEPROM survey, women had a higher rate of employment growth, and there was no difference in the third. But in the credit-only subsample of the CARE survey and in our own survey, men had higher employment growth.

INCOME. Income was measured largely by business growth, and there was virtually no difference by gender in any of the three data sources. None emerged in our own survey. In the UNEPROM survey, 85 percent of both men and women credit recipients reported growth; in the CARE survey there was no gender difference in business growth in five of the six foundations included (men led in the sixth). Intriguingly, in all three subsamples of the UNEPROM survey, women reported a higher propensity to reinvest income in their businesses than men. This may be considered the quintessential measure of entrepreneurial "seriousness."

PRODUCTIVITY. The only data I found on productivity came from a 1988 study of a foundation that was more or less following the Acción model of minimalist (no frills, almost no training), market-interest-rate credit (Buvinic, Berger, and Jaramillo 1988). There female credit recipients increased their productivity: they made more money while working fewer hours (cutting their business workday from 10.3 hours in 1984 to 9.3 hours in 1985, while increasing their hourly incomes significantly more than men borrowers). Presumably, these women, who averaged between five and six children per household and worked a "double day," used the extra time in "human capital formation" (i.e., childcare, but the former phrase gets much more respect).

"SERIOUSNESS." Our own microenterprise survey (Blumberg 1990a) found women to be at least as entrepreneurial as the men.

1. Men and women had similar
    — Perception that they could sell more
    — Desire to export
    — Satisfaction with the business
    — Desire for expansion
    — Perceived ability to compete with larger businesses
    — Perception that their greatest need for growth is working capital.
2. Women exceeded men in some business-related items, reporting
    — Fewer problems with selling their products
    — Fewer problems with marketing and competition
    — More optimistic views of their firm's future
    — More credit from suppliers
    — More use of a daily ledger
    — More of a tendency to like competition and risk-taking.
3. Concerning the scale of their businesses, although men had more employees and a larger monthly payroll, men and women microentrepreneurs proved alike with respect to
    — Level of fixed assets
    — Change in income from 1989 to 1990
    — Profit/loss of the business
    — Keeping a general ledger
    — Applying for business loans in the last year
    — Keeping a bank account.

None of these findings offers any justification to pass over women or the types of businesses they run.

Two notable differences emerged in our microenterprise survey that relate to the different worlds of men and women MEs. First, asked about why they started their own businesses, women, who have less access to better-paying jobs in the formal sector, stressed greater economic necessity to earn, where men stressed the independence motive. Second, asked about who they employed, women reported they were more likely to hire women and to use their own children part-time (when not in school); men were more likely to hire men and have their spouses work in the business. This second difference reflects both the high levels of gender segregation of microenterprise activities and the greater likelihood of women's businesses to be home-based and reliant on family labor.

A second example of reinventing the (wrong) wheel was the persistence in some of the programs we researched of subsidized rates of credit. The immediate result was to reduce the proportion of female clients. For example, the foundation that charged the highest rate of interest (market rates, plus charges for insurance, training, and even a health scheme) had the highest proportion of women clients (60 percent); the foundation that offered the lowest (subsidized) interest rates gave credit to only 35.6 percent of its women clients. The long-term result, as a voluminous literature attests, is decapitalization and a "trickle up" of benefits to those with more money and power than the originally intended target group.

A third example of a wrongheaded approach is almost too ludicrous to recount. Although the Acción model has demonstrated in a number of countries (including most Latin American ones) that what works best are loans that are issued quickly, involve frequent payments (weekly, if possible), and impose no collateral or co-signer requirements, one foundation in a secondary city was pursuing the exact opposite tack.

The foundation worked with a local bank that forwarded the money collected to the Central Bank only quarterly and that had a manager who distrusted poor people. He insisted that the loans be "renewed"—rolled over—quarterly and that not one but two guarantors be secured for the original loan and each renewal. The foundation and the bank also strictly interpreted an Ecuadorian law that has since been changed: that in loan matters, *both* partners in a legal or common-law marital union (even if separated) must sign. The foundation and the bank, therefore, required that each quarter up to six people come in person for the delivery of the payment and the loan renewal (if the loan period originally had been set at two years, for example, this would mean eight such ceremonies). If any of the six were absent, the payment would not be accepted and the borrower would be liable for the extremely stiff penalties for delinquency.

Aside from having an artificially inflated delinquency rate, the foundation also was disproportionately freezing out women: they had much less leverage in getting a separated husband to come and sign as a guarantor than vice versa (for example, if the woman had children, the husband could threaten to stop making contributions if she did not sign). And she certainly had less leverage in getting the spouses of female guarantors to sign.

GENDER AND REPAYMENT. Despite all these obstacles to the participation of women, they ranged from 20 to 60 percent of the clients in every organization we visited or included in our analyses. Only partial data on arrearage were available for the present research, but once again, with one complex exception, women proved to have lower rates of arrears. The exception occurred in one of the three CARE subsamples (in the other two, women had, respectively, arrearage rates of 7 percent vs. 12 percent for men, and 0 percent vs. 4 percent for men). In the exception, the subsample of those who received training, women had 13 percent arrears versus 7 percent for men. I visited one of the four foundations involved and found none of the women in arrears versus 10 percent of the men. Since the data lumped the four foundations in the subsample together, it proved impossible to know where the women's higher reported arrearage rate was coming from. Otherwise, in all other instances with data, women had lower arrears rates than men.

In sum, the Ecuadorian data, like the Dominican Republic results, seem to indicate that it makes economic sense for microenterprise credit project donors and foundations to encourage women clients as much as men.

Two positive achievements that helped women are worth describing. First, two foundations started health plans funded by tacking on a small surcharge to loans. One had been functioning for about a year and involved an afternoon medical and dental clinic. During several weeks of research visits I found that most of those waiting for attention were women microentrepreneurs with their children. The women interviewed were often emotional in their support of the clinics: unless they were married to men with formal sector jobs covered by social security, they had no access to low-cost medical care. But if anyone in their family got sick, *they* had to take care of them, regardless of the consequences to their business. The doctor told me the plan was financially solid, since not everyone used it. This idea is worth copying.

Second, one foundation in the most *machista* area of Ecuador, the province of Manabí, solved a recurrent problem: low proportions of women in training courses because of the opposition of husbands and fathers. The foundation offered "hands on" courses in clothing production (*corte y confección*) that resulted in immediate increases in income for their students. In the small but poor city where this took place, word spread. Men's need for income proved stronger than their attitude that "the woman is for the house." The courses were always filled, and many of the students were married women. But in training courses offering less of an immediate return, or a smaller likelihood of leading to microenterprise loans, almost no wives were allowed to attend; women students were mainly single or female household heads. Thus, even serious constraints to women's involvement in ME credit or training projects can be overcome if concerted efforts are made to work with, rather than against, the local gender culture.

The Strange Political Economy of the Guatemala SIMME Project, 1988 and 1989

In contrast to the private sector efforts in the Dominican Republic and Ecuador, the project in Guatemala involved a mixed public-private sector effort. The SIMME initiative (Urban Microenterprise Multiplier System) was conceived in 1987 to help the growth of established microenterprises in Guatemala's informal sector. After half a decade of economic crisis, 1980–85, the economy began to recover in 1986 under the first civilian government since the (CIA-supported) overthrow of the Arbenz regime in 1954.[6] The SIMME project worked through six private voluntary organizations (PVOs), but its overriding objective was to make forty thousand loans by December 31, 1990. Coincidentally, the next presidential election would take place shortly thereafter.

I carried out evaluation research on the SIMME project (as team leader) in 1988 (Blumberg and Reibel 1988) and in 1989 (Blumberg and Revere 1989). The project had several positive points, but political aspects intervened in two damaging ways. First, the government heeded a lone United Nations Development Programme (UNDP) consultant who advocated cheap credit, rather than everyone else's advice of charging market rates of interest. So it was decided that the SIMME project would have subsidized interest rates, at least initially. It did not prove politically possible to raise interest rates, however, even when the usual problems associated with subsidized credit began to surface. For one thing, more sophisticated borrowers, realizing that this was a government program attempting to maximize the number of low-cost loans before the election, decided that there would be no serious attempts to collect—so they went into delinquency or default on their loans.

Their gamble paid off, at least at the beginning, because of the second factor. This was the fact that the promoters (*asesores*) were under intense pressure to give out loans or lose their jobs. They had no time for the monthly client follow-up that is at the heart of the Acción model (SIMME management had had some Acción consulting but had not implemented some of the model's key features). Although their jobs were on the line if they failed to make their quota of loan applications, no sanctions were taken if they did not collect overdue loan payments. The *asesores'* attitude was that the executing bank's collection department was supposed to see to that. Unfortunately, the lawyers of this bank (a state entity) felt that these microenterprise loans were too tiny to pursue aggressively. If a collector failed to find a debtor on the first attempt, it took months for anything further to happen—and only a trivial proportion of delinquencies or defaults were followed up legally. Word soon spread.

It is against this background that we must measure the fact that women proved to have lower arrearages in 1988 and 1989. And it is against this background that we must evaluate the *asesores'* insistence that it was the poor, the women, and the Indians who had the best payback record. Perhaps they had not heard the word. Or perhaps they did not want to jeopardize the only chance at cheap credit they were likely to be offered in their lives. Since no records were kept on social class and ethnicity, only the women's performance could be assessed empirically.

For example, by August 1988, 1,623 individual loans averaging $1,300 had been granted. Only 17.7 percent had been given to women ($N = 287$). By that date 15.3 percent of loans were in arrears ($N = 248$). Yet only twenty-six women were behind in their payments. This means that women, 17.7 percent of the loan population, constituted only 10.5 percent of those in arrears. The difference is significant (Blumberg and Reibel 1988). By 1989 both arrears rates and the extent to which women had a better payback record had risen sharply (Blumberg and Revere 1989).

In both years my Rapid Rural Appraisal methodology picked up extraordinary stories of women (and men) who turned modest loans into life-changing opportunities. But by mid-1989 SIMME was in enough trouble with its donors to have to put more emphasis on better loan repayment. The geographically based *asesores* (this positive feature of the ADEMI model was adopted) were told to put more stress on loan follow-up and to look for better clients. The *asesores* knew their turf, so they began to seek out more women clients.

Swaziland Small Entrepreneurs, 1991: The Fear of "Too Many Women"

Swaziland is one of two remaining monarchies in Africa: South Africa, which surrounds Swaziland on three sides (the fourth is war-torn Mozambique) likes it that way. The other remaining monarchy (Lesotho) is also considered a South African client state. The legacy of the British colonialist policy of indirect rule through indigenous chiefs and the continuing South African influence have resulted in the institutionalization of a more patriarchal version of the traditional system. Women are jural minors in patrilineal, patrilocal Swaziland: they need husbands' written signatures to get loans or make contracts. Despite the fact that women do most of the farming and market trade, it would seem an unlikely place for them to rise in the informal sector pyramid. And unlike the other projects, the effort in Swaziland emphasized the upper reaches of that pyramid—small entrepreneurs rather than microentrepreneurs.

Both my Rapid Rural Appraisal data and my review of the literature on the Swazi informal sector led me to the conclusion that despite the legal restrictions under which they operated, women (the overwhelming number of them married) were a majority of small entrepreneurs and a substantial majority of microentrepreneurs. But within the donor agency one man had been told by one official in the Ministry of Commerce that this was not possible. Results from a large-scale survey were not yet in; when the data were analyzed, they showed women to be fully 84 percent of the owners of small enterprises in Swaziland (Downing 1992, 4).

The locus of contention was the project target for the proportion of women beneficiaries. Based on my research, I suggested "at least 40 percent" (Blumberg 1991b), instead of the project draft language of "at least 30 percent." In contrast, the official wanted this figure downgraded to "as much as 30 percent" of beneficiaries to be women.

Swaziland is a small country, and I had already had occasion to see how devastating word of mouth is in small cities (coastal Ecuador) or countries (Guatemala) when a microenterprise credit project starts to go sour. The women small entrepreneurs in Swaziland had achieved their position by virtue of an almost Darwinian process of selection: they had much less access to well-paid formal sector jobs, and they had to learn to get around not only their husbands but also the entire legal and institutional apparatus to succeed. They tended to be far more dynamic and risk-taking, and their businesswomen's association was exponentially more dynamic than the major male-dominated groups. After all, men with some education and initiative tended to become employees of white-owned companies, and the men in small and microenterprises in the informal sector had not had to overcome the challenges faced by the women. For example, in a secondary city of Swaziland I interviewed two small entrepreneurs located next door to each other.

The first was a woman who had a beauty salon and a fleet of taxis. She had persuaded her brother, who had a taxi license for a run-down car and had just bought a new vehicle, to let her have the old car and the license. She hired a good mechanic and launched her business, buying more cars with her profits. She didn't miss a trick with her beauty business either: nearby was a large agribusiness plantation that employed many women workers for the harvest, which was then in progress. She dispatched two of her operators to open a makeshift beauty salon in the field, correctly guessing that these women would want to spend some of the money they were making to get fixed up before returning to their families.

The man had worked as a manager for many years for a white-owned concern before going into business for himself. He ran a nice, clean carry-out restaurant and grocery business but said that government regulations and sanitary requirements were too onerous for him to want to stay in the business. His new idea, after attending a seminar in South Africa, was to open his own carpet-cleaning business. The firm that gave the seminar franchises operations and claimed to have the contract for cleaning the luxury South African chain hotels of Swaziland's beautiful Mlilane Valley. The company had told him they would give him the contract. He told me that he was just about to invest. When I asked him if he had contacted any franchisees of the company in either South Africa or Swaziland, he admitted that he had not. He also had not checked with the hotels in question to see if the franchising firm actually had the contract or if they would, indeed, award it to him if he bought the franchise. He said that the interview left him with food for thought.

In Swaziland it was a matter not of whether to adopt all or some elements of the best available model, but of whether to deal with women in proportion to their importance and level of performance in the small/microenterprise sector. This was a fledgling effort, so failure would probably complicate future attempts at small/microenterprise credit projects for some time to come. I failed to sway the person in question, but I hope a more positive end to this story will sometime be written.

The Consequences of Informal Sector Income—Less Empowering?

The criticism is sometimes made that supporting women's informal sector activities is counterproductive. This is because informal ventures—especially employment—generally offer a much lower rate of return than those in the formal sector. Also, women's informal sector activities often represent merely extensions of their domestic role. Are these women better off?

My argument recognizes the low-paid nature of most of women's informal sector activities. Such endeavors are almost always outside a country's social security or health system (such as it is) and almost never pay legally mandated fringe benefits.[7] Nor do they pay as much. Ecuadorian figures, which are probably representative, indicate that average income in the public and private formal sector is 60 percent higher than informal sector income, according to studies using the government's Permanent Household Survey data (Baca Carbo 1989). Moreover, one study of people working in small and microenterprises in the informal sector in five coastal cities found that men made 250 percent more than women (Samaniego and Mayguashca 1989).

Thus, my argument is based not on the characteristics or desirability of informal sector employment but on the fact that income, however earned, has certain fairly clear-cut effects on the relative power of recipients in general and women recipients in particular.

After presenting three hypotheses from my general theory of gender stratification, I offer a list of hypothesized consequences of income under female (vs. male) control. These are taken from my theories of gender stratification and gender and development.

My general theory of gender stratification has as its central hypothesis:

1. Women's economic power relative to men's (defined as control of key economic resources such as income, property, and other means of production) is posited as the most important and achievable[8] (though certainly not the sole) independent variable affecting gender stratification at a variety of "nested" micro- and macrolevels ranging from the couple to the state (Blumberg 1984).

A related proposition is the notion of net economic power:

2. A woman may not get a dollar's worth of economic power for every dollar she brings into the household. In particular, a woman's overall economic power is affected by a variety of macro- and microlevel "discount factors."

   The macrolevel factors are typically negative and measure the extent of gender inequality at the top, that is, the extent to which a society's political, economic, legal, and ideological systems disadvantage women.

   The microlevel factors may be either negative or positive and measure variables that can add to or erode the woman's hypothetical dollar's worth of economic power for every dollar she brings to the household (Blumberg 1984, 1991a; Blumberg and Coleman 1989). They include (a) the gender role ideology of each partner (Ross 1987; Blumstein and Schwartz 1991), (b) the woman's socialization to bargain less hard to realize economic leverage (England and Kilbourne 1988; Chafetz 1991), (c) each partner's relative attractiveness or local "market value" (Blumberg and Coleman 1989), (d) each partner's relative commitment, since the less committed partner has more leverage by the "principle of least interest" (Blumberg and Coleman 1989), (e) personality factors, such as each partner's relative assertiveness and, perhaps, dependency (Blumstein and Schwartz 1991), and (f) the man's felt economic dependence on the woman's economic contribution, regardless of its level (Blumberg 1991a).

An additional caveat is whether the income represents surplus or mere survival:

3. Allocating surplus provides more clout than allocating resources needed for bare subsistence (Blumberg 1984). Withholding food from hungry children is rarely an option at the microlevel and nowhere socially approved—especially for mothers. This may be why poor women do not get more power from the often high proportion of resources they provide the household.

Proposition 4 and its subpropositions also come from my general theory of gender stratification. In view of the various discount factors in 2 and the surplus versus subsistence income distinction in 3, I propose:

4. The greater a woman's absolute and/or relative control of economic resources—most commonly, income—the greater her efficacy and empowerment in a variety of areas, including:

—greater increase in self-esteem and self-confidence (see Blumberg 1988 for references);

—greater leverage in fertility decisions—that is, the more these reflect her *own* utilities versus those of her husband, the extended family, or the state (see Blumberg 1988, 1989a for references);

—greater leverage in other household economic and domestic decisions and a stronger overall voice and vote (leadership) in the relationship (Blumberg 1988, 1989a; Blumstein and Schwartz 1991).

Conversely, mere work in economic activities (or even ownership of economic resources) does not translate into the benefits above if the person derives no control of income or other economic resources thereby (Acharya and Bennett 1981, 1982, 1983; Blumberg 1988).

Three more propositions from my theory of gender and development round out the discussion of the consequences of income under women's control, however earned:

5. Women who have provider responsibilities (even as providers of last resort) spend income under their control differently than men, focusing more on children's well-being and family subsistence. Specifically, it is a mother's, rather than a father's, income (or food production) that tends to be more closely related to children's nutrition (see Blumberg 1988, 1989a, 1989b for references); and women tend to contribute a higher proportion of their income to family subsistence, holding back less for personal consumption (Blumberg 1988, 1989a, 1989b).

6. Women tend to allocate labor toward activities that put income (and/or food if they have provider obligations) under their control and, to the extent culturally feasible, away from activities that do not—even if these are (somewhat) more profitable for the household or husband (Blumberg 1988, 1989a, 1989b).

7. Women who lose income lose domestic power (proposition 4) more quickly and sharply than they gain it when income rises (Blumberg 1988, 1989a, 1989b, 1989c).

It is entirely possible that there is a smaller discount on the income of a woman who earns it in more prestigious activities, those that have neither the onus of the informal sector nor the implicit devaluation of being tasks that are extensions of women's "normal domestic chores." But that is accounted for in the propositions above.

If we compare the leverage in household decisions—and the ability to help her children and herself—of a woman with no income versus one whose income comes from operating or working in an informal sector microenterprise, the outcome is clear. The latter woman has more clout and more ability to enhance the well-being of her children. The price, however, is often a higher rate of self-exploitation than for the woman with no income: she earns the money by further lengthening her already bone-wearying day.

In my experience in gender-related activities in more than twenty countries and gender and development field research in more than a dozen, I have invariably found that women with even modest informal sector income have more say in their own lives and their family's decisions, as well as more impact on their children's nutrition, health, and education, than women with absolutely no income under their control. In sum, aside from the probably greater (negative) discount associated with income earned in the urban informal sector, the consequences of that income should not be notably different than those of income earned by other means. As the economists delight in telling us, income is fungible: no matter how you get it, there are few limits to how you can use it.

What's Good for Microenterprise Credit Projects Is Good for Women: Doing Well by Doing Good

Before delineating the factors that make for both good microenterprise credit projects and lots of women clients, it is relevant to note that in general, microenterprise credit projects with many women clients have proved among the most successful ever studied. Here are several examples.

Bangladesh: The renowned Grameen Development Bank has a minimal default rate, under 3 percent (Timberg 1988, 11), and as of August 1993 had provided loans to more than 1,500,000 borrowers (*Grameen Dialogue* 1993, 16). These people are among the poorest of the poor, primarily landless and near landless. Women receive smaller loans, on average, than men. As of December 31, 1986, the bank had 295 branches with 234,000 members. Of these, 60 percent were women, accounting for 55 percent of the cumulative loan amount (Timberg 1988, 10). Based on evaluation of relative male/female loan performance, those proportions have risen rapidly, as the bank's recent expansion has been almost entirely among women (Timberg 1988, 12). By 1989 women made up about 82 percent of borrowers (Helmore 1989). By August 1993 Grameen had reached 33,080, or almost half, of Bangladesh's 68,000 rural villages. Women made up 94 percent of the bank's 1,679,164 members, and its cumulative disbursements had surpassed U.S.$743 million (*Grameen Dialogue* 1993, 16). Islamic Bangladesh is one of the most restrictive societies in the world for women, with female seclusion (purdah) widely observed and women having much less access to education and income than men. This makes the bank's success even more notable.

Indonesia: The enormous BKK program made 2.7 million loans between 1972 and 1983, amounting to over $55 million. Loans averaged $20, targeted to "rural families for off-farm productive purposes." Interest rates were high enough (5.6 to 10.8 percent per month) for the program as a whole to make a profit of $333,000 in 1981, a 7 percent return on its portfolio. Yet delinquency was only 6 percent on current loans. Sixty percent of the loan clients were women, overwhelmingly traders (Timberg 1988, 14).

Meta-evaluation of one hundred LEIG (livelihood, employment, and income generation) projects: Judith Tendler's 1987 study found that microenterprise credit projects were among the most successful. She identified eight of the one hundred grantees as better performers. As Katherine McKee (1988) stresses, five of the eight dealt exclusively with women and the other three gave serious attention to women clients from the start. All eight were narrowly focused on economic rather than social welfare activities.

These cases, in combination with the material on the Dominican Republic, Ecuador, Guatemala, and Swaziland presented above, suggest that, first, experienced female microentrepreneurs, given what is usually their first opportunity to get credit at nonexploitative rates, are at least as good credit risks as men. Second, as explicated below, the microenterprise credit projects that succeed in reaching women are those that have eliminated the obstacles and constraints that often not only preclude women from getting such loans but also reduce the project's chances for success.

Many of the successful mixed-sex microenterprise credit projects did not initially seek out women as participants. But the better ones seem to have eliminated the up-front constraints that typically prevented *poor* people from receiving credit. When these constraints were eliminated in credit programs aimed at poor microentrepreneurs, women were able to take advantage of the programs. Slowly, some—but far from all—the programs became institutionally conscious of the positive attributes of women clients. Even if the executives are typically unaware of women's relative performance, loan promoters often know that women are reliable clients, especially if they are evaluated even in small part on the basis of the payback rates of their loans.

I have mentioned that the Acción model has worked in a number of countries. I am not advocating that only an Acción model be used. But its principal features can be seen in the ADEMI case. Here, based on the ADEMI experience and corroborating examples, are some of its features that seem associated with successful microenterprise credit programs—and with high proportions of women.

   1. *Low transaction costs.* ADEMI reduced the number of trips that a person had to make to the credit office in order to process a loan application (generally, to a single visit) and reduced the amount of paperwork. Similarly, the foundation in Ecuador that had the highest proportion (60 percent) of women (Fundación Ecuatoriana de Desarrollo, FED) had the least onerous paperwork and the fewest up-front requirements of all the foundations I studied there.

2. *Minimal collateral and co-signer requirements.* ADEMI did not require collateral for most of its loans (and it initially resorted to a group guarantee scheme, the Solidarity Group, for the poorest clients). Similarly, the only Ecuadorian foundation with an on-going Solidarity Group plan used it for its poorest clients, who turned out to be largely female and primarily engaged in commerce. The Solidarity Group component was quite successful. Before FED eliminated its Solidarity Groups as part of a reorganization in which the main advocate of the approach was replaced, this component was where the highest proportion of women were found. In 1984–86 women microvendors made up 65 percent of Solidarity Group members versus only 35 percent of microproducers receiving individual loans (Buvinic, Berger, and Jaramillo 1988). Women are much less likely to have the kinds of resources and friends that foundations requiring collateral and co-signers or guarantors are likely to accept.

3. *Streetwise promoters who are (a) geographically based and (b) have at least some accountability for the performance level of their loans.* ADEMI, Guatemala's SIMME, and several of the Ecuadorian foundations used the system of promoters. Since so much of informal sector microenterprise takes place behind closed doors and/or in the home (in part to evade formal sector regulation and costs), it is very hard to locate. A striking example took place during my Guatemala research: the promoters convinced me that an expensive and supposedly exhaustive census of informal sector businesses had missed a good proportion of their own clients. Their businesses just were not obvious from the street. These promoters soon learn the local reputations of the microentrepreneurs in their territories. If the performance evaluations and bonuses of the promoters suffer when their clients fall behind on payments, they make efforts to seek out MEs with better reputations for responsibility—and, provided they are not excluded by high transaction costs or burdensome collateral or co-signer requirements, the proportion of women loan recipients slowly rises.

4. *Fast turnaround time on loans.* Often, for poor MEs, the timeliness of credit is even more important than its price. Moneylenders offer instant, usually very short-term credit (daily loans are common, for example, in the case of market vendors). Their rates are generally astronomical, but they are fast, and for most poor microentrepreneurs, they are the only option. The speed of ADEMI loans was one of its most appreciated features: first loans would be approved and issued in days rather than weeks

or months, and subsequent loans typically were issued in about a day.

5. *Rewards for on-time payments in the form of guaranteed, slightly larger subsequent loans.* ADEMI made short-term loans, so it was able to turn over its portfolio quite frequently. It encouraged full, on-time repayment by guaranteeing another loan, for somewhat more money. This further strengthened the incentives of those who had no recourse to any form of formal sector credit.

6. *Frequent payments that correspond to the business cycle of microentrepreneurs.* Many Acción model programs require payments weekly or no less often than monthly. Except for a few types of microenterprise (e.g., carpentry/furniture) whose business cycle may be longer, frequent, small payments are easier for poor MEs to make. Moneylenders use this principle and probably have for millennia.

The next point is probably the most important of all for the health and survival of the microenterprise credit program, and it is also associated with a higher proportion of women clients:

7. *Positive real rates of interest so that the foundation does not decapitalize and the well-known "trickle up" effect of subsidized credit does not occur.* A clear relationship emerged in Ecuador between the rate of interest charged and the proportion of women loan beneficiaries of the foundation in question. The foundation with the highest interest, FED, as noted, has the highest proportion of women clients (60 percent). Over and above the market rate of interest, it adds fees for training, insurance, health care, and other items that are amortized with the loan. In contrast, UNEPROM, which offers a subsidized interest rate, gave credit to only 35.6 percent of the women who were its clients in other types of development assistance programs.

8. *A minimalist approach that provides virtually nothing except credit, to already experienced microentrepreneurs.* Although some models emphasize training or attempt to help people with no prior ME experience get started, they tend to be less successful. The most successful ME credit projects worldwide have almost all been minimalist (Tendler 1987; Timberg 1988), which is the approach of the Acción model.

9. *No arbitrary exclusion of particular types of enterprises such as commerce or services.* ADEMI, for one, did not exclude vendors in its Solidarity Groups. Many of the more successful credit programs follow the same policy and typically have more

women clients as a result. For example, FED was not allowed to loan IDB money to commerce MEs, but through Acción it obtained other donors. There was no restriction on these funds, so it was able to continue some loans to vendors.

Conclusion

Women tend to be much poorer than men and, increasingly, have provider responsibilities. The net result is that they have greater unmet income needs and, in economists' parlance, lower opportunity costs. This means that their time is worth less, so they tend to jump at opportunities that may not offer sufficient incentive to male counterparts with greater and more lucrative alternatives. In ME terms, once the successful programs reduced the constraints that prevented women from obtaining credit, they eagerly took advantage of nonsubsidized credit. And having so few alternatives, they tried to make the most of their microenterprise credit project opportunities.

Thus, microenterprise credit programs can be strategies for empowering poor women and men. The best ones operate by giving people additional means that enable them to take care of their immediate problems themselves. This is a major achievement, even if it does not solve the larger problems of class, gender, or racial/ethnic inequality.

In sum, the evidence indicates that when given a chance in an area where they already are economically active, women microentrepreneurs, spurred by their strong unmet need for income (especially if they have provisioning responsibilities for their children), tend to do their utmost to succeed. They benefit (although they may increase their work day and self-exploitation), their children benefit, the credit project benefits, and the planet's equity account becomes a little less tilted toward power, privilege, and patriarchy.

NOTES

1. Rapid Rural Appraisal (RRA) is a methodology used in the field of development that has evolved steadily since being named at a conference at the University of Sussex in 1978 (Beebe 1985; see Blumberg 1989d for references). Basically, it uses the technique of "triangulation" to study a limited list of variables with multiple methods and sources. The methods include group meetings, key informants, analysis of existing project and government documents, secondary analysis of relevant data sets, and, on occasion, small surveys—almost always done as a last step and more often using purposive than random samples. Time in the field is usually six weeks or less. Ideally, RRA involves a multidisciplinary team of

host-country nationals and highly experienced social scientist-development re-searchers. Although numbers generated by RRA are less precise than those generated by large-scale sample surveys, RRAs may reveal considerably more contextual information about a given delimited topic than the surveys and one to two years sooner. As numerous methodological critiques have demonstrated over the years, surveys are not appropriate when the range of variation is not known or the topic involves complex, sensitive issues and no incentives for telling the truth. The level of reliability and validity achieved by RRA's triangulation technique is not easily quantified, but most RRA researchers are painfully aware that they have a powerful moral obligation to be accurate: decisions on development projects that may profoundly affect the wealth and well-being of thousands of poor and vulnerable people may hinge on the findings. In sum, RRA is quick but not inherently "dirty."

RRA is particularly well suited for gender analysis. For example, within a small agroecological area the gender division of labor, resources, income, and time tend to vary only by social class and/or ethnicity, so group meetings with the appropri-ate subgroups of women and men can quickly and effectively give an overview. Many projects proceed in near-total ignorance of who does what and who gets the returns for the activities in question, and thus come to grief. Alice Stewart Carloni (1987) and I (Blumberg 1989a) have found that both the project and the women are likely to be undercut by such gender blindness, particularly when women are important in the activities promoted by the project but they and their incentives are not taken into account. In this black hole the information generated by RRA comes as a dazzling beacon of light. For example, in the summer of 1992 I did an RRA that showed why the men in one Ecuadorian village failed to plant addi-tional pasturage, which is the prerequisite to adopting the technologies of double milking and separation of cows and calves. These two technologies increase milk production. But the men make most of their income from crops, not dairy: milk money goes to the women, and land is scarce. Planting pasturage on scarce land would cut their income from crops. The men were not stupid or fatalistic, as thought by project personnel: they were acting rationally. But because no one had ascertained the gender division of labor and incentives beforehand, the project was promoting an activity doomed to failure.

2. In April 1985 Mirtha Olivares, then ADEMI's executive director, summa-rized the organization's activity and impact as follows: (a) It creates one job for every US$818 it lends (paying US$67, then RD$209, per month per employee [US$1.00 = RD$3.125]). (b) It creates an average additional monthly profit per microentrepreneur. (c) It rotates its portfolio 3.5 times a year. (d) Therefore, with a US$100,000 loan portfolio, ADEMI can lend US$350,000 and can generate US$1,184,000 in additional income per year, as follows: US$343,000 for new workers; US$841,000 in additional microentrepreneurs' income. (e) Thus, each dollar of the original US$100,000 generates almost US$12 of new income a year (Blumberg 1989c, 68–69).

3. ADEMI loans were issued within a few *days* after the application was received versus *months* for many typical credit programs, especially public sector ones offering subsidized credit.

4. According to analyses done by Steve Gross and Jeffrey Ashe, ADEMI may have been engaging in its own version of "trickle up" among individual ME clients. A comparison of the distribution of ADEMI loans in the last quarter of 1984 with the distribution of MEs surveyed in a large-scale 1980 study of the informal sector shows that the average ME in the 1980 research had 1.6 employees; ADEMI's late-1984 loan clients averaged 3.8 (Blumberg 1989c, 76–77).

5. The belief that most microenterprise ventures can be classified as pure "production, commerce, or service" is not borne out by the data. In my own Rapid Rural Appraisal research I found almost no such unmixed types. For example, one shoe producer and repairer also sold school supplies and stationery out of a glass counter on the left side of his shop and women's and children's clothes out of another glass counter on the right; the shoe business occupied the center counter and the back room. One shirt manufacturer sat in a market stall he maintained with his sisters as often as several days a week when excess unsold merchandise threatened to swamp his business. Another market vendor set up neighbors as employees who produced the items she sold from her kiosk. Moreover, although commerce MEs create fewer jobs than such labor-intensive production sectors as clothing, and create less value-added than such capital-intensive sectors as metalworking, they report increases in sales sometimes at a *higher* rate than production businesses (see, for example, data in Gomez 1990). In 1992 the Inter-American Development Bank stopped prohibiting microenterprise loans for commerce and service.

6. The Christian Democrat government was not wholly independent of military pressures; death squad activity continued, although at a lower pace than in 1979–84, when it is estimated that thirty thousand to fifty thousand people— mainly poor Indian noncombatants—were killed in a brutal counterinsurgency campaign by successive military governments (Krueger and Enge 1985).

7. One of the reasons for such high rates of informality is the very progressiveness of the labor codes in many Third World countries. Only a small aristocracy of labor, largely employed by import-substitution enterprises or foreign companies, and public sector workers benefited from the expensive provisions for overtime, holidays, severance pay, maternity benefits, and the like. Other enterprises avoided the law, often by avoiding the formal sector—which also saved them from expensive bureaucratic regulation. This was partially offset by payoffs to remain unregistered, in many instances.

8. Empirically, for women, economic power is the most achievable of the four major sources of power discussed by Gerhard E. Lenski (1966): economic, political-hierarchical, force, and (slightly less important) ideological. Over the range of human history and human societies we find that the power of force clearly is the least achievable for women, who are more likely to be its victims than its wielders. This is so at both the individual violence level (domestic abuse, for example) and the organized force level (police-military power). With respect to political power, we have no data on even one society where women have a fifty–fifty split. Regarding the power of ideology, we know of a few groups or societies that proclaim women's ideological equality with men but none where women are deemed ideologically superior. Only with respect to *economic* power does women's position run the full gamut from near zero (e.g., the Azande of the

Sudan) to near total control of the local economy (e.g., the Iroquois of colonial North America); in general, however, women's predominance is more common at the microlevels of family and community, with macrolevels dominated by males. A fifth source of power, information, is becoming increasingly important, as Alvin Toffler (1990) argues.

REFERENCES

Acharya, Meena, and Lynn Bennett. 1981. *The Rural Women of Nepal: An Aggregate Analysis and Summary of Eight Village Studies.* Vol. 2, part 9. Kathmandu, Nepal: Centre for Economic Development and Administration, Tribhuvan University.

———. 1982. *Women's Status in Nepal: A Summary of Findings and Implications.* Washington, D.C.: Agency for International Development, Office of Women in Development.

———. 1983. *Women and the Subsistence Sector: Economic Participation in Household Decision-Making in Nepal.* Working Paper no. 526. Washington, D.C.: World Bank.

Baca Carbo, Raúl. 1989. "Plan nacional y masivo de apoyo a las Unidades Populares Económicas." In *Programas de micro y pequeña empresa en el Ecuador.* Quito, Ecuador: INSOTEC.

Beebe, James. 1985. *Rapid Rural Appraisal: The Critical First Step in a Farming Systems Approach to Research.* Networking Paper no. 5, Farming Systems Support Project. Gainesville, Fla.: University of Florida.

Berger, Marguerite, and Mayra Buvinic, eds. 1988. *La mujer en el sector informal.* Quito, Ecuador: Instituto Latinoamericano de Investigaciones Sociales, Editorial Nueva Sociedad.

Blumberg, Rae Lesser. 1984. "A General Theory of Gender Stratification." In *Sociological Theory 1984,* ed. Randall Collins, 23–100. San Francisco: Jossey-Bass.

———. 1988. "Income under Female vs. Male Control: Hypotheses from a Theory of Gender Stratification and Data from the Third World." *Journal of Family Issues* 9 (March): 51–84.

———. 1989a. *Making the Case for the Gender Variable: Women and the Wealth and Well-being of Nations.* Washington, D.C.: Agency for International Development, Office of Women in Development.

———. 1989b. "Toward a Feminist Theory of Development." In *Feminism and Sociological Theory,* ed. Ruth A. Wallace, 161–199. Newbury Park, Calif.: Sage.

———. 1989c. "Entrepreneurship, Credit, and Gender in the Informal Sector of the Dominican Republic: The ADEMI Story." In *Women in Development: A.I.D.'s Experience, 1973–1985, Vol. 2, Ten Field Studies,* ed. Paula O. Goddard, 65–84. Washington, D.C.: Agency for International Development.

———. 1989d. "Work, Wealth, and a Women in Development 'Natural Experiment' in Guatemala: The ALCOSA Agribusiness Project in 1980 and 1985."

In *Women in Development: A.I.D.'s Experience, 1973–1985. Vol. 2, Ten Field Studies,* ed. Paula O. Goddard, 85–106. Washington, D.C.: Agency for International Development.

———. 1990a. "Gender and Microenterprise in Ecuador." In *Ecuador Micro-Enterprise Sector Assessment: Key Characteristics of the Micro-Enterprise Sector,* ed. John H. Magill, Robert G. Blayney, Rae L. Blumberg, Joseph Burke, Peter D. Livingston, and Jennifer L. Santer, chap. 2. Gemini Technical Report no. 12. Bethesda, Md.: Gemini-Development Alternatives, Inc.

———. 1990b. *Gender and Development in Ecuador.* Quito, Ecuador: USAID/Ecuador.

———, ed. 1991a. *Gender, Family, and Economy: The Triple Overlap.* Newbury Park, Calif.: Sage.

———. 1991b. "Social Soundness and Gender Analysis: Swaziland Small Business Development Project." Washington, D.C.: Weidemann Associates; Mbabane, Swaziland: USAID/Swaziland.

———. 1993. "The Political Economy of the Mother-Child Family: New Perspectives on a Theory." In *Where Did All the Men Go: Female-Headed/Female-Supported Households in Cross-Cultural Perspective,* ed. Joan P. Mencher and Anne Okongwu, 13–52. Boulder, Colo.: Westview.

Blumberg, Rae Lesser, and Marion Tolbert Coleman. 1989. "A Theory-Guided Look at the Gender Balance of Power in the American Couple." *Journal of Family Issues* 10 (June): 225–249.

Blumberg, Rae Lesser, and Jaime Reibel. 1988. *Guatemala's Urban Microenterprise Multiplier System (SIMME): Program Appraisal.* Washington, D.C.: Arthur Young/Management Systems International.

Blumberg, Rae Lesser, and Elspeth Revere. 1989. *Evaluation of Guatemala's Urban Microenterprise Multiplier System (SIMME).* Guatemala City: USAID/Guatemala.

Blumstein, Philip, and Pepper Schwartz. 1991. "Money and Ideology: Their Impact on Power and the Division of Household Labor." In *Gender, Family, and Economy: The Triple Overlap,* ed. Rae Lesser Blumberg, 261–288. Newbury Park, Calif.: Sage.

Bruce, Judith, and Cynthia Lloyd. 1992. "Beyond Female Headship: Family Research and Policy Issues for the 1990s." Paper presented at the Workshop on Intrahousehold Resource Allocation: Policy Issues and Research Methods, Washington, D.C., International Food Policy Research Institute, February 12–14.

Buvinic, Mayra, Marguerite Berger, and Cecilia Jaramillo. 1988. "Impacto de un proyecto de crédito dirigido a microempresarios en Quito, Ecuador." In *La mujer en el sector informal,* ed. Marguerite Berger and Mayra Buvinic, 331–362. Quito, Ecuador: Instituto Latinoamericano de Investigaciones Sociales, Editorial Nueva Sociedad.

Carloni, Alice Stewart. 1987. *Women in Development: A.I.D.'s Experience, 1973–1985. Vol. 1, Synthesis Paper.* A.I.D. Program Evaluation Report no. 18. Washington, D.C.: Agency for International Development.

Chafetz, Janet Saltzman. 1991. "The Gender Division of Labor and the Reproduction of Female Disadvantage: Toward an Integrated Theory." In *Gender,*

Family, and Economy: The Triple Overlap, ed. Rae Lesser Blumberg, 74–96. Newbury Park, Calif.: Sage.

Downing, Jeanne. 1992. *The Growth and Dynamics of Women Entrepreneurs in Southern Africa.* GEMINI Technical Report no. 47. Bethesda, Md.: Gemini-Development Alternatives, Inc.

England, Paula, and Barbara Stanek Kilbourne. 1988. "Markets, Marriages, and Other Mates: The Problem of Power." Paper presented at the Conference on Economy and Society, University of California, Santa Barbara, May.

Folbre, Nancy. 1991a. "Women on Their Own: Global Patterns of Female Headship." In *The Women and International Development Annual,* vol. 2, ed. Rita S. Gallin and Anne Ferguson. Boulder, Colo.: Westview.

——. 1991b. "Mothers on Their Own: Policy Issues for Developing Countries." New York/Washington, D.C.: Population Council/International Center for Research on Women.

Gomez, Arelis. 1990. *Informe de evaluación de impacto programa USAID/MTRH.* Washington, D.C.: Nathan Associates.

Grameen Dialogue. 1993. Dacca, Bangladesh: Computer Unit, Grameen Bank, no. 16, October.

Hagen, Margaret, and Tamara Tiffany. 1990. *Small Enterprise Development Project Credit Strategy Study.* Quito, Ecuador: CARE-Ecuador.

Helmore, Kristin. 1989. "Banking on a Better Life." *Christian Science Monitor,* March 15, pp. 12–13.

Krueger, Chris, and Kjell Enge. 1985. *Security and Development Conditions in the Guatemalan Highlands.* Washington, D.C.: Washington Office on Latin America.

Lenski, Gerhard E. 1966. *Power and Privilege: A Theory of Social Stratification.* New York: McGraw-Hill.

McKee, Katherine. 1988. "Micro Level Strategies for Supporting Livelihoods, Employment, and Income Generation of Poor Women in the Third World: The Challenge of Significance." Paper presented at the World Conference on Support for Microenterprises, Washington, D.C., June 6–9.

Magill, John H., Robert G. Blayney, Rae L. Blumberg, Joseph Burke, Peter D. Livingston, and Jennifer L. Santer. 1990. *Ecuador Micro-Enterprise Assessment: Key Characteristics of the Micro-Enterprise Sector.* GEMINI Technical Report no. 12. Bethesda, Md.: GEMINI-Development Alternatives, Inc.

O'Brien, Stephen. 1991. "Structural Adjustment and Structural Transformation in Sub-Saharan Africa." In *Structural Adjustment and African Women Farmers,* ed. Christina H. Gladwin. Gainesville, Fla.: University of Florida Press.

Rakowski, Cathy A., ed. 1995. *Contrapunto: The Informal Sector Debate.* Albany: State University of New York Press.

Ross, Catherine E. 1987. "The Division of Labor at Home." *Social Forces* 65 (3): 816–833.

Samaniego, Pablo, and Lincoln Mayguashca. 1989. *Situación y perspectivas de la micro y pequeña industria en cinco ciudades secundarias de la costa ecuatoriana: Esmeraldas, Quevedo, Manta, Portoviejo y Santo Domingo de los Colorados.* Quito, Ecuador: INSOTEC.

Tendler, Judith. 1987. *Whatever Happened to Poverty Alleviation?* Report prepared for the mid-decade review of the Ford Foundation's Programs on Livelihood, Employment, and Income Generation. New York: Ford Foundation.

Timberg, Thomas A. 1988. "Comparative Experience with Microenterprise Projects." Paper presented at the World Conference on Support for Microenterprises, Washington, D.C., June 6–9.

Toffler, Alvin. 1990. *Powershift.* New York: Bantam Books.

World Bank. 1989. *Sub-Saharan Africa: From Crisis to Sustainable Growth.* Washington, D.C.

CHAPTER 9

✳

Women's Social Movements in Latin America

HELEN ICKEN SAFA

The 1980s witnessed a marked increase in participation by women in social movements in Latin America. Latin American women are struggling for their rights as workers in trade unions, as housewives in squatter settlements, and as mothers defending human rights against state repression. Although undoubtedly influenced by the feminist movements that developed earlier and were largely middle-class in origin, these social movements are distinguished by the widespread participation of poor women, who focus their demands on the state in their struggle for basic survival and against repression.

Many studies trace the origin of these movements to the current economic and political crisis in the region, but I believe they are indicative of a broader historical trend toward the breakdown of the traditional division between the private and public spheres in Latin America.[1] The private sphere of the family has always been considered the domain of women, but it is increasingly threatened by economic and political forces. Industrialization and urbanization have reduced the role of the family and strengthened the role of the state. There have been marked occupational changes, including a growing incorporation of women into the labor force. The importance of women as wage earners has been made even more acute by the economic crisis gripping Latin America, in which the state services on which women have come to depend have been reduced or curtailed. Authoritarian military regimes have invaded the very heart of the family by taking children and other loved ones and subjecting them to terror and repression.

Nevertheless, women in Latin America are not just defending the private domain of the family against increasing state and market intervention. They are also demanding incorporation into the state, so that their rights as citizens will be fully recognized. In this sense, these movements not only are symptomatic of the breakdown between the public and private spheres in Latin America but are themselves furthering this process. Women are demanding to be recognized as full participants in the public world and no longer wish to have their interests represented solely by men, as male heads of households, barrio leaders, or politicians and union officials.

At the same time, as Elizabeth Jelin (1987) notes, Latin American women are insisting on distinct forms of incorporation that reaffirm their identity as women, and particularly as wives and mothers. This form of incorporation differs from the contemporary U.S. and western European experience in which women seek a gender-neutral participation in the public sphere. Latin American women, in contrast, think that their roles as wives and mothers legitimize their sense of injustice and outrage, since they are protesting their inability to carry out these roles effectively, as military governments take away their children or the rising cost of living prevents them from feeding their families adequately. In short, they are redefining and transforming their domestic role from one of private nurturance to one of collective, public protest, in this way challenging the traditional seclusion of women in the private sphere of the family.

The prominence of women in these new social movements challenges Marxist theory in at least two fundamental ways. In the first place, participation in these women's movements is based primarily on gender rather than on class, which Marxists have emphasized as the principal avenue for collective action. The bulk of poor women who participate in these movements are conscious of both class and gender exploitation but tend to legitimize their concerns over issues such as human rights or the cost of living primarily in terms of their roles as wives and mothers rather than as members of a subordinated class. This points out the weakness of Marxist theory in addressing the importance of gender, racial, or religious differences within the working class. Second, and as a consequence of their gender emphasis, the primary arena of confrontation for women's social movements in Latin America has been not with capital but with the state, largely in terms of women's reproductive roles as wives, mothers, and consumers, both of state services and of private consumer goods. The state has assumed a major role in social reproduction in Latin America, particularly in terms of the provision of basic services such as health, education, and transportation. At the same time, the need for these services has grown with the rapid increase in urbanization and industrialization in the postwar period.

Women are not the only subordinated group to challenge the state, and social movements have arisen as well among youth, peasants, the urban poor, and broader-based human rights groups. Latin American women have also demanded greater participation in labor unions, political parties, and peasant movements that have attempted to make the state more responsive to their needs. They have worked with feminists in establishing daycare centers or in developing ways to cope with sexual violence and other problems. Here, however, I focus on Latin American women's movements for human rights and those centering on consumer issues.

The Bases of Women's Social Movements in Latin America

Women's social movements in Latin America are commonly seen as a response to military authoritarian rule and the current economic crisis, both of which create particular hardships for the working class. In an attempt to address the growing debt crisis, many Latin American governments have set up structural adjustment programs designed by the International Monetary Fund. These programs, which have resulted in increased unemployment and underemployment, a decline in real wages coupled with accelerated inflation, the elimination of state subsidies for basic foods, as well as cuts in government expenditures for social services, such as health and education, have had a devastating impact on women and children (Cornia 1987).

The economic crisis has reinforced the need for collective action, particularly among poor urban women who organize primarily on a neighborhood basis. The urban poor in Latin America have a long history of collective action, as demonstrated by the development of squatter settlements and other neighborhood actions to improve urban services (see, e.g., Safa 1974). Women have always played a prominent role in these neighborhood forms of collective action, though their importance has seldom been explicitly acknowledged (Caldeira 1987, 77). At the same time, women commonly resort to informal networks of mutual aid, including extended family and neighbors, to help stretch the family income and resolve community problems. Women also add to the family income through participation in the informal economy as domestic servants, street vendors, and industrial homeworkers and through other forms of self-employment. With the economic crisis these survival strategies have been intensified and institutionalized into formal organizations, such as the *comedores populares* or *ollas comunes* (communal kitchens) for food distribution or *talleres productivos* (workshops) for making garments or doing other types of piecework. In the metropolitan region of Santiago, Chile, in 1986, there were an estimated 1,383 Organizaciones Económicas Populares, or OEP (Popular Economic Organizations), of which 1,208 were self-help organizations with almost exclusively female leadership and participants (Valdés and Weinstein 1989, 11).

The participation of women in social movements in Latin America is also a product of demographic changes among Latin America women, especially since 1960. Fertility has been declining steadily in most countries of the region, so that by 1980–85 only three Latin American countries registered average fertility rates in excess of six children per woman, while eight countries had rates of fewer than four children per woman (Economic Commission for Latin America and the Caribbean 1988a, 2). Fertility decline was associated with women's higher educational levels and increased labor force participation, as well as with greater access to contraceptives and the promotion of family planning programs in several Latin American countries. Women's educational levels rose at a faster rate than men's as part of the enormous expansion in primary and, in particular, secondary education between 1950 and 1970. The number of women in higher education rose from 35 percent to 45 percent from 1970 to 1985 (Economic Commission for Latin America and the Caribbean 1988a, 3–4). The growth of urbanization and the service sector resulted in a threefold increase in the Latin American female labor force between 1950 and 1980, with overall participation rates rising from almost 18 percent to over 26 percent in the same period (Economic Commission for Latin America and the Caribbean 1988b, 15). Workforce participation rates for women grew faster than those for men, and while all age groups experienced growth, single women between the ages of twenty and twenty-nine continued to have the highest level of paid employment among women.

Increasing workforce participation rates for women and decreasing participation rates for men coupled with higher male unemployment has meant that women are now making a major contribution to their household economies, particularly where there has been a high demand for women's labor, as in the export processing zones of the Dominican Republic or among garment workers in Puerto Rico (Safa 1990). Women's larger economic contribution has resulted in a shift toward more egalitarian conjugal relationships in some Dominican and Puerto Rican households, but women are still struggling for greater legitimacy at the level of the workplace or the state, where they continue to be regarded as supplementary wage earners.

The higher educational and occupational levels of Latin American women also contributed to the growth of a feminist movement among middle-class women, who felt their exclusion from the public sphere even more sharply than poor women did. These feminists have devoted a great deal of attention to the poor through research and involvement in action projects such as daycare, health services, and centers for raped and battered women. Such programs helped transmit feminist concerns for greater gender equality and have stimulated poor women to challenge their traditional role. The visibility these gender issues received during the UN Decade for the Equality of Women through numerous conferences, publications, and projects reinforced their appeal.

Poor women in Latin America also received considerable support from the church (Alvarez 1989, 20–26). Women played a major role in the Catholic church's organization of ecclesiastic base communities (CEBs) in Brazil and other Latin American countries. The CEBs were part of the church's efforts to give more support to social justice for the poor in Latin America, emanating from liberation theology, which is now under attack from the Vatican. The CEBs were also an attempt by the church to reinforce grassroots support, which was weakening with the growth of Protestantism and the church's elitist stance. Women were organized into mothers' clubs for the provision of food, sewing classes, and other traditional domestic tasks. Many of women's collective consumption strategies, such as communal kitchens, have received church support. Though based on traditional women's roles, these clubs provided an additional organizational base from which women could challenge the existing order.

Under military rule, the church often provided the only legitimate umbrella under which women and other groups could organize, since all other forms of mobilization were prohibited. In some Latin American countries, such as Chile and Brazil, women from all class levels, with church support, organized into human rights groups to protest the disappearance or killing of their loved ones or to seek amnesty for political prisoners or exiles. Catholic doctrine played an important role in the self-definition and quest for legitimacy of these women, and they rarely questioned traditional gender roles. On the contrary, the women often appealed to Catholic symbols of motherhood and the family in legitimizing their protest—values these authoritarian states also proclaimed but destroyed in the name of national security. Women themselves were often victims of this repression: they were systematically sought out for violent sexual torture designed to destroy their femininity and human dignity (Bunster-Burotto 1986).

In sum, many factors have contributed to the growing participation of women in social movements in Latin America. Women have long been active at the neighborhood level, through both informal networks and more organized forms of collective action such as establishing squatter settlements and barrio committees. With the economic crisis and military rule, these activities took on added importance and also received the support of key groups such as the Catholic church and nongovernmental agencies. Increased educational and occupational opportunities made women more aware of previous restrictions and more vocal in protesting them. Poor women became more receptive to the largely middle-class feminist movement in Latin America and began to redefine their traditional role, including their relationship to the state.

Women's Social Movements and the State

Women's social movements have been described as a new form of doing politics (*nueva forma de hacer política*) in Latin America, but the impetus for most of these movements has not come from traditional political parties and labor unions in the region. Most women's movements have consciously avoided partisan political connections, in part because of the weakness of these traditional avenues of political action during the period of authoritarian military rule when most of these movements arose. The attempt of these regimes to limit legitimate political action contributed to the politicization of women and other groups that had not been participating actively in the public arena (Jelin 1987).

The other reason women's social movements took place largely outside the realm of traditional political parties is that politics is seen as men's sphere, particularly by poor women. Latin American political parties traditionally have been dominated by men and have been seen as struggles for power in which the poor are essentially clients. Poor people's loyalty to the party is exchanged for favors such as paving a road, providing state services, guaranteeing title to land, or getting jobs. The Centros de Madres, or Mothers' Centers, in Chile, which had begun to acquire some autonomy during the governments of Frei and Allende, under the military dictatorship of Augusto Pinochet were completely subverted to the needs of the state for the control and co-optation of poor women (Valdés et al. 1989). Although the Mothers' Centers were privatized, they were run by a staff of volunteers appointed by the government and headed by Pinochet's wife, who offered such services to both rural and urban women as training courses that focused largely on improving their domestic role. Political participation was discouraged as "unfeminine," although members were often called on to display their loyalty to the regime by participating in rallies and other activities. As a result, membership in the Mothers' Centers declined drastically from the premilitary period, and new, unofficial women's groups arose, in the areas of human rights and collective survival strategies, in response to Chile's severe economic crisis and rising rates of unemployment (Arteaga 1988, 573). These unofficial groups provided the base for the women's movement against Pinochet starting in 1983.

Latin American women appear to have chosen the state as the principal arena of their collective action rather than the workplace, as men traditionally have, partly because industrial capitalism transformed the organization and social relations of production and the gender division of labor. Industrial capitalism initially drew women into the paid labor force in many areas, but they were never as fully incorporated as men, who became the chief breadwinners. Women were relegated to the role of supplementary wage earners, while their reproductive roles of housewives and consumers assumed new importance. Despite recent significant increases in women's labor force participation in Latin America, this image of women as supplementary workers persists and helps explain women's comparatively low level of consciousness as workers per se. Most poor women are relatively recent and less stable entrants to the formal labor force in Latin America and work primarily to support themselves and their families, obtaining little gratification or self-fulfillment from their jobs. Their primary identification, even when they are working, is as wives and mothers.

The gendered division of labor in the workplace may reinforce gender hierarchies rather than weaken them, by relegating women to inferior jobs. Even in São Paulo, Brazil, where the spectacular industrial boom of the 1970s led to an 181 percent increase in women's employment in manufacturing between 1970 and 1980, women workers were largely concentrated in exclusively women's jobs at the bottom of the job hierarchy (Humphrey 1987). These gender asymmetries in the workplace were reflected in the conflict between male-dominated unions and working women. Elizabeth Souza Lobo's study (1991) of the metallurgy industry found that although women formed union committees and some individually active women were integrated into the union structure, women continued to see the union as a men's sphere that remained largely unresponsive to their demands.

As a result of their frustration in working through political parties and labor unions, the recognized channels for collective action, Latin American women presented their demands to the state directly. One of the principal demands was for the provision of public services, such as running water, electricity, and transportation, all of which are sorely lacking in the squatter settlements in which most of these poor women live. Women's reproductive role as housewives and mothers has tended to push them into the foreground as champions of these collective consumption issues, and they have been at the forefront of protests against the cost of living and demands for programs to provide daycare, health services, and even food.

One of the most successful and unique collective consumption strategies to combat the economic crisis is the *comedores populares,* or communal kitchens, organized by women in Lima, Santiago, and other Latin American cities. Groups of fifteen to fifty households buy and prepare

234 HELEN ICKEN SAFA

food collectively for the neighborhood, with each family paying according to the number of meals requested. Many of these *comedores* sprang up spontaneously; others were started or at least supported by the church, the state, and other local and international agencies. UNICEF-Peru in 1985 estimated that there were three hundred in Lima (Cornia 1987, 99), and Cecilia Blondet (1989) recently estimated their number between one thousand and twelve hundred. Their growth is evidence of women's collective response to the increasing severity of the economic crisis in Peru and other Latin American countries in the 1980s.

In Lima popular organizations may be the only alternative to acquire basic services such as health, education, and food, yet the *asistencialismo* (welfare dependency) this policy encourages may be exploited by the government, political parties, and other agencies (Blondet 1989). Traditional district and neighborhood organizations are controlled by male leaders who attempt to usurp the popular support enjoyed by women's groups for their own partisan ends. Blondet (1989) recounts, for example, how the popular women's federation in Villa El Salvador, a large shantytown in Lima, split and was partially absorbed through pressure brought by the traditional men's organization. The political fragmentation then occurring among leftist political parties in Peru was reproduced within the women's organizations, further weakening their base of support.

Some feminists have been critical of these women's self-help organizations because they focus almost exclusively on traditional women's tasks and do not challenge the traditional gender division of labor. I argue that the collectivization of private tasks, such as food preparation and childcare, is transforming women's roles even though they are not undertaken as conscious challenges to gender subordination. These women never reject their domestic role but use it as a base to give them strength and legitimacy in their demands on the state (Caldeira 1987, 97; Alvarez 1989, 20). In moving their domestic concerns into the public arena, they are redefining the meaning associated with domesticity to include participation and struggle rather than obedience and passivity.

Nowhere is this new militancy more apparent than in the demands Latin American women have placed on the state for the recognition of human rights. One of the best-known cases in contemporary Latin America involves the Mothers of the Plaza de Mayo, who played a decisive role in the defeat of the military dictatorship that ruled Argentina from 1976 to 1983. Composed mostly of older women with no political experience, the Mothers take their name from the Plaza de Mayo, the principal seat of government power in Buenos Aires, in which they march every Thursday, wearing white kerchiefs and carrying photographs of their missing children as a symbol of protest. Although the military government attempted to discredit them as madwomen or mothers of subversives, they continued to march, publish petitions in the newspaper, organize trips abroad, and seek cooperation with other human rights groups and youth movements, with whom they organized larger demonstrations in 1981 and 1982. The publicity they received from the foreign media and the support given them by certain European countries and the United States during the Carter administration contributed to their popularity (Reimers 1989). In order to maintain their legitimacy during the military regime, they refused any identification with political parties or feminism. They maintained, "Nosotros no defendemos ideologías, defendemos la vida" (We don't defend ideologies, we defend life) (Feijoo and Gogna 1987, 155). Their demands were not political power for themselves but a guarantee from the state for the return of their loved ones (or their remains) and for the punishment of the military who had violated the sanctity of the home and family. These demands remain largely unfulfilled. Though some high-ranking officers were prosecuted, most of the military were granted amnesty, and even those imprisoned were later released.

After the end of military rule the Mothers were weakened by internal conflict regarding the democratically elected government's human rights policy and the prosecution of the military, and split in two. Although similar women's human rights groups have arisen in Uruguay, Chile, Brazil, Honduras, El Salvador, Guatemala, and other Latin American countries subject to military rule, the decline in popular support for the Mothers of the Plaza de Mayo reflects the difficulty women's social movements have in converting political mobilization into institutional representation (cf. Jaquette 1989, 194).

The Transformative Potential of Women's Social Movements in Latin America

Most participation by women in social movements arises out of women's immediate perceived needs and experiences, or out of what Maxine Molyneux (1986) terms women's practical gender interests. Molyneux claims these practical gender interests do not challenge gender subordination directly, unlike strategic gender interests, which question or transform the division of labor. As we have seen, women's social movements are often based on women's role as wives and mothers and may reinforce or defend women's domestic role. As these practical gender interests are collectivized and politicized, however, they may also lead to a greater consciousness of gender subordination and the transformation of practical into strategic gender interests.

Although neither women's movements for human rights nor collective consumption were designed as challenges to gender subordination, participation in these movements has apparently led to greater self-esteem and recognition by women of their rights, as the following statement by a Brazilian woman, leader of a neighborhood organization, underlines: "Within the women's movement, as a woman, I discovered myself, as a person, as a human being. I had not discovered that the woman always was oppressed. But it never came to my mind that the woman was oppressed, although she had rights. The woman had to obey because she was a woman. It was in the women's movement that I came to identify myself as a woman and to understand the rights I have as a woman, from which I have knowledge to pass on as well to other companions" (Caldeira 1987, 95–96; my translation).

Women's participation in grassroots economic organizations has also given Chilean working-class and poor women a greater sense of self-worth apart from their role as wives and mothers and has led to greater awareness that their own poverty and other problems are not unique but extend to their communities and beyond (Soles 1992). It seems that as a result of participation in social movements, women are building a new collective gender identity, based not just on their private responsibilities as wives and mothers but on their public rights as citizens. Such changes are the best guarantee that these women will resist any attempt to reestablish the old order and will continue to press for their rights. They imply a redefinition of women's identity away from a purely domestic image as guardians of the private sphere into more active participants in the public arena struggling to gain greater legitimacy. This redefinition must occur not only in the minds of women themselves, however, but in the society at large, so that women are no longer treated as supplementary wage earners and pawns in the political process. For such goals to be achieved, there must be unity within the women's movement, across class, ethnic, and ideological lines. Women must also gain support from other groups in the society, such as political parties and labor unions, which often try to use women's movements for their own ends.

A glaring example of co-optation comes from an earlier period in Bolivia, where both the women's committee within the party then in power and the housewives' committee of the miners' union were used for partisan politics, and neither the party nor the union ever addressed demands specific to women (Ardaya 1986). Neither of these women's committees had sought autonomy, since they saw themselves serving class rather than gender interests.

Tension between the primacy of class and gender interests in women's organizations throughout Latin America produces differences between women who are feminists and those who are *políticas* (party militants of the left) (Kirkwood 1986, 196). Whereas feminists view politics as a way of furthering their own interests, *políticas* subordinate women's needs to a political program in the hope of their future incorporation. Those who profess to uphold both feminist and partisan political goals are said to be practicing *doble militancia,* or double militancy.

This tension between feminists and *políticas* has become more apparent with the end of military rule in Latin America and the reemergence of political parties, which reactivate divisions within the women's movement formerly united in opposition. The women's movement in Chile suffered less partisan fragmentation than other social sectors opposing the military dictatorship and was an important force in the plebiscite to oust General Pinochet. With the return to democratic rule, however, umbrella women's groups such as Memch 1983 have splintered. Although political parties have recognized the importance of women's electoral support and have integrated some women's demands into their platforms, few women candidates have been elected to public office. Only two women senators and seven women deputies out of 120 were elected in the first democratic elections in 1989. No woman held a position in the first cabinet of President Patricio Aylwin, although a woman was later appointed to the cabinet to head the Servicio Nacional de la Mujer (SERNAM), or the National Women's Office (Valenzuela 1990).

The Brazilian liberal, democratic state that supplanted military rule has been more successful in addressing women's needs and electing women to public office, including twenty-six women in the 1986 congressional elections (Alvarez 1989, 58). The initial impetus given by the Catholic church through the development of base communities (CEBs) and by feminist groups for the women's movement was critical in building a wider base of support, even though these groups remain divided on some issues such as family planning. Women also gained greater representation within the state through the government-appointed Council on the Status of Women in São Paulo, which was subsequently established in twenty-three other states and municipalities, and through the National Council on Women's Rights, which played an important role in developing women's proposals for the new Brazilian constitution. But the election of a conservative president weakened the National Council through budget cuts and the appointment of women who were less responsive to women's interests. The continuing economic crisis also diminishes the possibility of implementing women's demands.

Nevertheless, certain gains have been made and even institutionalized into legal codes. The Brazilian constitution adopted in 1988 facilitates divorce, extends maternity leave, and eliminates the prohibition on abortion (without legalizing it). Argentina has also legalized divorce and modified *patria potestad* (feudal father-right law) to give women more equality in the family and joint custody of children (Jaquette 1989,

199–200). Nongovernmental organizations (NGOs) staffed largely by middle-class feminists and addressing such issues as income generation, health care, and domestic violence have proliferated throughout Latin America and the Caribbean and are pressuring authorities to channel needed resources to the grassroots women's groups they represent (Lebon 1993). Despite the political and economic problems Latin American countries are facing in the transition to democracy, important gains in women's rights have been made as a result of women's social movements.

Conclusion

What is the future of women's social movements in Latin America? Are we to conclude with Jelin (1987) that Latin American women participate more frequently in short-term, sporadic protest movements than in long-term, formalized institutional settings? Or does women's political mobilization represent part of a progressive longer-term trend that may suffer setbacks but not total eclipse?

I argue for the latter perspective. Latin American women have been too far incorporated into the public sphere to retreat into the private domestic sphere. They have become increasingly important members of the labor force and contributors to the household economy, they have organized social movements for human rights and social welfare, and they are trying to voice their demands in labor unions and political parties. Even if these activities are not undertaken as conscious challenges to gender subordination, they show that women have broken out of the domestic sphere and that gender roles are changing. Latin American women's emergence into the public sphere interacts with profound cultural changes in the private sphere, and women are demanding more "democracy in the home" as well as in the state. These changes in Latin American women's gender identity are most likely to endure and to give women the confidence to continue to bring pressure on public authorities for greater recognition of women's rights.

When women's demands are confined to such domestic issues as childcare, communal kitchens, or even human rights, they pose less of a threat than when women attempt to gain leverage in traditional men's power structures such as political parties or labor unions. In short, as women move away from practical to strategic gender interests, they are likely to encounter more opposition along both gender and class lines from established interest groups that are unwilling to grant them the same legitimacy as men in the public arena.

Latin American women are attempting to establish a new relationship to the state, one based not on subordination, control, and dependency but on rights, autonomy, and equality (Valdés and Weinstein 1989). They have passed beyond the stage in which women's needs were largely invisible and ignored, to one in which women are now heard, even if some may be co-opted for partisan political ends. By politicizing the private sphere, women have redefined rather than rejected their domestic role and have extended the struggle against the state beyond the workplace into the home and community. This shift does not invalidate the Marxist theory of class struggle but calls for its reinterpretation to accommodate these new political voices. As Julieta Kirkwood (1986, 65) reminds us, the issue is not simply one of women's incorporation into a male-defined world but one of transforming this world to do away with the hierarchies of class, gender, race, and ethnicity that have so long subordinated much of the Latin American population, men as well as women.

NOTES

Acknowledgments: The ideas for this chapter were first presented at a 1985 conference supported by the Wenner-Gren Foundation entitled "Anthropological Perspectives on Women's Collective Action," co-organized by Constance Sutton and myself in Mijas, Spain. I wish to thank Constance Sutton, Teresa Valdés, and other colleagues, as well as the reviewers of *Gender & Society,* for their helpful comments on an earlier version of this chapter.

1. Although the concept of public-private spheres has been criticized by many feminists and has been largely replaced by the notion of production and reproduction, I believe it has particular validity for Latin America, the Caribbean, and Mediterranean Europe, where it has been widely used in the study of gender roles. The reasons for its particular validity for this region lie beyond the scope of this chapter, but it should be noted that I am using the concept of public-private spheres as poles of a continuum rather than as a dichotomy between mutually exclusive categories (cf. Tiano 1988, 40). It is this fluidity that makes possible the domination of the private by the public sphere.

REFERENCES

Alvarez, Sonia. 1989. "Women's Movements and Gender Politics in the Brazilian Transition." In *The Women's Movement in Latin America: Feminism and the Transition to Democracy,* ed. Jane Jaquette, 18–71. Winchester, Mass.: Unwin Hyman.

Ardaya, Gloria. 1986. "The Barzolas and the Housewives' Committee." In *Women and Change in Latin America,* ed. June Nash and Helen I. Safa, 326–343. Westport, Conn.: Bergin and Garvey.

Arteaga, Ana María. 1988. "Politización de lo privado y subversión de lo cotidiano" (Politicization of the private and subversion of everyday life). In *Mundo de mujer: continuidad y cambio* (Woman's world: Continuity and change). Santiago, Chile: Centro de Estudios de la Mujer.

Blondet, Cecilia. 1989. "Women's Organizations and Politics in a Time of Crisis." Paper presented at a workshop at the Helen Kellogg Institute for International Studies, University of Notre Dame, Notre Dame, Ind.

Bunster-Burotto, Ximena. 1986. "Surviving Beyond Fear: Women and Torture in Latin America." In *Women and Change in Latin America*, ed. June Nash and Helen I. Safa, 297–325. Westport, Conn.: Bergin and Garvey.

Caldeira, Teresa. 1987. "Mujeres, cotidianeidad y política" (Women, daily life, and politics). In *Ciudadanía e identidad: Las mujeres en los movimientos sociales latino-americanos* (Citizenship and identity: Women and Latin American social movements), ed. Elizabeth Jelin, 47–78. Geneva: United Nations Research Institute for Social Development.

Cornia, Giovanni. 1987. "Adjustment at the Household Level: Potentials and Limitations of Survival Strategies." In *Adjustment with a Human Face*, ed. Giovanni Cornia, Richard Jolly, and Francis Stewart, 90–104. New York: UNICEF; Oxford: Clarendon Press.

Economic Commission for Latin America and the Caribbean. 1988a. *Women, Work, and Crisis.* LC/L.458 (CRM.4/6). Santiago, Chile.

————. 1988b. *Latin American and Caribbean Women: Between Change and Crisis.* LC/L.464 (CRM.4/2). Santiago, Chile.

Feijoo, María del Carmen, and Mónica Gogna. 1987. "Las mujeres en la transición a la democracia" (Women in the transition to democracy). In *Ciudadanía e identidad: Las mujeres en los movimientos sociales latino-americanos* (Citizenship and identity: Women and Latin American social movements), ed. Elizabeth Jelin, 79–114. Geneva: United Nations Research Institute for Social Development.

Humphrey, John. 1987. *Gender and Work in the Third World: Sexual Division in Brazilian Industry.* London: Tavistock.

Jaquette, Jane. 1989. "Conclusion: Women and the New Democratic Politics." In *The Women's Movement in Latin America: Feminism and the Transition to Democracy*, ed. Jane Jaquette, 185–208. Winchester, Mass.: Unwin Hyman.

Jelin, Elizabeth, ed. 1987. *Ciudadanía e identidad: Las Mujeres en los movimientos sociales Latino-Americanos* (Citizenship and identity: Women and Latin American social movements). Geneva: United Nations Research Institute for Social Development.

Kirkwood, Julieta. 1986. *Ser política en Chile: Las feministas y los partidos* (To be political in Chile: Feminists and parties). Santiago, Chile: Facultad Latinoamericana de Ciencias Sociales.

Lebon, Nathalie. 1993. "The Brazilian Feminist Movement in the Post-Constitutional Era: Assessing the Impact of the Rise of Feminist Non-Governmental Organizations." *Florida Journal of Anthropology* 18:17–26.

Molyneux, Maxine. 1986. "Mobilization without Emancipation? Women's Interests, State, and Revolution." In *Transition and Development: Problems of Third World Socialism*, ed. Richard Fagen, Carmen Diana Deere and José Luis Corragio, 280–302. New York: Monthly Review.

Reimers, Isolde. 1989. "The Decline of a Social Movement: The Mothers of the Plaza de Mayo." Master's thesis, Center for Latin American Studies, University of Florida, Gainesville.

Safa, Helen I. 1974. *The Urban Poor of Puerto Rico: A Study in Development and Inequality.* New York: Holt, Rinehart and Winston.

———. 1990. "Women and Industrialisation in the Caribbean." In *Women, Employment, and the Family in the International Division of Labour,* ed. Sharon Stichter and Jane L. Parpart, 72–97. Philadelphia: Temple University Press.

Soles, Diane R. 1992. "The Making of Actors for Social Change: Women, Collective Action, and the Transition to Democracy in Chile." Master's thesis, Center for Latin American Studies, University of Florida, Gainesville.

Souza Lobo, Elizabeth. 1991. "Brazilian Social Movements, Feminism, and Women Workers' Struggle in the São Paulo Trade Unions." In *A classe operaria tem dois sexos* (The Laboring Class Has Two Sexes). São Paulo: Editorial Brasilense.

Tiano, Susan. 1988. "Women's Work in the Public and Private Spheres: A Critique and Reformulation." In *Women, Development, and Change: The Third World Experience,* ed. M. F. Abraham and P. S. Abraham. Bristol, Ind.: Wyndham Hall Press.

Valdés, Teresa, and Marisa Weinstein. 1989. *Organizaciones de pobladoras y construcción democrática en Chile* (Organizations of squatter settlements and democratic reconstruction in Chile). Working Paper 434. Santiago, Chile: Facultad Latinoamericana de Ciencias Sociales.

Valdés, Teresa, Marisa Weinstein, M. Isabel Toledo, and Lilian Letelier. 1989. *Centros de Madres, 1973–1989: ¿Solo disciplinamiento?* (Mothers' Centers, 1973–1989: Only imposed discipline?). Working Paper 416. Santiago, Chile: Facultad Latinoamericana de Ciencias Sociales.

Valenzuela, María Elena. 1990. "Mujeres y política: Logros y tensiones en el proceso de democratización" (Women and politics: Successes and tensions in the democratic process). In *Proposiciones 18: Chile, sociedad y transición* (Propositions 18: Chile, society, and transition). Santiago, Chile: Ediciones Sur.

CHAPTER 10

✳

Revolutionary Popular Feminism in Nicaragua

Ideologies, Political Transitions,
and the Struggle for Autonomy

NORMA STOLTZ CHINCHILLA

On February 25, 1990, Nicaraguans went freely to the polls to elect a president, vice-president, and delegates to the National Assembly for the second time in their history as an independent nation. To the surprise of everyone—supporters and opponents of the ruling Sandinista Front, independent pollsters, and election observers alike—the revolutionary political party that had been in power for more than a decade since the successful overthrow of the Somoza dictatorship lost the elections to a conservative opposition coalition headed by Violeta Barrios de Chamorro.

Some observers saw this defeat as simply another nail in the coffin of socialism, or at least Soviet and East-bloc style state socialism. Others saw it as evidence of the unacceptability of even moderate, relatively democratic Third World attempts at revolution, including those based on a mixture of ideologies and economic forms, to the world's dominant economic and political power, the United States. Neither explanation alone adequately captured the complex mix of factors—internal conditions, such as political and ideological weaknesses in the leadership and strategy of the revolution, and externally influenced conditions, primarily the devastation caused by the U.S.-financed Contra war, economic boycott, and political opposition—that contributed to the unexpected change in regime.

The Nicaraguan women's movement, conceived in the womb of the Sandinista revolution before the overthrow of the dictatorship, experienced the same disorientation as other Sandinista-affiliated organizations

in the immediate postelectoral period. Over time, however, sectors of this ←
movement have emerged with greater creativity, dynamism, visibility,
and diversity than before, despite meager resources, the loss of direct
access to the state, and sharp disagreements with elements of Sandinista
Front leadership.

This outcome stems from the models, strategies, ideologies, and practices that framed activities of the Nicaraguan women's movement at each
stage of the postdictatorship Sandinista revolutionary decade and the
strengths and weaknesses manifested in them. The strengths included the (1)
privileges associated with a women's movement having direct access to
state power and intimately linked to a broad-based political party capable
of mobilizing masses of people, and a party and government more
sympathetic to women's equality than any in Nicaraguan history. Other (2)
strengths were the impressive political and organizing skills women
activists learned in the heat of the struggle against the dictatorship and the
Contras and in the process of attempting mass mobilization and social
change.

The weaknesses included restrictions on the autonomy of party-affili-
ated women's organizations, the subordination of gender-specific demands when "national unity" was seen as a priority, and the party *weakness*
leadership's tendency alternately to embrace and then suppress a more
explicitly feminist discourse. Some of the weaknesses derived from the
overthrow of a dictatorship without a clear understanding of the roots of
women's oppression or a consensus about strategies for overcoming it.
Others originated in outdated Marxist conceptions about the relationship
of politics to economics in strategies for change (conceptions the Sandinistas attempted to challenge in practice more than in theory) and a lack of
models for revolutionary women's organizations in the Third World
context.

For every women's movement that aspires to state power as part of a
broader movement for fundamental change, whether through elections or
revolution, the Nicaraguan experience is rich in theoretical and political
insights. The case is important as well for a broader understanding of the
relationship of feminism to political parties and democracy.

The Nicaraguan Revolution and the Marxist Tradition

An important watershed of the Nicaraguan women's movement during
the Sandinista period was the announcement of the Sandinista Front's
programmatic position on women's organizing on International Wom-
en's Day, March 8, 1987. The statement, or "Proclama," as it was
known, was the culmination of two years of discussion and debate at

every level of the Front as well as in the popular organizations affiliated with it (rural and urban trade unions, professional and student associations, the military, the women's association, and so on) and by the public at large (McArthur 1987a, 1987b; Murguialday Martínez 1987).

Within the Proclama were implicit theoretical assumptions and concepts about politics, gender, and economic change. It accepted the view, put forth by Sandinista feminists, that political and ideological gains can be made by women even in the context of material shortages and the need for broad political unity. Implicitly, it seemed to accept the argument that, at each stage of the revolutionary process, some form of gender-specific or feminist struggle could and should be waged, even if the economic conditions did not exist to solve many of women's problems.[1] This position was consistent with a more basic Sandinista principle that political and ideological struggles can themselves become material forces in the process of revolutionary transformation (Núñez 1981).

In according importance to politics and ideology in addition to the economic infrastructure, the leadership of the Nicaraguan revolution departed from the economism and mechanical "stageism" of Stalinist-period Marxist thinking (Anderson 1976; Vogel 1981, 1983) in favor of a more dialectical approach influenced by European Marxists such as Antonio Gramsci, and Latin American socialists such as José Carlos Mariátegui and Carlos Fonseca Amador, cofounder of the Frente Sandinista de Liberación Nacional (Sandinista Front for National Liberation, or FSLN) (Hodges 1986). This more flexible version of Marxism, based on an awareness of the complexity and unevenness of Latin American societies and a commitment to pluralism, democracy, and mass participation in the transition to socialism (Bengelsdorf 1986; Lowy 1986; Saul 1986), was seen by Nicaraguan feminists as more compatible with modern feminists' arguments about the dialectical nature of production and reproduction, class and gender, and the ideological and economic spheres of social reality (Barrett 1980), and with women's right to self-organization (Brenner 1980; Molyneux 1982), than traditional Marxist thought.

Some elements of the new Marxism in Latin America were embraced by the Cuban revolution, but the emphasis on political pluralism and popular democracy became an important foundation of the Nicaraguan revolution, in part because it came to power through a more prolonged grassroots struggle against the dictatorship that required high levels of mass organization and in part because of lessons learned from the Cuban experience. In addition, the Latin American and world political climate was much different in 1979 than it was in 1959 (Burbach and Núñez 1987). These factors combined with the numerically and strategically important role Nicaraguan women played in the last two years of the anti-Somoza struggle, compared to a minimal role in Cuba, and the willingness of the revolution to interact with feminists from other countries. The situation in Nicaragua in the first part of the Sandinista decade seemed unique in the history of Third World revolutions. Important changes in the social structure beginning before the dictatorship's overthrow (a high proportion of female-headed families) and in the gendered division of labor associated with the anti-Contra war (women assuming "male" jobs and public sphere roles) seemed, more than in any previous Third World revolution, to favor a form of feminism that was both consistent with the revolutionary process and supported by a wide variety of women, including the majority who were poor.

The Proclama seemed to support the view of revolutionary feminists that an apparently universal tendency for women to demobilize politically after a revolutionary movement takes power, even when urged by official policy to do otherwise, can be combated by a political will on the part of the leadership of revolutionary movements to take on the difficult and potentially controversial issues of sexist ideology and practices. Though such a commitment can conceivably arise voluntarily within the ranks of the high-level (mostly male) political leadership, it probably will be deeper and more long-lasting when it is the result of a struggle by women themselves from inside and outside the "vanguard" revolutionary organization. As part of this struggle, a political space must be created where women themselves can define their interests. Here what Maxine Molyneux (1986) calls "practical gender interests" (those interests that arise out of the prevailing gendered division of labor) can be politicized and transformed into "strategic gender interests" (those that challenge prevailing forms of gender subordination) and articulated with other aspects of women's interests (including class, race, ethnicity, and national identity) to form a platform for women's attempts to influence the process of revolutionary transition. This articulation of practical and strategic gender interests and their integration with other aspects of women's identity and structural location is what Molyneux argues constitutes "a central aspect of feminist political practice" (1986, 285) in revolutionary transformations such as the one attempted in Nicaragua.

By the time the electoral campaign that ultimately resulted in defeat was begun, however, these principles of women's revolutionary organizing were no longer dominant in the Front's leadership (if they ever were), and women were pressured to close ranks to participate in a campaign heavily laced with male symbols and generic appeals to greater sacrifices for the survival of the revolution. To understand some of the ambiguities and contradictions inherent in the Nicaraguan revolutionary experience, we must retrace the development of the Nicaraguan women's movement and the role of women within it, both those who had or developed an explicitly feminist perspective and those who were reluctant to advance feminism within a poor, Third World context.

Women against the Dictatorship

The massive participation of Nicaraguan women in the overthrow of the Somoza dictatorship was unprecedented not only in the history of Nicaragua but in the Western Hemisphere (Maier 1980; Ramírez-Horton 1982; Chinchilla 1983, 1985–86). Some of this participation was indistinguishable in form and motive from the general population's uprising against repression, corruption, poverty, and unemployment. But during the last two years of the dictatorship a large part of women's grassroots involvement in the revolution in urban neighborhoods and towns was stimulated and coordinated by the FSLN-sponsored women's organization, the Association of Women Confronting the National Problem (AMPRONAC). The significance and limitations of this first cross-class Nicaraguan women's organization become apparent in an overview of its origins, composition, and positions.

AMPRONAC emerged in late 1977 with the goal of bringing together women of different social classes and sectors, united in a basic demand of respect for human rights. As time went on, the perspective as well as the tactics of AMPRONAC grew more radical, and by the summer of 1978 the majority faction supported the broad-based FSLN-influenced coalition (the MPU, or United People's Movement) that called for the overthrow of the Somoza dictatorship (Randall 1981; Ramírez-Horton 1982; Murguialday Martínez 1988).

AMPRONAC was the most successful women's organization linked to a left revolutionary party in Latin America up to that time. A key factor in its success was its ability to take up a general issue—human rights—that affected women in a particular way and pursue it with tactics and organizational forms that came out of women's particular experiences. It was based not on the assumption that women's political consciousness was a derivative of men's, that is, the hand-me-down consciousness concept that feminists have rightly criticized (Rowbotham 1974; Rowbotham, Segal, and Wainwright 1979; Hartmann 1981) but on the assumption that women have gender-specific experiences, some of which are class-specific but others of which are shared across social classes. On the other hand, it did not have an explicitly "feminist" analysis of women's oppression, that is, one that departs from an analysis of the specificity of women's experience and proposes solutions based on this analysis. The political mobilization of women around demands based on the existing gendered division of labor reflected practical rather than strategic gender interests (Molyneux 1986), or "women's consciousness" as distinguished from "feminist consciousness" (Kaplan 1981).

The organization's founding statement did include a section titled "Women's Struggles for Their Own Emancipation" (following the section titled "Women's Struggles for the General Emancipation of the People"), which stated that in addition to the poverty and repression that women share with the population in general, women carry "a double burden of discrimination on the basis of sex . . . dependence and submission to men" (AMPRONAC program, quoted in Maier 1980, 155–56).

The primary blame for this situation of oppression was placed on the Somoza dictatorship (and implicitly capitalism), and the primary way to overcome it was for women to broaden their horizons beyond the domestic sphere and participate in AMPRONAC's struggle against the dictatorship. Only full participation of women in the political, economic, and social life of the country, the statement concluded, could guarantee "the total destruction of the system of discrimination against and oppression of women."

In theory, then, AMPRONAC criticized the isolating and alienating effect of unpaid domestic work in the home and the assumption that women's natural sphere should be narrowly equated to it. The organization argued instead that women should extend their vision beyond the family or neighborhood to the nation and struggle militantly, through a gender-specific association, to bring about an improvement in their lives, as well as the lives of others, by overthrowing the dictatorship. No vision of the future beyond this point or strategy for achieving it, however, was mentioned, nor was it acknowledged that women's economic participation in the public sphere had already been increasing significantly for some time.

In practice, many, perhaps most, of the women who responded to AMPRONAC's call to mobilize for human rights and against the dictatorship did so, at least originally, more out of a strong identification with their roles as mothers, grandmothers, and spouses than out of any critique of the gendered division of labor or their circumstances as women (Maier 1980; Randall 1981). The strength of many women's identification with their role as self-sacrificing defenders of their families, especially their children, seemed to give them the courage to violate traditional gender-role prescriptions against public activity (outside work and church) and to march into the dictatorship's jails and military barracks to demand the release of sons, daughters, husbands, lovers, and other family members (Randall 1981). While some quietly used their networks of friends and relatives to collect medical supplies or organize clinics and safe houses for armed combatants, others baked home-made explosives in their ovens and carried them in market baskets filled with fruits and vegetables to their intended targets. Still others gave interviews and made speeches (Maier 1980; Randall 1981).

In the process, the image of what women, particularly mothers, could do changed in the consciousness of the general public and in the minds of the women themselves. Together with the younger women who left home to take up arms as FSLN militants, the women in AMPRONAC won an undisputed right to participate in the process of transforming Nicaragua after the dictatorship was overthrown. The full exercise of this right, however, turned out to be limited not only by concrete conditions in women's lives (i.e., economic survival and the "double shift" for women who worked both inside and outside the home) but by a failure consistently and directly to challenge the ideology of male privilege and power reproduced in the context of the revolution. Inconsistent efforts at consciousness raising among women themselves about the roots of their subordinate status contributed to these limitations.

The Euphoria of the First Two Years

After the victory of the revolution on July 19, 1979, AMPRONAC became the Luisa Amanda Espinoza Association of Nicaraguan Women (AMNLAE), but the overall perspective of integrating women into the revolution, primarily on the basis of their existing gender roles with little explicit critique of that position, remained the same. This strategy, seemingly successful against the dictatorship, proved insufficient for sustaining the momentum of women's mobilization, let alone for transforming their subordinate status, even in the political sphere. AMNLAE and most Sandinista leaders believed in a position, later referred to as "integrationist," that women's traditionally devalued image would be transformed among men and women as a result of women's dedicated and even heroic contributions to reconstruction, resulting in greater equality. On the basis of this strategy, AMNLAE mobilized its energy behind campaigns of national reconstruction that the FSLN had defined as primary for the period. There was little discussion of how AMNLAE's efforts might be distinguished from those of other mass organizations and no theoretical discussion of the roots and specific manifestations of women's subordination in the Nicaraguan context.

AMNLAE sought to maximize women's participation in the community trials of the Somoza guardsmen, the voluntary community clean-up campaign, and the cotton and coffee harvests, and mobilized large numbers of young women as teachers for the Literacy Crusade with their mothers for logistical support. When the Literacy Crusade was over, many of the same women participated in vaccination campaigns and in nutrition, hygiene, and preventative medicine brigades. AMNLAE persuaded thousands of women to join the popular militias, and as a result of its persistence, several women's infantry battalions were formed (Deighton et al. 1983; Chinchilla 1985–86).[2]

AMNLAE also played an important role in the creation of Sandinista Defense Committees (the majority of whose members were women),[3] the production collectives and sellers' cooperatives, and childcare centers in rural and urban areas. Its delegates to the Council of State played an active and visible role in that body after its creation in May 1980, especially in the struggle to change parts of the old legal code and constitution that restricted the rights of women (McArthur 1986).

By October 1981 AMNLAE claimed a national membership of twenty-five thousand women (Deighton et al. 1983), but there were already concerns about an apparent demobilization of women on behalf of the revolution. AMNLAE defined itself as a mass-based popular organization parallel to other popular organizations, such as the Sandinista trade unions and peasant organizations, but it was unclear about any specific focus other than mobilizing women on behalf of the revolution. Throughout 1980 AMNLAE's membership grew among housewives, market women, mothers of the combatants or Sandinistas killed in the insurrection, and health and education workers who had been drawn in as a result of specific campaigns. It drew only lukewarm support, however, from Sandinista women professionals, government employees, and members of the party apparatus. Women agricultural and industrial wage workers, young women, and women in the army were noticeably absent from its ranks (Murguialday Martínez 1987).

In some cases, women activists' lack of identification with AMNLAE represented a tolerance of discrepancies between women's public and private roles among those who, in the words of one of the FSLN's highest-ranking women members, Comandante Dora María Téllez, "are members or militants eight or ten hours a day, and the rest of the time ideologically assume the traditional role of the oppressed woman and some even like it" (speech made at the First Conference of Women Leaders of the Sandinista Popular Revolution, August 1981, quoted in Fried 1981). But in other cases, the lack of enthusiasm reflected a theoretical and political difference with the strategy, a belief that the organization was not feminist or militant enough in the defense of women's rights and its critique of machismo or autonomous enough from the FSLN hierarchy in initiating ideas about strategy and tactics. AMNLAE's structures, these women argued, were more ratifying than decision making. For them, AMNLAE become equated in the popular mind with an organization of housewives and mothers of the combatants and martyrs rather than one that could lead the way in changing women's roles. What had been a source of strength in the prerevolutionary period, they believed, was now the cause of ideological and organizational weakness. AMNLAE leadership, in turn, viewed the critique of its timidity in its relationship with the FSLN as "too radical and too feminist," or "out of sync with the needs of women from the popular classes," an expression used interchangeably with "feminist" by some FSLN leaders (Murguialday Martínez 1987).

Looking back, a few women who were AMNLAE activists during this period say they were feminists from the beginning but did not feel they could or should argue the point publicly, since feminists had often been portrayed negatively as antifamily, antimale, or sexually libertine by the Latin American mass media during the 1970s (Portugal 1985). The traditional left party conception of feminism, including that of the Cuban revolutionary government since 1959, was equally negative—a bourgeois or petty bourgeois movement interested only in formal legal rights, appropriate perhaps for more developed societies, or, in its more radical forms, a movement that pitted women against men and diverted the class struggle, the success of which depended on unity (Chinchilla 1977; Maier 1985, 82–85). Others, however, say they began to identify as feminists much later as a result of their own experiences in the revolution and discussions with other feminists through conferences and international exchanges (Criquillón 1993).

The Cuban Model

The AMNLAE critics' expectation that a left revolutionary women's organization should chart an explicitly feminist agenda, take initiatives of its own, and assertively make demands on the leadership of a revolutionary party or government in the fragile early years after taking power was a relatively new one in Latin America. The Cuban Women's Federation had been organized in 1960 on the initiative of Fidel Castro himself, a year after the revolutionary government took power (Azicri 1985), without a prerevolutionary base of women's networks and organizing experience such as occurred in Nicaragua. The Cuban conception of the proper role for such an organization reflected the generally conservative international context at the time, as well as traditional Latin American and Soviet understandings of the function of a women's association. The Cuban Women's Federation was organized to carry out the directives of the revolution and to convince women that they would achieve liberation by integrating themselves into the labor force and the general revolutionary process (Rowbotham 1974; Azicri 1985). Despite the high level of consciousness about feminist issues reflected in a number of Cuban films and animated debates throughout Cuban society leading up to the adoption of the pioneering Family Code on March 8, 1975, there was never really a full-scale campaign against sexist ideology and practice. Key assumptions underlying government policy on women's work outside the home, child-bearing, the nuclear family, sexuality, and popular notions of masculinity and femininity escaped critical examination, and a tradition of top-down initiatives meant that when campaigns were undertaken to transform gender roles, they sometimes encountered resistance from women as well as men (Rowbotham 1974; Murray 1979; Greer 1985; Padula and Smith 1985; Torrents 1988).

During the first two years of its existence AMNLAE took an approach resembling the Cuban model of involving women in the overall tasks of the revolution without prior discussion of possible alternative strategies and organizational forms. By 1981, despite the hard work of its leaders and activists to attract a wide spectrum of members and increase women's participation in different sectors of society, the results were discouraging. Women in urban neighborhoods who had participated in the insurrection complained that they had less time for political activity because, now that the immediate crisis was over, their families expected them to wash and iron clothes and prepare meals on time. In some cases, these demands were made by husbands or children who were themselves actively partici-pating in the revolution. Women who were heads of households—some 34 percent of families nationally and 60 percent of those in Managua (Chinchilla 1985–86)—complained that the need to provide for their families through petty vending and informal services, as well as formal jobs, made it difficult to sustain political activity. Factory women, profes-sional women, and peasant women were participating in unions and work-related associations and, in some cases, the FSLN itself. For all these women, involvement in AMNLAE meant a double or triple militancy, for which they had little time.

The New Model

After a period of critical reevaluation AMNLAE's leadership an-nounced a change in organizing strategy and self-definition. AMNLAE no longer would be a direct membership organization parallel to other mass organizations, such as trade unions and peasant associations, but would be instead a "political-ideological social movement," a catalyst to build a broad mass movement to promote a women's agenda and women's leadership in all the revolutionary institutions and organizations. Rather than devoting its energy to building and maintaining its own organiza-tional structures, AMNLAE would encourage, support, and reinforce the efforts of women in each sector and organization and would pressure other organizations and governmental bodies to facilitate greater involvement on the part of women and support for women's issues and campaigns. It would also continue to mobilize public opinion on behalf of reforms and programs related to women (AMNLAE 1981, 1982; Fried 1981). AMNLAE did not, however, reexamine its fundamental conception of what women should be mobilized for (i.e., its relationship to feminism) or raise the issue of greater democracy and autonomy in its relationship to the FSLN.

Although no one was sure at the beginning what structures to create to implement the new approach, the change was widely applauded, since it increased the probability that AMNLAE would have a broader and more secure social base. Over the next year AMNLAE made proposals to the Council of State (the precursor of the National Assembly, the main legislative body) regarding legal-code reforms in relation to divorce, responsibility for children, familial relations, discrimination, exploitation of women in advertising, maternity leave, the conditions of women workers, and the decriminalization of abortion. It used the occasion of the proposed changes to stimulate widespread discussion about the ideology and practice of traditional male-female relations in Nicaragua, including responsibility for children and domestic labor. Extensive use was made of radio, newspapers, and television to promote public debate, and open assemblies and meetings of practically every organization and sector in the country discussed the proposals and offered feedback. During this period AMNLAE also encouraged *Barricada*, the official newspaper, to feature women who did nontraditional jobs, agitated for the inclusion of women in the draft (believing that it was the participation of women in combat alongside of men in the period of the insurrection that had most dramatically changed women's and men's attitudes about what women could do), and made extensive efforts to promote international solidarity with the Nicaraguan revolution through participation in international conferences and contacts with women from other countries.

Of these activities, the efforts to promote changes in the law governing children and families, the decriminalization of abortion, and the inclusion of women in the draft were the most controversial. Though numerous modifications were made in AMNLAE's original proposals for family law reform as a result of the grassroots discussion, the basic principles of the original proposals prevailed or were strengthened. The feudal father-right law, *patria potestad*, which gave men property rights over wives and children, was replaced by the Law of Nurturing, which mandated shared parental responsibility (*guardia compartida*) for children born in and out of wedlock and the responsibility of men living in a family unit to share domestic labor (Fried 1981; Chinchilla 1983, 1985–86; Deighton et al.

1983). This law made it possible for the court to order wages garnished for child support in cases where men were employed and formally inscribed on a payroll, but it did little to relieve the burden of domestic labor in female-headed households or traditional nuclear family units. The importance of a public debate regarding the social value of work women do in the home and the lack of a biological mandate for women's domestic labor and parenting, however, should not be underestimated. The real issue was the definition of a new standard for how men thought of women and what women expected or demanded of men.

AMNLAE lost, however, in its attempt to have women included in the draft. Many parents already objected to the mandatory conscription of young sons after so many lives had been lost in the insurrection, and it was felt that the Catholic church and the opposition political parties who were attempting to erode Sandinista support might exploit this issue to their advantage. The base committees of AMNLAE had enthusiastically supported the proposal, but the lack of broad popular support made it difficult to get solid backing from the Sandinista leadership. AMNLAE did succeed in negotiating an agreement that women could, in principle, volunteer for active duty in all-female army units, but such units were not actually formed until 1986 (Montenegro 1986). Nevertheless, large numbers of women did receive military training as members of the army reserves (there were seven all-women reserve battalions in 1982 that were later gradually dissolved into mixed units) and through service in the civilian militia, where they were trained to take over and run factories, installations, and offices in the event of war (Molyneux 1986). Almost 45 percent of an estimated fifty thousand militia members in 1984 were women. This proportion may have increased as the war against the Contras intensified.

AMNLAE also had to back off its attempt to stimulate greater discussion on the explosive issue of abortion for fear of losing support on other issues. Even more than the draft, the proposal to replace a Somoza-era law criminalizing abortion with one making it legal had to be postponed because of strong opposition from the Catholic church, conservative opposition parties, and within the ranks of Sandinista supporters who opposed abortion for religious or practical reasons.

Legalized abortion was available in most socialist countries and was not a major point of controversy in Cuba. In the Nicaraguan context, however, where the institutional Catholic church was historically stronger and more influential as a shaper of secular laws and popular culture, the issue of abortion rights for women was highly divisive, including among women themselves. This tradition, combined with many women's strong positive identity with motherhood, the desire to replace lives lost in the overthrow of the dictatorship, the association of family-planning programs with U.S. imperialism and the Somoza dictatorship, the contention of some revolutionary leaders that abortion rights were of interest only to middle- and upper-class women, and the "pronatalist" bias of some Sandinista leaders (based on positions taken by certain other postrevolutionary socialist or nationalist states [Molyneux 1982]), made it difficult for an open debate on the desirability of abortion reform to occur spontaneously. In addition, the Sandinista leadership was unwilling to risk alienating its antiabortion Catholic supporters, given the need to consolidate the heterogeneous forces supporting the revolution.

By 1983 the euphoria that followed the 1979 victory started to fade, and women's discontent with their lives was more frequently expressed. Mobilization for war against the Contras meant that the refuge in a tranquil "normal" personal life that some women had dreamed of would not be possible and that the early gains in women's health care and literacy, derived from the revolution, began to pass from memory. As a result of mobilization for the war, women's daily burdens increased without any clear promises or concrete plans for improvement in the future. Eventually, AMNLAE activists were encouraged to respond to this discontent by trying to combine women's specific demands with campaigns for national defense, but this encouragement was withdrawn when electoral campaigns began toward the end of the decade as the war was coming to a close.

A Women's Movement in the Context of War

The war took its toll on the national economy and on human and material targets in the zones of combat. Shortages appeared as a result of the U.S.-imposed blockade, internal sabotage, and diversion of resources for the war. Casualties mounted and lives were lost, some forty-six thousand between 1982 and 1987, according to official statistics (Instituto Histórico Centroamericano 1988). Previous gains in literacy and health care began to erode as a result of the fighting and population relocation in the zones of conflict.

A second massive grassroots mobilization of the population, similar to that achieved against the dictatorship, was necessary if the revolution was to survive, and the FSLN called for all popular organizations to make defense of the revolution their principal task. Early on, AMNLAE leaders interpreted this mandate to mean that public debate on a specific women's agenda for change in the legal code or on housework, domestic violence, sexuality, abortion, or the socialization of children had to be postponed. AMNLAE focused its attention once again on moral support for the mothers of combatants (who this time around were virtually all men), political work with mothers who opposed military conscription of their sons, and logistical and material support of the war (collection of materials for recycling, campaigns for saving energy and scarce goods, and so on). With most young and some older men serving as soldiers in the war zones, women became the backbone of the rear guard of the war, key links in the neighborhood civilian defense network, and increasingly important in some areas of production, particularly agriculture. At the same time, the war meant that many women faced greater demands on their time and more contradictions in their lives than ever before. Whether or not they had formal jobs or sources of income, women continued to carry out their traditional responsibilities for the daily reproduction of families; now, however, their job was made more difficult by frozen wages, inflation, black-market speculation, shortages, the continuing scarcity of childcare and maternity care, and the persistence of machismo.

During the fall 1984 campaign for Nicaragua's first national elections since the revolution, women expressed their discontent to FSLN representatives in urban neighborhoods and rural towns. The FSLN was aware that frustrated housewives had lent support to right-wing efforts to reverse progressive change elsewhere in Latin America (Crummett 1977), and there were indications that support among women working outside their homes might also be weakening. Women constituted 62 percent of the electorate and were the mainstay of the domestic front of the anti-Contra war. Since sacrifices on behalf of the war effort depended on voluntary efforts, and since the Sandinistas still had to compete within a pluralistic political system for hegemony over the revolutionary process, the discontent that women were beginning to express was taken seriously. The FSLN called for a critical reevaluation of its approach to organizing women in the context of the war, with the primary focus on the strategy guiding the work of AMNLAE.

Although AMNLAE was defined from the beginning as organically autonomous from the government and the FSLN, in reality the relationship between AMNLAE and the Sandinista Front was a relatively hierarchical one, possibly even more so than that between the Front and other mass organizations. Critics have suggested that AMNLAE leaders usually were chosen de facto by the Front and that campaigns and priorities were often dictated by it, even though some degree of consultation between the leadership and the base was always characteristic of the Front's style. In return, the leadership was, not surprisingly, passive in pushing the concerns of AMNLAE activists when they differed from perceived leadership perspectives, even when an aggressive campaign might have modified those views (Criquillón 1993; Quandt 1993).

Some women affiliated with the FSLN who were strongly committed to women's organizing and consciously identified as feminists maintained their affiliation with AMNLAE and periodically waged campaigns to revitalize it, but also fought for women's agendas in other (usually male-female) organizations. They, along with some men, wanted a more explicitly feminist strategic perspective in AMNLAE and criticized what they saw as too passive a relationship among AMNLAE's leadership, the government, and the FSLN. These women, also Sandinista cadre of long duration, often worked in governmental offices, organs of the Front, or as professional staff in other mass organizations of young people, professionals, or industrial or agricultural workers. Increasingly, their perspective was echoed by some of the women peasants, workers, and young people who were emerging as leaders in their respective mass organizations.

Significantly, the strongest critique came from women who had worked with the Association of Agricultural Workers (ATC) as members or professional staff. Two years before AMNLAE convened assemblies calling for a reevaluation of its strategy, the ATC's mostly male leadership embarked on a program to "make women's rights a union priority and to promote programs to help women enter 'male only' jobs and deepen their participation in union affairs" (Jaquith and Kopec 1987). Since women in the Nicaraguan countryside had traditionally been the most subordinated and marginalized, the ATC campaign's initial successes in encouraging women's leadership and activism where virtually none had existed before, and its beginning analysis of how gender relates to class and feminism to social revolution, served as persuasive evidence that a feminist strategy consistent with the goals of the revolution and appropriate for the Nicaraguan context could be developed (CIERA 1984; Nebbia 1986a; Zalaquett 1987; McArthur 1988; White 1989).

Based on the ATC experience, feminists argued that mobilization for the war effort and feminism could and should be combined: women would be much more willing to sacrifice for the revolution if they could be assured that the importance of their contributions to defense were recognized and the gains they had made in transcending traditional gender roles would not be reversed once the soldiers came home. Mobilizing for war should not rule out meetings of women to discuss the concrete conditions of their daily lives and might also be a source of creative solutions to problems. More generally, feminist revolutionaries urged that priorities for the work of the revolution should be decided more democratically, so that women of different social sectors and personal situations could influence the agenda before it was formulated (Murguialday Martínez 1987; Criquillón 1993).

The AMNLAE leaders were reportedly surprised to discover how critical their constituency was of the failure to discuss fully issues such as domestic violence, machismo, rape, contraception, and abortion. They agreed, in principle, to adopt a new approach to the work, one that would be based on groups of women with similar interests meeting together to discuss their problems and proposing concrete actions to the organization as a whole. In short, the demands of different sectors of women would set the organization's priorities, not the leadership.

In April 1985 AMNLAE called an assembly to discuss women's demands related to sexuality, workplace discrimination, and domestic violence. Tensions with the FSLN were evident as its representatives urged AMNLAE not to abandon its work with the mothers of combatants. As a compromise, AMNLAE established "interest groups," each of which would have a specific focus of work. Betweeen April and September more than forty thousand women in six hundred base assemblies met to generate proposals, discuss ideas, and elect the more than one thousand delegates who would attend the Second National Assembly in September 1985. During this period it seemed that, for the first time, women constituted a real pressure group capable of making demands on governmental agencies, mass organizations, and the FSLN. One participant in the Assembly called it the "birth of the Nicaragua women's liberation movement . . . its entrance onto the political stage of the Sandinista revolution" (Murguialday Martínez 1988, 63). Another called it "the first time in the history of the women's movement in Nicaragua [where] we discussed our problems and obstacles in terms of gender . . . a beautiful moment" (Criquillón 1993, 18–19).

Forging a Women's Agenda within the Revolution

Energized by new leadership and armed with the enthusiastic mandate it had received at the Second National Assembly for integrating more explicitly feminist demands into its overall strategy, AMNLAE began to play a more aggressive and visible role in educating Nicaraguan society about workplace discrimination, sexual harassment, rape, domestic violence, and the need for sex education, contraception, and greater institutionalization of avenues for women's power and influence. One of these new avenues was the creation of an Office on Women, strategically located in the president's office so that it could have input into all stages of national planning. Data collected and publicized through the Office on Women as of 1988 showed that women's labor outside the home had increased as a result of the war to the point that women were the majority of workers in the textile, clothing, leather and shoes, food, and pharmaceutical industries and constituted up to 80 percent of the labor force of many factories, although generally in the lowest-paid, least-skilled jobs. Women made up 34 percent of all agricultural labor and more than half the harvest-time workforce in coffee, cotton, and tobacco, three of the most important foreign-exchange-earning, agricultural export crops. Women made up 40 percent of the membership of the ATC but only 15 percent of its local leadership and less than 10 percent of farm cooperative and collective members. They were also a substantial proportion of workers in the informal sector, primarily petty vendors and domestic workers. Women who worked outside the home spent 56 percent of their total work day in domestic labor, compared to only 9 percent for male workers, resulting in an average eighteen-hour work day for women agricultural workers and a sixteen-hour day for women industrial workers. Most working women did not have access to childcare centers (Jaquith 1987; Galinsky 1988, 1989).

Of the women who sought assistance at AMNLAE's new legal office for women, 51 percent were victims of domestic violence. The rate of female-headed households continued to be high, especially among women who worked outside the home, and women still complained of men's lack of responsibility for the children they helped conceive, despite the new constitution that made both biological parents equally responsible (Jaquith 1986a, 1986b; Oficina Legal de la Mujer—AMNLAE 1986; Pérez Alemán and Siu 1986; Rodríguez 1987; Pérez et al. 1988).

This documentation of the reality of Nicaraguan women's situation seven years after the revolution began to be discussed by popular organizations, governmental institutions, and soldiers in the army. As a result of these discussions, many men were surprised to discover that the Nicaraguan revolution had arrived on their doorsteps. Just as important, women at all levels were confronting their organizations and government officials with the need to act more deliberately, especially on the problems that did not require major outlays of nonexistent resources (White 1988a; DelGadillo 1989; Galinsky 1989).

The confrontations occurred in open assemblies and sometimes on national television. Armed with documentation from the medical community, for example, AMNLAE began to publicize the increasing number of women being admitted to the Women's Hospital as a result of complications from self-induced or lay midwife–assisted abortions.[4] Advocates of a liberalized abortion policy pointed out that saving these women's lives and repairing the damage from botched abortions were already adding to the shortage of public health facilities and supplies.

Such arguments were not without their opponents among the Sandinista leadership, however. As late as 1987, in a "Face the People" meeting with President Daniel Ortega and Minister of Health Dora María Téllez, called to mark the tenth anniversary of the founding of AMNLAE and held just six months after the much-praised official statement by the FSLN on women, Ortega's response to audience comments in favor of abortion upset many women activists. The president said, "The ones fighting in the front lines against this aggression are young men. One way of depleting our youth is to promote the sterilization of women in Nicaragua—just imagine what would happen then—or to promote a policy of abortion. The problem is that the woman is the one who reproduces. The man can't play that role . . . some women, aspiring to be liberated, decide not to bear children. A woman who does so negates her own continuity and the continuity of the human species" (Jaquith and Kopec 1987, 9).

The remarks, although personal rather than official, were disturbing not only for their moralism but for the seeming implication that "women have been passive bystanders in the revolutionary process and must now therefore discharge their debt to the nation by having babies" (Molyneux 1988, 123). Other high-ranking Sandinista leaders, however, such as Carlos Núñez, president of the National Assembly, made it clear that they supported decriminalization of abortion and also stricter penalties for sexual abuse (White 1988b).

Throughout this period (1985–87), the high point of women's organizing during the Sandinista decade, conflicts and tensions between AMNLAE and the FSLN remained in the background, and lack of clarity continued on the part of AMNLAE leadership as to how to transform the new perspective on working with women in the different sectors into an efficient and effective practice. These were the worst years of the Contra war, and its pressures were keenly felt. It was not immediately obvious which short-term feminist strategies would be viable and attractive for different sectors of women affected by the war as well as by class and gender inequality. AMNLAE suffered from an unwieldy internal bureaucracy, and women organized in the different sectors resented the suggestion that AMNLAE organizers would be sent out to "guide" them when some of them already had experience in promoting women's demands in that sector (in the ATC and the Sandinista Workers' Confederation [CST], for example). By June 1988, at the Assembly of AMNLAE Leaders, it was clear that the organization once again was experiencing paralysis. An important part of the solution, AMNLAE leaders finally concluded, was greater internal democracy within the women's movement. Political and electoral processes would be opened up, culminating in the convening of AMNLAE's national assembly and the first open election of a new leadership committee by the membership. During the following year it became clear that women with an explicitly feminist orientation were destined to capture most if not all the leadership positions to be voted on. But in May 1989, shortly before AMNLAE's national assembly and elections were scheduled, the order came down from the FSLN that all priorities and decision making would be subordinate to the FSLN's new emphasis on unity as a result of its decision to move up presidential and legislative elections. AMNLAE's elections never took place, and temporary leaders named by the FSLN were announced for the organization.

The Conservative Agenda and Women's Struggle for Equality

Although the lack of exit polls and the ideological heterogeneity of the opposition coalition parties in the 1990 elections make it difficult to draw any definitive conclusions about which subgroups of the population voted for which candidate and why, most observers cite two issues above all others as common denominators in coalescing the opposition: the precarious state of the economy and the continuing war against the Contras. But embedded in these two overarching concerns are other important political questions, particularly the ambivalence of women about the sacrifices they were being asked to make for the revolution and criticisms of the style of leadership of the FSLN and its relationship to the organized and unorganized masses it was supposed to represent. Both these issues echoed criticisms previously raised by Sandinista feminists in the context of strategies for women's organizing.

Surveys conducted throughout the campaign up to the thirty-day preelection limit suggested an important gender dimension in the vote. Young women (twenty-five years old and younger), particularly professional urban working women, were among the Sandinista Front's strongest supporters. Conversely, women who did not work outside the home, particularly those who were older, lived in rural areas (especially in zones of conflict or the Atlantic coast), or were strongly religious, were among the weakest in their support for the Sandinista government. Controls for other variables, such as age and level of education, might have reduced (or even erased) these differences, but anecdotal evidence seemed to corroborate the existence of weak Sandinista support among the groups of women identified by the pollsters.[5]

Although the winning coalition's platform was vague on most points and silent altogether on issues of women's equality and liberation, sections of the "social program" outlined in its platform suggested a traditional conservative ideology of the family and women's roles. It called for "greater respect for parents on the part of children" and "the recuperation of the moral and social function of the Nicaraguan family." The only specific reference to women urged that "programs be directed to women with the purpose of strengthening their sense of dignity and integration into family, economic, social, and political functions."

Once the Chamorro government came to power, its fundamentally conservative and antifeminist character on issues relating to women, sexuality, and the family became more visible and concrete. It blamed the FSLN for "the destruction of the family," "loose" sexuality, a high divorce rate, and the increase in women working outside the home, and it advocated instead, through government programs and school textbooks, traditional family gender roles, the rhythm method as the only acceptable form of contraception, and procreation as the fundamental purpose of sex. Government economic policies have resulted in extra hardships for female-headed families (81.4 percent of which live in poverty, 37.5 percent of them in extreme poverty), and the imposition of fees on previously free public education will disproportionately affect the education of young women, particularly in rural areas. The message to feminists, poor women, and progressive women in general was clear: "The Frente lost and so did you" (Quandt 1990).

At the same time, the removal of the Sandinistas from government relieved them of the dual and frequently contradictory role of controlling and reactivating the economy while attempting to pursue redistributive goals of economic and social justice and of having to conciliate a hostile Catholic church hierarchy. Thus, the possibility increased of their playing a leadership role in a revitalized mass movement.

While the mass movement, and particularly the women's movement, has grown and diversified (partially through the establishment of a multiplicity of institutes and service centers supported by external public and private institutions, mostly from western Europe and Canada), the Front has lost its hegemonic leadership role because of internal divisions over strategy, tactics, and party reform combined with widespread public criticism over the *piñata* (the scramble of top government officials for individual titles to government-owned property and automobiles). Criticisms of top-down leadership styles, sectarianism, past infringements on autonomy, and the failure of the Front to extend internal democracy through direct elections of the National Directorate have emboldened grassroots movements to experiment with new forms of organizing and expanded notions of democracy and autonomy. A wide variety of new women's groups, centers, and institutes, including gay rights groups and women's cultural groups with an explicitly feminist focus, have led the way in asserting their right to determine their own agendas and leadership even while supporting the general goals and ideals of the original revolution. This boldness sometimes has led to serious tensions in their relationship to the FSLN and to those groups that remain more closely tied to the FSLN leadership position. In the case of women, the polarization between AMNLAE and independent feminists is particularly acute. AMNLAE remains closely affiliated with the FSLN, asserts virtually no autonomy, and continues to blame women's problems on the government or "unequal gender roles" rather than on machismo or patriarchy. Independent feminists believe women's resistance to male domination must be at the center of their work, whether in autonomous or mixed organizations. AMNLAE, together with the ATC and the CST, important Sandinista-affiliated organizations that once had a leadership role in the women's movement, accuses the feminist radicals of not focusing their efforts primarily on the desperate economic concerns of women from the "popular sectors," while independent feminists charge AMNLAE with subordinating women to the leadership of men opposed to or, at best, unschooled in the importance of feminist organizing strategies.

Toward an Autonomous Nicaraguan Women's Movement

While AMNLAE responded to the Sandinistas' electoral loss with calls for unity and an affirmation of its existing vision, AMNLAE's critics demanded new discussions about the relationship of gender to citizenship and democracy and a major reassessment of strategies for building a Nicaraguan women's movement. When AMNLAE held a tense Fourth Assembly, on March 9 and 10, 1991, some five hundred women who were not invited to the assembly (either because they were not affiliated with AMNLAE or because they worked with women's centers or autonomous groups rather than unions or grassroots organizations) made their first public appearance as an independent women's movement through the "52 percent festival," a three-day event with exhibits of the groups' work, forums for debate, music, and theater, attended by an estimated three thousand people. The event marked "the existence of two women's movements . . . on the one side AMNLAE, no longer an 'umbrella' where all the women's groups congregate, but the expression of only a section of working class women, marketplace vendors and mothers of heroes and martyrs; on the other, the rest of the women's groups, open to constructing their own forms of organization and struggle" (Vásquez and Murguialday, 1991).

The power of convocation of the new, loosely knit network of centers, programs, groups, and individuals was demonstrated a little less than a year later in the February 1992 national conference to prepare for the First Central American Women's Encounter, to be held in Nicaragua on March 23 to 27. Under the banner of "Unity in Diversity," more than eight hundred women gathered to voice criticisms of the past and discuss the future of the Nicaraguan women's movement. The gathering, almost three times the size expected by organizers, provided a truly open forum in which women of different political positions and affiliations, including individuals affiliated with AMNLAE and the governing UNO coalition, could put forth their views, one without a predetermined agenda and leadership slate. Although some of the participants wanted to concretize the new direction in an organization with formal leadership, others argued that it was better to proceed slowly in order to transcend the cynicism and mistrust left from the past. Conference participants agreed to establish seven action networks and work together on three national actions. Women who had come to the conference despite their suspicions that it was just "another party activity" left enthusiastic about the possibility of building a more autonomous women's movement, one that encourages creativity, diversity, and grassroots participation.

Despite the enthusiasm generated by the conference, which was officially boycotted by AMNLAE, ATC, and CST (although individuals from those organizations attended), relations among different sectors of the post-Sandinista Nicaraguan women's movement have been tense, making it difficult to work in stable coalitions. Nevertheless, the vitality of the movement in this period of extreme economic crisis and political confusion cannot be denied.

Implications of the Nicaraguan Experience for Feminism

Progress in unraveling complex theoretical problems, such as the relationship of class to gender and race or ethnicity, is often connected to the acceleration of experience that occurs in the course of social movements, in particular the breaking of old patterns and the experimentation with new relationships or linkages that happen in the course of a revolution. The efforts of feminist revolutionaries in Nicaragua to forge a feminism that is both popular and revolutionary raises important questions about the relationship of feminism to the state, political parties, and democracy, and about the theoretical and political assumptions underlying strategies for women's organizing.

Nicaraguan feminism has, for example, shown that the seemingly contradictory dichotomy between material conditions and politics and ideology, such that the latter two can advance only as a mechanical response to the former, is more apparent than real. There is no question that material conditions are a limiting factor or parameter for the character of societies, classes, and individual lives, but politics and ideology can, in their own ways, be transformed into a material force that increases the possibility and probability of finding solutions to material problems. In a study of the effects of change on rural women, for example, Nicaraguan women scholar-activists concluded: "We are convinced that the contradictions between production and reproduction, and class struggle and the struggle for women's liberation must and can be resolved. Capitalism is patriarchal, the life of a woman is an integrated whole, and women's struggle for emancipation is an irreducible part of all peoples' struggle for their right to self-determination, democracy, and peace" (Padilla, Murguialday, and Criquillón 1987, 141).

Feminism, though often appearing to intensify social conflict over the short run, has the potential to strengthen the class struggle over the long run without being reduced to it. The Nicaraguan ATC made this point during the Sandinista period in its call for a strategic alliance between the women's movement and working-class organizations such as unions: "This revolutionary thinking of the women helps us a lot. They want a society without patriarchy, without relations of power between men and women, where political leadership is given under conditions of equality where it does not matter whether one is man or woman . . . we believe that the antipatriarchal struggle will be a contribution when we define this socialism of ours, our own socialism" (Criquillón 1988, 35).

This attempt to specify the relationship between class and gender, between antipatriarchal struggle and socialism, brings to mind the comments Sheila Rowbotham made in the conclusion to her book on women, feminism, and social revolution two decades ago:

> The connection between the oppression of women and the central discovery of Marxism, the class exploitation of the worker in capitalism, is still forced. It is still coming out of the heads of women like me as an idea. . . . I believe that the only way in which their combination will become living and evident is through a movement of working-class women, in conscious resistance to both, alongside black, yellow and brown women struggling against racialism and imperialism. We are far from such a movement now. But when the connection between class, colonial and sexual oppression becomes commonplace we will understand it, not as an abstract imposed concept, but as something coming out of the experience of particular women. (1974, 247)

Conclusion

Neither socialism nor revolution appears to be on the immediate agenda in Nicaragua. It shares with many Third World countries a rapidly deteriorating economy, external debt, and a high degree of political and personal insecurity. But the revolution has left Nicaragua with a unique political culture that continues to influence public policies and social movements. Two decades of effort by some Nicaraguans to forge a feminism that is both popular and revolutionary have had a lasting effect on Nicaraguan society and on other women's movements in Central

America and the world. Many important concepts and relationships, such as the interaction of popular organizations and political parties, and the character of democracy in the context of a revolutionary transition, have not yet been fully defined, not only for Nicaragua but for other movements as well. The future of a popular revolutionary feminist movement in Nicaragua depends, in part, on the outcome of these discussions and social experiments. Twenty years of revolutionary experience in Nicaragua can serve as a basis, I believe, for beginning the synthesis Rowbotham sought.

NOTES

1. The recognition of a need to wage a conscious campaign against sexist ideology and practice in government policies as well as in the daily practice of revolutionaries clearly differentiated the Sandinista Front's position from a traditional Latin American left argument that sexism is a problem of "ideologically and culturally backward sectors of society" but is "on its way to being solved among 'advanced revolutionaries.' " The Front also departed from the notion that potentially explosive discussions about sexism, especially in personal relations, should be avoided until a revolutionary movement is no longer under external attack or until the economic conditions exist to incorporate women fully into paid labor and to socialize household labor (i.e., until socialism has been fully established). The Front's position deviated from those formulations that assume that women's current lack of equal participation is wholly due to their "backwardness," which, in turn, is the product of a history of exclusion. Here the Front ignored or underestimated the continuing obstacles represented by machismo and sexism.

2. Men and women fought side by side during the insurrection, but after the overthrow army officials complained that an overall relaxation of discipline led to problems in mixed units, including a large number of young women with unplanned pregnancies. On their recommendation, and perhaps as a result of Cuban military trainers' advice, training for men and women in the regular army became separate. After some initial protests that they were now being assigned to infrastructure and support tasks rather than combat, the women's units received battlefield assignments. Nicaragua was apparently the only socialist country in which women served in combat units. Because promotions to positions of higher political responsibility often come as a result of military service in times of war, many women activists in Nicaragua were concerned about the effect that lower numbers of women in active-duty service might ultimately have on their representation in top-level leadership.

3. Sandinista Defense Committees (CDS) have their origins in the period of the insurrection when people organized by blocks or neighborhoods to give concrete support to efforts to overthrow the dictatorship. After the overthrow they carried out a wide variety of tasks: distribution of relief supplies, housing reconstruction, reestablishment of services, and vigilance against the Somocistas, speculation, hoarding, high prices, and high rents. They also provided voluntary labor to

repair streets and build schools, established community drugstores and clinics, and conducted campaigns against delinquency and prostitution and on behalf of the census, first aid, and other health education, and for neighborhood beautification. The defense committees were open to anyone above the age of thirteen. In 1985 45 percent of CDS members were women; in 1987 67 percent were women.

4. The national chief of police, Doris Tijerno, took the position that no one would be prosecuted for performing or undergoing an abortion, but abortions performed in public hospitals were legal only in the case of rape or danger to the mother's life, and the illegal status of abortion contributed to its continued stigma. The same doctors who refused to do abortions in public hospitals often did them in private practice for fees that poor women could not afford.

5. In a poll conducted by the U.S. agency Greenberg & Lake in January 1990, for example, 41.6 percent of the polled homemakers who did not work outside the home indicated support for Ortega, compared to 51 percent of men polled. Women who worked outside the home, however, indicated the highest level of support for the Sandinista candidate of any of the three groups: 59 percent. Correspondingly, housewives expressed the highest level of support for Chamorro (28 percent, compared to 22 percent for men and working women) and represented the highest level of undecided voters (20 percent, compared to 16 percent for men and 12 percent for working women). The remaining percentages making up the total reflect nonresponses or support for minor parties.

Although this poll, like the majority of those conducted, did not accurately predict the outcome of the campaign, and although controls for age and education might have reduced the differences, the significant variations it found among these three categories of voters are replicated consistently in all the polls that were conducted, so much so that the inside joke among pollsters was that in Nicaragua there were not two genders but three.

REFERENCES

AMNLAE. 1981. *Balance presentado en el IV anniversario* (Balance presented on the fourth anniversary). September.

———. 1982. Documentos de la Primera Asamblea Nacional (Documents from the First National Assembly). December.

Anderson, Perry. 1976. *Considerations on Western Marxism.* London: NLB.

Azicri, Max. 1985. "Women's Development through Revolutionary Mobilization." In *The Cuba Reader: The Making of Revolutionary Society,* ed. Philip Brenner, William M. Leogrande, Donna Rick, and Daniel Siegel, 457–471. New York: Grove Press.

Barrett, Michèle. 1980. *Women's Oppression Today: The Marxist Feminist Encounter.* London: Verso.

Barricada Internacional. 1987. "Emancipation for Everyone." March 26.

Bengelsdorf, Carollee. 1986. "State and Society in the Transition to Socialism: The Theoretical Legacy." In *Transition and Development: Problems of Third World Socialism,* ed. Richard Fagen, Carmen Diana Deere, and José Luis Coraggio, 192–211. New York: Monthly Review.

Brenner, Johanna. 1980. "Women's Self-Organization: A Marxist Justification." *Against the Current* (Fall): 24–32.

Burbach, Roger, and Orlando Núñez. 1987. *Fire in the Americas: Forging a Revolutionary Agenda.* New York: Verso.

Chinchilla, Norma Stoltz. 1977. "Mobilizing Women: Revolution in the Revolution." *Latin American Perspectives* 4:83–102.

———. 1983. "Women in Revolutionary Movements: The Case of Nicaragua." In *Revolution in Central America,* ed. Stanford Central America Action Network, 422–434. Boulder, Colo.: Westview.

———. 1985–86. "Women in the Nicaraguan Revolution." *Nicaraguan Perspectives* 11 (Winter): 18–26.

CIERA. 1984. *La mujer en las cooperativas agropecuarias en Nicaragua* (Women in agricultural cooperatives in Nicaragua). Managua, Nicaragua: MID-INRA.

Criquillón, Ana. 1988. "Acabemos con el mito del sexo débil" (Ending the myth of the weaker sex). *Terra Nuova Forum* 13 (June): 31–35.

———. 1993. *The Nicaraguan Women's Movement: Feminist Reflections from Inside.* Washington, D.C.: EPICA.

Crummett, María de los Angeles. 1977. "El poder femenino: The Mobilization of Women against Socialism in Chile." *Latin American Perspectives* 4 (Fall): 103–113.

Deighton, Jane, Rossana Horsley, Sarah Stewart, and Cathy Cain. 1983. *Sweet Ramparts: Women in Revolutionary Nicaragua.* Birmingham, England: War on Want/Nicaraguan Solidarity Campaign.

DelGadillo, Theresa. 1989. "Nicaragua Seminar Discusses Problems Facing Young People." *The Militant,* April 21.

Fried, Harry. 1981. "Nicaraguan Women Demand Rights: Battling Sexism Remains a Key Task." *The Guardian,* December 21.

FSLN. 1987. *El FSLN y la mujer en la revolución popular Sandinista* (The FSLN and women in the Sandinista popular revolution). Managua, Nicaragua: Editorial Vanguardia. (Excerpts in English in *The Militant,* May 22.)

Galinsky, Seth. 1988. "Women Farmworkers Meet in Nicaragua: Conference Urges Fight against Sexual Harassment, for Low Cost Contraception." *The Militant,* December 16.

———. 1989. "Inside a Nicaraguan Garment Factory." *The Militant,* March 10.

Greer, Germaine. 1985. "Cuba." In *Women: A World Report,* ed. Debbie Taylor, 271–292. London: Methuen.

Hartmann, Heidi. 1981. "The Unhappy Marriage of Marxism and Feminism: Toward a More Progressive Union." In *Women and Revolution: A Discussion of the Unhappy Marriage of Marxism and Feminism,* ed. Lydia Sargent, 1–42. Boston: South End Press.

Hodges, Donald C. 1986. *Intellectual Foundations of the Nicaraguan Revolution.* Austin: University of Texas Press.

Instituto Histórico Centroamericano. 1988. *Envío.* Washington, D.C.

Jaquith, Cindy. 1986a. "Debaten el derecho al aborto legal" (Debate over legalization of abortion). *Perspectiva mundial,* January.

————. 1986b. "Legalization of Abortion Discussed." *Intercontinental Press,* February 10.

————. 1987. "The Status of Women in Nicaragua Today." *The Militant,* February 20.

Jaquith, Cindy, and Roberto Kopec. 1987. "Advances, Challenges for Women in the New Nicaragua." *The Militant,* November 20.

————. 1988. "¿Cómo impulsar derechos de la mujer?" (How can the rights of women be advanced?). *Perspectiva mundial,* January.

Kaplan, Temma. 1981. "Female Consciousness and Collective Action: The Case of Barcelona, 1910–1918." In *Feminist Theory: A Critique of Ideology,* ed. Nannerl Keohane, Michele Rosaldo, and Barbara Gelphi, 55–76. Chicago: University of Chicago Press.

Lowy, Michel. 1986. "Mass Organization, Party, and State: Democracy in the Transition to Socialism." In *Transition and Development: Problems of Third World Socialism,* ed. Richard R. Fagen, Carmen Diana Deere, and José Luis Coraggio, 264–279. New York: Monthly Review.

McArthur, Harvey. 1986. "El pueblo debate una nueva constitución" (The people debate a new constitution). *Perspectiva mundial,* September.

————. 1987a. "Nicaraguan Women Hold National Assembly." *The Militant,* May 1.

————. 1987b. "Debaten lucha por derechos de la mujer" (Debate over the struggle for women's rights). *Perspectiva mundial,* July.

————. 1988. "Brigade Is a First for Peasant Women." *The Militant,* February 19.

Maier, Elizabeth. 1980. *Nicaragua: La mujer en la revolución* (Nicaragua: Women in the revolution). Managua, Nicaragua: Ediciones de Cultura Popular.

————. 1985. *Las Sandinistas* (The Sandinistas). Managua, Nicaragua: Ediciones de Cultura Popular.

Militant, The. 1987. "Revolution Opens Door to Women's Equality." May 22.

Molyneux, Maxine. 1982. "Socialist Societies Old and New: Progress toward Women's Emancipation?" *Monthly Review* 34 (3): 56–100.

————. 1986. "Mobilization without Emancipation? Women's Interests, State, and Revolution." In *Transition and Development: Problems of Third World Socialism,* ed. Richard R. Fagen, Carmen Diana Deere, and José Luis Coraggio, 280–302. New York: Monthly Review.

————. 1988. "The Politics of Abortion in Nicaragua: Revolutionary Pragmatism or Feminism in the Realm of Necessity?" *Feminist Review* 29:114–132.

Montenegro, Sofía. 1986. "Integran a las mujeres en el ejército" (Women join the army). *Perspectiva mundial,* June 23.

Murguialday Martínez, Clara. 1987. *Ser mujer en Nicaragua: Testimonios de mujeres haciendo revolución* (To be a woman in Nicaragua: Testimonies of women who are making revolution). Montevideo, Uruguay: Imprenta Cunatai.

————. 1988. "Una brecha en el muro del machismo: Diez años de lucha de las mujeres nicaragüenses" (A break in the wall of machismo: Ten years of struggle by Nicaraguan women). *Terra Nuova Forum* 13 (June): 9–65.

Murray, Nicola. 1979. "Socialism and Feminism: Women and the Cuban Revolution, Part Two." *Feminist Review* 3:99–108.

Navas, María Candelaria. 1985. "Los movimientos femeninos en Centroamérica: 1970–1983" (Feminist movements in Central America). In *Movimientos populares en Centroamérica* (Popular movements in Central America), ed. Danile Camacho and Rafael Menjívar, 200–237. Centroamérica: EDUCA.

Nebbia, Ruth. 1986a. "Encuentro de trabajadoras del campo" (Encounter for women agricultural workers). *Perspectiva mundial,* November.

———. 1986b. "La mujer en la defensa por conciencia" (Women join the national defense out of sense of duty). *Perspectiva mundial,* July 7.

Núñez, Orlando. 1981. "La ideología como fuerza material" (Ideology as a material force). In *Clases sociales en Nicaragua* (Social classes in Nicaragua) (no editor listed). Managua, Nicaragua: Ediciones Blas Real Espinales.

Oficina Legal de la Mujer—AMNLAE. 1986. *Aportes al análisis del maltrato en la relación de pareja* (Notes for the analysis of domestic violence). Managua, Nicaragua.

Padilla, Martha Luz, Clara Murguialday, and Ana Criquillón 1987. "Impact of the Sandinista Agrarian Reform on Rural Women's Subordination." In *Rural Women and State Policy: Feminist Perspectives on Latin American Agricultural Development,* ed. Carmen Diana Deere and Magdalena León, 124–141. Boulder, Colo.: Westview.

Padula, Alfred, and Lois Smith. 1985. "Women in Socialist Cuba, 1959–1984." In *Cuba: Twenty-Five Years of Revolution, 1959–1984,* ed. Sandor Halebsky and John M. Kirk, 79–92. New York: Praeger.

Pallais, Desiree. 1988. "Para la plena paridad se necesitará más tiempo" (For complete equality more time is needed). *Terra Nuova Forum* 13 (June): 66–68.

Pérez, Paola, et al. 1988. "Mujer campesina y organización en Nicaragua: ¿Participación productiva sin participación social?" (Peasant women and organization in Nicaragua: Productive participation without social participation?). Paper presented at the Eighth Central American Sociology Congress, Guatemala City, October.

Pérez Alemán, Paola, and Ivonne Siu. 1986. "La mujer en la economía nicaragüense: Cambios y desafíos" (Women in the Nicaraguan economy: Changes and challenges). Paper presented at the Fifth Nicaraguan Social Science Congress, Managua, Nicaragua, October.

Portugal, Ana María. 1985. *On Being a Feminist in Latin America.* Santiago, Chile: ISIS International Women's Information and Communication Service.

Quandt, Midge. 1990. "Nicaragua's Feminists: Beyond Self-Sacrifice." *The Guardian,* September 26, p. 13.

———. 1993. *Unbinding the Tie: The Popular Organizations and the FSLN in Nicaragua.* N.P.: Nicaragua Network Education Fund.

Ramírez-Horton, Susan E. 1982. "The Role of Women in the Nicaraguan Revolution." In *Nicaragua in Revolution,* ed. Thomas W. Walker, 147–160. New York: Praeger.

Randall, Margaret. 1981. *Sandino's Daughters.* Vancouver: New Star Books.

Rodríguez, Ileana. 1987. *Obstáculos a la promoción y aplicación de la con-*

vención sobre la eliminación de todas las formas de discriminación contra la mujer: Caso de Nicaragua (Obstacles to the promotion and application of the convention on the elimination of all forms of discrimination against women: The case of Nicaragua). Managua, Nicaragua: Oficina Legal de la Mujer—AMNLAE.

Rowbotham, Sheila. 1974. *Women, Resistance, and Revolution: A History of Women and Revolution in the Modern World.* New York: Vintage.

Rowbotham, Sheila, Lynne Segal, and Hilary Wainwright. 1979. *Beyond the Fragments: Feminism and the Making of Socialism.* London: Merlin Press.

Saul, John S. 1986. "The Role of Ideology in the Transition to Socialism." In *Transition and Development: Problems of Third World Socialism,* ed. Richard R. Fagen, Carmen Diana Deere, and José Luis Coraggio, 212–230. New York: Monthly Review.

Torrents, Nissa. 1988. "*Mujeres Magazine:* The First Twenty-Five Years." Paper presented at the Fourteenth International Congress of the Latin American Studies Association, March 17–19, New Orleans.

Vásquez, Norma, and Clara Murguialday, 1991. *FEM,* no. 102 (June).

Vogel, Lise. 1981. "Marxism and Feminism: Unhappy Marriage, Trial Separation, or Something Else?" In *Women and Revolution: A Discussion of the Unhappy Marriage of Marxism and Feminism,* ed. Lydia Sargent. Boston: South End Press.

———. 1983. *Marxism and the Oppression of Women: Toward a Unitary Theory.* New Brunswick, N.J.: Rutgers University Press.

White, Judy. 1988a. "Nicaragua's Atlantic Coast: How Miskito Indian Women Organize, Make Gains." *The Militant,* December 9.

———. 1988b. "Human Toll Is High from Illegal Abortions in Nicaragua." *The Militant,* December 30.

———. 1989. "Women's Brigade Helps Bring in Nicaragua's Coffee Harvest." *The Militant,* February 10.

Zalaquett, Monica. 1987. "Rural Women Forge Ahead." *Barricada Internacional,* August 27.

Zimmerman, Matilde. 1987. "1500 Women Attend Latin American Feminist Conference in Mexico." *The Militant,* November 20.

*

About the Editors and Contributors

Index

ABOUT THE EDITORS
AND CONTRIBUTORS

Editors

Edna Acosta-Belén is a Distinguished Service Professor of Latin American and Caribbean Studies and Women's Studies and Director of the Center for Latino, Latin American, and Caribbean Studies (CELAC) at the University at Albany, SUNY. Her publications include *The Puerto Rican Woman: Perspectives on Culture, History, and Society* (1979, 1986), *La mujer en la sociedad puertorriqueña* (1980), *The Hispanic Experience in the United States* (with Barbara Sjostrom) (1989), and *Researching Women in Latin America and the Caribbean* (with Christine E. Bose) (1993). She received her PhD from Columbia University and has been a postdoctoral fellow at Princeton and Yale universities. Her book in progress, *In the Shadow of the Giant: Colonialism, Migration, and Puerto Rican Culture,* is under contract with Temple University Press.

Christine E. Bose is an Associate Professor of Sociology, Women's Studies, and Latin American and Caribbean Studies and was the founding Director of the Institute for Research on Women (IROW) at the University at Albany, SUNY. Some of her publications are *Jobs and Gender: A Study of Occupational Prestige* (1985), *Hidden Aspects of Women's Work* (with Roslyn Feldberg and Natalie Sokoloff) (1987), *Ingredients for Women's Employment Policy* (with Glenna Spitze) (1987), and *Researching Women in Latin America and the Caribbean* (with Edna Acosta-Belén) (1993). She received her PhD from Johns Hopkins University.

Contributors

Luz del Alba Acevedo is an Assistant Professor of Latin American and Caribbean Studies and Women's Studies at the University at Albany, SUNY. She has published articles on the division of labor by gender in the manufacturing and service sectors of the Puerto Rican economy, gender identity and political power in the formulation of development policy, and power relations among women in the construction of feminist theory and praxis. Currently, she is working on a book about the political economy of gender relations in Puerto Rico. She received her PhD from the University of Illinois at Chicago.

Rae Lesser Blumberg is a Professor of Sociology at the University of California, San Diego. Her recent books include *Making the Case for the Gender Variable: Women and the Wealth and Well-Being of Nations* (1989), *Gender, Family, and the Economy: The Triple Overlap* (1991), and *Engendering Wealth and Well-Being* (with Cathy A. Rakowski, Irene Tinker, and Michael Monteon) (1994). She has researched gender and development in more than twenty countries around the world, guided by her general theory of gender stratification. She received her PhD from Northwestern University.

Norma Stoltz Chinchilla is Director of the Women's Studies Program at California State University, Long Beach. She has published extensively on the impact of development on women's work, social and political change in Guatemala, feminism and Marxism, and the interrelationships among social movements, women's movements, and feminist movements in Latin America. She is currently working on a book of oral histories of Guatemalan women who have participated in movements for social change. She received her PhD from the University of Wisconsin, Madison.

M. Patricia Fernández Kelly is a Research Scientist at the Institute for Policy Studies and an Associate Research Professor in Sociology at Johns Hopkins University. She has also been a Visiting Scholar at the Russell Sage Foundation. She is the author of *For We Are Sold, I and My People: Women and Industry in Mexico's Frontier* (1983) and coeditor of *Women, Men, and the International Division of Labor* (with June Nash) (1983), as well as coproducer of the Emmy Award–winning documentary "The Global Assembly Line" (with Lorraine Gray). She has written extensively on international development, U.S. industrial restructuring, migration, and the employment of Hispanic women in the garment and electronics industries of California and Florida. Her most recent research is on the conditions surrounding impoverished African American families in West Baltimore. She received her PhD from Rutgers University and also holds a doctoral degree from the Universidad Iberoamericana in Mexico City.

June Nash is a Distinguished Professor of Anthropology at City College of CUNY. Her books include *Sex and Class in Latin America: Women's Perspectives on Politics, Economics, and the Third World* (with Helen I. Safa) (1976), *We Eat the Mines and the Mines Eat Us: Dependency and Exploitation in a Bolivian Tin Mining Community* (1979), *Women, Men, and the International Division of Labor* (with M. Patricia Fernández

Kelly) (1983), *Women and Change in Latin America* (with Helen I. Safa) (1986), *From Tank Town to High-Tech: The Clash of Community and Industrial Cycles* (1989), *Crafts in the World Market: The Impact of Global Integration on Middle American Artisans* (1993), and *I Spent My Life in the Mines* (1993). She is currently synthesizing her work with the Maya on the advancing frontiers of capitalist penetration and neoliberal reforms. She holds a PhD from the University of Chicago.

Jean Larson Pyle is an Associate Professor of Economics at the University of Massachusetts, Lowell. Her research and teaching interests span the areas of economic development, labor, gender, and policy. She is the author of *The State and Women in the Economy: Lessons from Sex Discrimination in the Republic of Ireland* (1990) and numerous articles and book chapters. She is currently working on a new book analyzing the effect of state employment, family, and reproductive rights policies on women's labor force participation in Singapore since the 1960s. Other research projects include an interdisciplinary study of the levels of factors that facilitate diversity within the workplace. She holds a PhD from the University of Massachusetts, Amherst.

Palmira N. Ríos is an Assistant Professor of Urban Policy at the New School for Social Research. She has published extensively on Puerto Rican women's employment in the United States and Puerto Rico, on Dominican migration, and on the sociology of ethnic relations in the Caribbean and the United States. In 1992–93 she was a Fulbright Scholar to the Dominican Republic. She received her PhD from Yale University.

Frances Abrahamer Rothstein is a Professor of Anthropology at Towson State University, Towson, Maryland. She publishes in the areas of anthropological political economy and gender, industrialization, and development. Her publications include *Three Different Worlds: Women, Men, and Children in an Industrializing Community* (1982) and *Anthropology and the Global Factory: Studies of the New Industrialization in the Late Twentieth Century* (with Michael Blim) (1992). She is currently studying the consequences of economic restructuring on women's employment in Mexico with a particular interest in women from Indian peasant families who are entering the professions. She received her PhD from the University of Pittsburgh.

Helen Icken Safa is a Professor of Anthropology and Latin American and Caribbean Studies at the University of Florida, Gainesville, where she is past Director of the Center for Latin American Studies and current Director of the Rockefeller Resident Humanities Fellowship in Afro-American Identity and Diversity. She is also a former President of the Latin American Studies Association. She is author or editor of many books, including *The Urban Poor in Puerto Rico* (1974), *In the Shadows of the Sun: Caribbean Development Alternatives and U.S. Policy* (with Carmen Diana Deere et al.) (1990), *Migration and Development: Implications for Ethnic Identity and Political Conflict* (with Brian H. du Toit) (1975), *Towards a Political Economy of Urbanization in Third World Countries* (1982), *Sex and Class in Latin America: Women's Perspectives on Politics, Economics, and the Third World* (with June Nash) (1976), *Women's Work: Development and the Division of Labor by Gender* (with Eleanor Leacock) (1986), and *The Myth of the Male Breadwinner: Women and Industrialization in the Caribbean* (1995). She received her PhD from Columbia University.

Saskia Sassen is a Professor of Urban Planning at Columbia University. She is the author of *The Mobility of Labor and Capital: A Study in International Investment and Labor Flow* (1988), *The Global City: New York, London, Tokyo* (1991), and *Cities in a World Economy* (1994). She is currently writing a book on immigration in a world economy, which compares key issues in the United States, western Europe, and Japan, and she has begun work on a five-year project entitled "Governance and Accountability in a World Economy." She received her PhD from the University of Notre Dame.

Kathryn B. Ward is a Professor of Sociology at Southern Illinois University at Carbondale. She is the author of *Women in the World System: Its Impact on Status and Fertility* (1984), *Women Workers and Global Restructuring* (1990), and numerous articles on women and the global economy. Other research interests include feminist critiques of sociology, the effects of gender and race on mentoring in science, macromodels of the U.S. women's movement, and oral histories of the civil rights movement in Cairo, Illinois. She received her PhD from the University of Iowa.

INDEX

Abortion, 237, 252, 253, 254, 257, 258, 259, 266n. 4

Acción Internacional, 197, 198, 200, 204, 206, 207, 217, 219–220

Accumulation, 71; capital, 18, 20, 22, 30, 78, 152, 153, 162; crisis of, 162; flexible, 38; pillars of, 27; process of, 152

ADEMI. *See* Association for the Development of Microenterprise (Dominican Republic)

Agriculture, 72; collective actions in, 33; development in, 19; diversification in, 159; employment in, 132 table 5-2; and level of education, 178, 179 table 7-9; mechanization of, 114; subsistence, 5, 154, 167, 171, 175; women in, 22, 32, 184; working conditions in, 29

Aid to Families with Dependent Children (United States), 161

AITEC. *See* Acción Internacional

Allende, Salvador, 157, 232

American Development Bank, 154

American Popular Revolutionary Alliance (APRA), in Peru, 157

AMNLAE, 248–260, 261–263

AMPRONAC (Nicaragua), 246–248

Androcentrism, 81, 87

APRA, 157

Argentina, 24; female labor in, 69; feminist movements in, 30; human rights movements in, 234–235; social movements in, 234–235

Arpilleras (Chile), 157

Asesores (Guatemala), 209–210

Asistencialismo (Peru), 234

Association for the Development of Microenterprise (Dominican Republic), 196–204, 217–220, 221nn. 2, 3, 222n. 4

Association of Agricultural Workers (ATC), in Nicaragua, 256, 258, 262, 263, 264

Association of Women Confronting the National Problem (AMPRONAC), in Nicaragua, 246–248

ATC. *See* Association of Agricultural Workers (Nicaragua)

Authoritarianism, 19, 24, 227, 229

Automation, 8, 40, 43, 45, 46, 105, 117

Autonomy, 4, 31, 65, 118, 119, 157, 161

Aylwin, Patricio, 237

Bangladesh: export processing zones in, 41; female labor in, 41; microenterprises in, 196, 216; subcontracting in, 45; wage remittances in, 49; working conditions in, 45

Banking sector, 10, 41

Barbados, 143; export processing workforce in, 143; resistance activities in, 52

Barriadas, 152

Barricada (newspaper), 252

Barrios de Chamorro, Violeta, 242, 261, 266n. 5

Bolivia, 27, 154; economic trends in, 158–160; foreign debt in, 158; housewives' committees in, 29

Brazil: class relations in, 79; ecclesiastic base communities in, 237; female labor in, 68, 72, 73, 233; foreign debt in, 158; gender division of labor in, 75; gender relations in, 81;

Mothers of the Plaza de Mayo, 234–235

Movements: bases of, 229–232; democratic, 45; feminist, 28, 29, 30, 162, 230, 232; grassroots, 1, 30, 236, 238, 246, 254; militant, 125; national liberation, 31; political, 155; resistance, 51–53; revolutionary, 29; self-determination, 31; social, 5, 89n. 8, 227–239; women's, 5; women's liberation, 31; and working-class organizations, 30

MPU (Nicaragua), 246

Muchachas, 3, 23

Muñoz Marín, Luis, 142

NAFTA, 8, 131

National Council on Women's Rights (Brazil), 237

Nationalization, 157, 159

National Women's Office (Chile), 237

Nicaragua, 7, 24; feminist activity in, 29–30; revolution in, 242–265; women's equality in, 32; women's movement in, 242–265

Nigeria, 186

Nongovernmental agencies, 231, 238

North American Free Trade Agreement (NAFTA), 8, 131

Núñez, Carlos, 259

Obreros (Mexico), 171

Office on Women (Nicaragua), 257

Ollas comunes, 229

Operación Manos a la Obra. *See* Operation Bootstrap (Puerto Rico)

Operation Bootstrap (Puerto Rico), 9, 19, 128–131, 138, 140, 142, 144

Oppression, 78; and gender, 32; male, 31; privatized, 152; sites of, 86; sources of, 79, 86; systems of, 26

Organizaciones Económicas Populares (Chile), 229

Organization of Petroleum Exporting Countries, 141

Organizations: economic, 229; forms of, 70; self-help, 229, 234 (*see also* Collective actions); working-class, 264

Ortega, Daniel, 258, 259, 266n. 5

Paternalism, 18

Patria potestad, 237, 252

Patriarchy, 4, 20, 21, 27, 31, 43, 69, 84, 118, 128, 139, 144, 160, 161, 170, 176, 189n. 6, 211

Paz Estenssoro, Victor, 158

Peru, 23, 154; collective actions in, 158; economic trends in, 157–158; female labor in, 69; informal sector in, 50, 71, 195; resistance activities, 53; transnational corporations in, 41

Petrochemical industry, 9, 131, 134–135 table 5-3, 140–142

Pharmaceutical industry, 131, 141, 257

Philippines, 45; economic roles of women in, 43; export processing workforce in, 143; female labor in, 41, 42; union membership in, 52; wage remittances in, 49

Piñata, 261

Pinochet, Augusto, 156, 232, 237

Pobladores, 158

Policy: development, 17, 18, 27, 28, 138–140; economic, 138; employment, 80; export-oriented, 144; and gender, 139–140; industrialization, 4; patriarchal, 4; state, 4, 42

Political alliances, 187

Political co-optation, 236

Political democracy, 18

Political economy, 2–5

Political mobilization, 160

Political movements, 155

Political parties, 7, 29, 30, 228–229, 232, 233, 236, 238

Political pluralism, 244

Political reform, 24

Political repression, 17, 24

Políticas, 236–237

Popular Economic Organizations (Chile), 229